Ruach HaKodesh
God the Holy Spirit

Messianic Jewish Perspectives
on Pneumatology

Other Books by Dr. Arnold G. Fruchtenbaum

A Passover Haggadah for Jewish Believers
An Historical and Geographical Study Guide of Israel: With a Supplement on Jordan
Ariel's Harmony of the Gospels
Faith Alone: The Condition of Our Salvation (An Exposition of the Book of Galatians and Other Relevant Topics)
God's Will & Man's Will: Predestination, Election, and Free Will
Ha-Mashiach: The Messiah of the Hebrew Scriptures
Israelology: The Missing Link in Systematic Theology
Jesus Was a Jew
The Feasts and Fasts of Israel – Their Historic and Prophetic Significance
The Footsteps of the Messiah: A Study of the Sequence of Prophetic Events
The Historical and Geographical Maps of Israel and Surrounding Territories
The Remnant of Israel: The History, Theology, and Philosophy of the Messianic Jewish Community
The Sabbath
What the Bible Teaches About Israel: Past, Present, and Future (An Abridged Version of Israelology: The Missing Link in Systematic Theology)
Yeshua: The Life of Messiah from a Messianic Jewish Perspective, Volumes 1-4 & The Abridged Version

Ariel's Bible Commentary Series:

The Messianic Jewish Epistles (Hebrews, James, I & II Peter, Jude)
Judges and Ruth
The Book of Genesis
Biblical Lovemaking: A Study of the Song of Solomon

Ariel's Come and See Series:

The Word of God: Its Nature and Content
What We Know About God: Theology Proper
Messiah Yeshua, Divine Redeemer: Christology from a Messianic Jewish Perspective

Ruach HaKodesh
God the Holy Spirit

Messianic Jewish Perspectives on Pneumatology

Arnold G. Fruchtenbaum
Th.M., Ph.D.

Ruach HaKodesh – God the Holy Spirit:
Messianic Jewish Perspectives on Pneumatology
(Arnold G. Fruchtenbaum, Th.M., Ph.D.)
Volume 4 in Ariel's "Come and See Series"
© 2019 by Ariel Ministries

ISBN 978-1-935174-82-0

Library of Congress Control Number:
2019909152
REL101000 RELIGION / Messianic Judaism / Jesus / Holy Spirit

Contributor and editor: Christiane K. Jurik, M.A.
Copy Editors: Pauline Ilsen, Joni Bohannon
Proofreader: Udaya Thangasamy
Printed in the United States of America
Cover illustration by Jesse and Josh Gonzales (*http://www.vipgraphics.net*)

All rights reserved. No part of this publication may be reproduced, distributed, or transmitted in any form or by any means, including photocopying, recording, or other electronic or mechanical methods, without the prior written permission of the publisher, except in the case of brief quotations embodied in critical reviews and certain other noncommercial uses permitted by copyright law. For permission requests, write to the publisher at the address below.

All Scripture quotations, unless otherwise noted, are from the *1901 American Standard Version* (Oak Harbor, WA: Logos Research Systems, Inc., 1994). However, the archaic language has been changed with one exception: The archaic *ye* has been retained in order to distinguish the second person plural from the singular *you*. The words "Jesus" and "Christ" have been replaced with "Yeshua" and "Messiah."

Published by Ariel Ministries
P.O. Box 792507
San Antonio, TX 78279-2507
www.ariel.org

This volume is dedicated to

Archie and Jo Ann Jones

Who have contributed so much effort to Ariel Ministries in its early days of service.

Contents

PREFACE 1

CHAPTER I
INTRODUCTION TO PNEUMATOLOGY

A. BIBLICAL PNEUMATOLOGY 3
B. FALSE VIEWS ABOUT THE RUACH HAKODESH 4
    1. Montanism 4
    2. Sabellianism 5
    3. Arianism 6
    4. Macedonianism 7
    5. Pelagianism 8
    6. From the Council of Ephesus to the Time of the Reformation 8
    7. Socinianism 10
    8. Arminianism 10
    9. Neo-Orthodoxy 11
    10. Neoliberalism 11
    11. Pentecostalism 12
C. QUESTIONS AND STUDY SUGGESTIONS 13

CHAPTER II
THE PERSON OF THE RUACH HAKODESH

A. NAMES AND TITLES 15
    1. Names and Titles in Relation to the Father 16
    2. Names and Titles in Relation to the Son 16
    3. Names and Titles in Relation to the Ruach Himself 16
B. THE PERSONALITY OF THE RUACH HAKODESH 17
    1. The Ruach Possesses the Characteristics of a Person 18
        a. Intellect 18
        b. Emotion 19
        c. Will 19
    2. The Ruach HaKodesh Performs the Works of a Person 19
        a. He Creates 19
        b. He Restrains Sin 20
        c. He Empowers 20
        d. He Teaches 21

		e.	He Comforts 21

- e. He Comforts 21
- f. He Guides and Leads 21
- g. He Convicts 21
- h. He Testifies and Witnesses 22
- i. He Issues Orders 22
- j. He Performs Miracles 22
- k. He Sends 22
- l. He Speaks 23
- m. He Prays and Intercedes 23
- 3. The Ruach HaKodesh as Personal Object of Faith 23
- 4. Unusual Grammar in Relation to the Ruach HaKodesh 24
- 5. Distinction Between the Spirit's Power and His Person 25
- C. QUESTIONS AND STUDY SUGGESTIONS 25

CHAPTER III
THE DEITY OF THE RUACH HAKODESH

- A. DIVINE TITLES 27
  - 1. Holy Spirit 27
  - 2. God 28
  - 3. Lord 28
  - 4. Another Comforter 28
- B. DIVINE ATTRIBUTES 29
  - 1. Omnipotence 29
  - 2. Omnipresence 29
  - 3. Omniscience 30
  - 4. Holiness 30
  - 5. Eternity 31
  - 6. Life 31
  - 7. Truth 31
- C. DIVINE WORKS 32
  - 1. Creation 32
  - 2. He Generated Messiah 33
  - 3. Inspiration 34
  - 4. Regeneration 35
  - 6. Impartation of Life 36
  - 5. Sanctification 37
- D. EQUAL ASSOCIATIONS 38
  - 1. With *YHVH* or *YHWH* (Jehovah) 38
  - 2. With God 39
    - a. II Samuel 23:2-3 39
    - b. I Corinthians 3:16-17 39
    - c. I Corinthians 6:19-20 40

		3. With the Son 40

- 3. With the Son 40
  - a. Luke 4:18-19 40
  - b. Romans 8:9-10 41
  - c. II Corinthians 3:17-18 41
  - d. Philippians 1:19 41
- 4. With the Father and the Son 42
  - a. Matthew 3:16-17 42
  - b. Matthew 28:19 43
  - c. I Corinthians 12:4-6 43
  - d. II Corinthians 13:14 43
- E. THE PROCESSION OF THE RUACH HAKODESH 44
  - 1. The Fact of Procession 45
  - 2. The Aspect of Eternality 46
  - 3. From the Father and the Son 47
- F. QUESTIONS AND STUDY SUGGESTIONS 48

CHAPTER IV
THE RUACH HAKODESH IN TYPOLOGY

- A. OIL 52
  - 1. Exodus 27:20-21 52
  - 2. Exodus 40:9-16 53
  - 3. Leviticus 8:10-12, 30 54
  - 4. I Samuel 10:1 55
  - 5. I Samuel 16:13 55
  - 6. I Kings 1:39 55
  - 7. Psalm 23:5 56
  - 8. Isaiah 61:1-2a and Luke 4:16-21 56
  - 9. Acts 10:38 57
  - 10. II Corinthians 1:21-22 57
  - 11. I John 2:20 58
  - 12. Significance 58
- B. WATER 58
  - 1. John 4:14 59
  - 2. John 7:37-39 60
  - 3. Significance 61
- C. FIRE 62
  - 1. Acts 2:1-4 62
  - 2. Revelation 4:5 63
  - 3. Significance 64
- D. WIND 65
  - 1. John 3:8 66
  - 2. Acts 2:1-4 68

  3. II Peter 1:21 68
  4. Significance 69
E. DOVE 69
  1. Scriptures 69
  2. Significance 72
F. EARNEST 72
  1. II Corinthians 1:21-22 72
  2. II Corinthians 5:5 73
  3. Ephesians 1:13b-14 73
  4. Significance 73
G. SEAL 74
H. CLOTHING 74
I. QUESTIONS AND STUDY SUGGESTIONS 75

CHAPTER V
THE WORKS OF THE RUACH HAKODESH

A. THE WORKS IN RELATION TO SCRIPTURE 77
  1. The Ministry of Revelation 77
  2. The Ministry of Inspiration 78
  3. The Ministry of Illumination 78
B. THE WORKS IN THE HEBREW SCRIPTURES 79
  1. The Ministry of the Holy Spirit in Relation to Creation 79
  2. The Ministry of the Holy Spirit in Relation to the World 79
  3. The Ministries of the Holy Spirit in Relation to Humanity 80
C. THE WORKS IN THE LIFE OF MESSIAH 83
  1. The Agent of Conception 84
  2. Other Activities in the Life of Messiah 86
   a. Anointing 86
   b. Being Upon the Messiah 88
   c. Filling 88
   d. Sealing 88
   e. Leading 89
  3. Messiah's Response to the Ruach HaKodesh 89
   a. Rejoicing 89
   b. Empowered 89
    (1) For Prophetic Ministry 89
    (2) To Cast Out Demons 91
    (3) To Perform Miracles 92
  4. In Relation to the Death of Messiah 92
  5. In Relation to the Resurrection of Messiah 93
   a. Romans 1:4 93
   b. Romans 8:11 94

		c.	I Peter 3:18 95	
D.	THE WORKS IN THE NATURAL WORLD 96
E.	THE WORKS IN THE LIFE OF THE BELIEVER...97
	1.	The Ministries of the Holy Spirit in Relation to Salvation 97
		a.	The Ministry of Regeneration 97
			(1)	The Means of Regeneration 98
			(2)	Faith is the Basis of Regeneration..99
			(3)	The Figures of Speech for Regeneration 99
			(4)	Two Aspects of the Work of Regeneration 99
			(5)	The Results of Regeneration..100
		b.	The Ministry of Indwelling 101
			(1)	Scriptures Concerning the Ministry of Indwelling....................101
			(2)	The Means of Indwelling 102
			(3)	The Universality of Indwelling 102
			(4)	The Permanence of Indwelling 103
			(5)	The Results of Indwelling...103
		c.	The Ministry of Spirit Baptism 104
			(1)	Several Reasons for the Confusion Regarding Spirit Baptism....104
			(2)	Scriptures Concerning the Ministry of Spirit Baptism...............105
			(3)	The Beginning of Spirit Baptism...107
			(4)	The Agent of Spirit Baptism 108
			(5)	The Universality of Spirit Baptism..108
			(6)	When Spirit Baptism Occurs 109
			(7)	The Frequency of Spirit Baptism...109
			(8)	The Results of Spirit Baptism 110
			(9)	Summary of the Spirit's Ministries in Relation to Salvation.......110
			(10)	The Delay of Spirit Baptism in the Book of Acts........................111
			(11)	The Transitional Nature of the Book of Acts.............................118
			(12)	The Danger of Deriving Doctrine from Historical Accounts 119
			(13)	Summary of Spirit Baptism 120
		d.	The Ministry of Sealing 120
			(1)	Scriptures...120
			(2)	The Ramifications of the Ministry of Spirit-Sealing...................121
			(3)	The Concept of the Seal in the Hebrew Scriptures 122
			(4)	The Significance of the Ministry of Spirit-Sealing 122
		e.	The Ministry of Anointing 123
		f.	Summary..124
	2.	The Ministries of the Ruach HaKodesh in Relation to Spiritual Growth ..125
		a.	The Ministry of Spirit-Filling 125
			(1)	The Greek Words 125
			(2)	The Meaning of Spirit-Filling 126
			(3)	The Nature of Spirit-Filling...126
			(4)	The Conditions for Living a Spirit-Filled Life..............................127

		(5) The Results of Spirit-Filling 129
		(6) Summary of Spirit-Filling 130
	b.	The Ministry of Teaching 130
	c.	The Ministry of Guiding 131
	d.	The Ministry of Assurance 132
	e.	The Ministry of Praying and Interceding 132
	f.	The Ministry of the Witness of the Spirit 134
	g.	The Ministry of the Fellowship of the Holy Spirit 138
F.	The Works in the Future 139
	1.	During the Great Tribulation 139
	2.	On Behalf of the Nation of Israel 140
	3.	During the Messianic Kingdom or the Millennium 142
G.	Questions and Study Suggestions 142

CHAPTER VI
SINS AGAINST THE RUACH HAKODESH

A.	Sins Committed by Unbelievers 145
	1. The Vexing or the Grieving of the Ruach HaKodesh 145
	2. Blasphemy of the Ruach HaKodesh 146
	a. The Rejection (Mt. 12:22-24) 146
	b. The Defense (Mt. 12:25-29) 149
	c. The Judgment (Mt. 12:30-37) 149
	d. The Conclusion 153
B.	Sins Committed by Believers 154
	1. The Grieving of the Holy Spirit 154
	a. Sins of Speech 154
	b. Other Sins 155
	c. The Remedy 156
	2. The Quenching of the Holy Spirit 156
	a. The Preventing of the Exercise of Spiritual Gifts 156
	b. The Remedy 158
C.	Conclusion 158
D.	Questions and Study Suggestions 159

CHAPTER VII
THE GIFTS OF THE RUACH HAKODESH

A.	The Greek Words 161
B.	Attributes of Spiritual Gifts 163
	1. What Spiritual Gifts Are 163
	2. What Spiritual Gifts Are Not 164

- C. MAIN BIBLE PASSAGES 165
  1. I Peter 4:10 165
  2. Romans 12:4-8 166
     a. The Body Doctrine (Rom. 12:4-5) 166
     b. The Gifts of the Spirit (Rom. 12:6-8) 166
  3. Ephesians 4:11-16 168
     a. The Gifts 168
        (1) The Gift of Apostleship 168
        (2) The Gift of Evangelism 170
        (3) The Gift of Pastor-Teacher 171
     b. The Purposes and Goals of the Gifts 171
     c. The Means of Maturity 173
  4. I Corinthians 7:1 and 7 174
  5. I Corinthians 12-14 174
     a. The Doctrine of the Gifts of the Spirit: I Corinthians 12 174
        (1) The Topic of Gifts and the Test (I Cor. 12:1-3) 175
        (2) The Distribution of the Gifts (I. Cor. 12:4-6) 176
        (3) The Gifts of the Spirit (I Cor. 12:7-11) 177
        (4) One Body and Many Members:
            Unity in Diversity (I Cor. 12:12-31) 181
        (5) Summary of the Doctrine of the Gifts 188
     b. Love and the Gifts of the Spirit (I Cor. 3:1-13) 189
        (1) Love and the Gifts (I Cor. 13:1-3) 189
        (2) The Attributes of Love (I Cor. 13:4-7) 190
        (3) The Relation to Time (I Cor. 13:8) 191
        (4) The Relation to Maturity (I Cor. 13:9-12) 192
        (5) The Present State (I Cor. 13:13) 194
     c. Practical Rules for Tongues and Prophecy (I Cor. 14:1-40) 194
        (1) The Contrasting of Tongues and Prophecy (I Cor. 14:1-5) 195
        (2) Tongues in the Public Assembly (I Cor. 14:6-19) 198
        (3) The Problems of Tongues in the Assembly (I Cor. 14:20-25) 201
        (4) Further Rules for Tongues and Prophecy (I Cor. 14:26-33a) 204
        (5) Conclusion (I Cor. 14:33b-40) 207
- D. THE END OF THE GIFTS OF APOSTLESHIP AND PROPHECY 210
  1. Laying the Foundation of the Church 210
  2. Recording New Testament Revelation 211
  3. Conclusion 212
- E. QUESTIONS AND STUDY SUGGESTIONS 213

Ruach HaKodesh – God the Holy Spirit

Preface

What is Come and See?

Come and See is a multi-volume collection of Messianic Bible studies transcribed from Dr. Arnold Fruchtenbaum's original radio broadcasts. For the book series, the manuscripts made from these transcripts were edited and expanded, and text based on his sermon notes was added.

Each study is a solid foundation upon which you can stand—a whiteboard from which you can teach or a podium from which you can preach the uncompromised truth to your congregation. This extensive collection is replete with expert knowledge of Hebrew, Greek, the Talmud, the history of the Jews, the geography of *Eretz Yisrael* (the land of Israel); a scholar's command of the Word; and the illumination of the *Ruach HaKodesh* (the Holy Spirit). *Come and See* will edify you in your personal devotion or small group Bible study regardless of which topic you choose.

What Will You Discover in This Volume?

Volume four of *Come and See* examines what we know about God the Spirit. In systematic theology, this topic is called "pneumatology," or "the doctrine of the Holy Spirit." This is a major section of systematic theology and is a further study in the *Come and See* series we have been developing for you.

Systematic theology is, of course, a logical development of what the Bible teaches about various subjects. The first main division is bibliology, which is the study of the Scriptures. We addressed the topic in volume one of *Come and See*, *The Word of God*. This is a logical beginning, since what we know about theology comes from the Scriptures themselves.

The second main division of systematic theology is called "theology proper," which is the doctrine of God. We addressed this topic in volume two of this series, *What We Know About God*. The study developed our understanding of God the Father and emphasized the deity, the theism, and the trinitarianism of God.

The third main division of systematic theology is Christology, also called "the doctrine of the Son" or "the doctrine of the Messiah." We covered this topic in volume three of our Come and See series, *Messiah Yeshua, Divine Redeemer: Christology from a Messianic Jewish Perspective*.

Questions and Study Suggestions for the Course

At the end of each chapter, you will find questions and study suggestions which provide application that is relevant to the subject.

The goal of this collection is for disciples of *Yeshua* (Jesus) to grow in their faith and to live out their calling to make disciples. We hope you enjoy the *Come and See Series*!

Chapter I

Introduction to Pneumatology

This book is devoted to the doctrine of God the Holy Spirit, or in Hebrew, the *Ruach HaKodesh*. Theologians call this doctrine "pneumatology." The term is essentially derived from two Greek words: *pneuma* and *logos*. *Pneuma* means "breath" or "spirit." *Logos* means "word" or "doctrine." So, pneumatology is "the word of the Spirit" or "the doctrine of the Spirit."

A. Biblical Pneumatology

The study of biblical pneumatology is predominantly a study of the Scriptures themselves. A plain reading of the passages that speak of the Spirit is enough to identify Him as who He is: God the Spirit, equal in nature and essence with God the Father and God the Son.

There are two key factors which we must always keep in mind in order to develop a true biblical pneumatology, a true doctrine of the Holy Spirit of God.

- ✡ The first factor is a **true and proper deity**. The deity of the Spirit must be emphasized and understood in all of the aspects that that term demands.
- ✡ The second factor is **the personality (or personhood) of the Spirit**. For a true pneumatology, the Ruach HaKodesh must always be viewed as a separate and distinct person of the triune Godhead.

Many in church history have failed to keep these two essential factors in mind and have developed various heresies, which we will now look at.

B. False Views About the Ruach HaKodesh

As far as a definition is concerned, pneumatology did not receive a lot of attention from the early church, which may be the reason why several false views developed not even a century after the last apostle died. The following is a condensed overview of the history of pneumatology, with a focus on the heresies that haven arisen.

1. Montanism

The first heresy found in early Christian writings is called Montanism (also "Cataphrygian heresy" or "New Prophecy"). While the original works of the adherents of this doctrine have been lost, several early church authors, such as Eusebius, Tertullian, and Epiphanius, recounted the history of the movement. According to their writings, Montanism was founded in the second century by a man named Montanus. Soon after Montanus converted to Christianity, he appeared in Ardabau, a small village in Phrygia (see map below). There, he fell into a trance and began prophesying—allegedly under the influence of the Holy Spirit. Two women by the name of Prisca and Maximilla joined this self-proclaimed prophet and began prophesying themselves.

At first, the teachings of Montanus and his followers did not seem to deny the foundational doctrines of the Bible. Their theology was characterized by legalism, which demanded a high morality of its followers. While this aspect of Montanism appealed to writers such as Tertullian, it soon became clear that the doctrine deviated from the Scriptures on important points. Montanus and his followers declared that the "Age of the Paraclete" had begun and that new revelations from God could be expected. They claimed that the end of the world was near and emphasized the experience of the Spirit over the truth of the Scriptures.

By the early 170s, the "New Prophets" had attracted a sizeable following, forcing their opponents to deal with the doctrine on a broader level. Eventually, the church officially rejected Montanism because of its focus on the experience of the Spirit and its insistence on additional revelation. From that time forward, the general teaching of the church was that apart from the Scriptures, there are no new revelations by the Spirit.

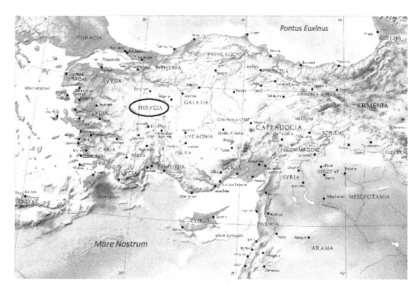

Above: Phrygia in Asia Minor (modern-day Turkey; map by Jesse Gonzales)

2. Sabellianism

The fallacy of Montanism was followed by Sabellianism. This heresy was based on two false doctrines called Modalism and Monarchianism. Modalists claimed that God, being one person, can switch between three expressions or "modes." They said that in the Hebrew Scriptures, God manifested Himself primarily as the Father; in the Gospels, He took on the form of the Son; and after His ascension, He switched to Spirit mode. Monarchians also denied the trinity but interpreted the oneness of God to the extreme of altogether denying His triune nature. According to their view, "Father," "Son," and "Spirit" are only different names for the same person.

Around the year 215, a man named Sabellius began to spread the heresies of Modalistic Monarchianism, preaching the oneness of God and denying the eternal distinctions among the persons of the Trinity. One outworking of his false view was that when he baptized people, he did so on one name only, thus ignoring Yeshua's words in Matthew 28:19 to baptize them *in the name of the Father and of the Son and of the Holy Spirit*.

As was the case with Montanism, the original writings of Sabellius have been lost. Hence, what we know has been passed on to us through the ages by those who refuted his heresy. One such opponent was Hippolytus of Rome, who addressed Sabellianism in his *Refutation of All Heresies*. Another opponent was Tertullian, who especially criticized the heresy of Patripassianism. According to this teaching, the Father suffered with the Son on the cross.

3. Arianism

The term "Arianism" refers to the teachings of Arius (256-336), a priest or presbyter from the Egyptian city of Alexandria. Arius believed in the monotheistic principle of Monarchianism. However, his teaching went further than the preceding heresy, as he claimed that God the Father had created the Son. Using verses such as John 3:16 and Romans 8:29 which speak of Yeshua as the begotten, firstborn Son, he would propound a riddle along these lines: "How can the Son be equal with the Father? If He is a son, then before He was begotten He was not in existence. If He was in existence, why was He begotten?" Arius then went on to say that the Son created the Holy Spirit. This made the Ruach HaKodesh the *ktisma ktismatos*, meaning "the creature of a creature" or the creation of a created being. The Spirit's personality was entirely denied by Arius, and He was considered the exerted energy of God. While Arius assigned some divine attributes to the Son (such as the power to create), he denied the deity of both the Son and the Spirit.

The teachings brought Arius into conflict with a bishop named Alexander (died ca. 326), who together with his assistant Athanasius (296-373) staunchly defended the Trinitarian view. The dispute between the presbyter and the bishop occurred at the beginning of the fourth century and became known as the "Arian controversy." From Alexandria, the controversy spread to the east. Roughly a quarter century after the debate erupted in Egypt, it had affected the entire church of the Roman Empire. One historian reported: "Bishop was contending against bishop, and the people were contending against one another, like swarms of gnats fighting the air."[1] After an extended period of fierce debate at various church councils, the heresy was finally condemned by the church in the year 325 at the First Council of Nicea. The Nicene Creed was adopted, explicitly affirming the divinity of the Son. The key term the council used to express that God the Father and God the Son are of the same substance was the Greek word *homoousios*. As to the essence, personhood, and deity of the Ruach HaKodesh, the creed remained rather vague. The text simply ended with the words "We believe in the Holy Spirit."

4. Macedonianism

The council's hopes that the Nicene Creed would once and for all establish the place of the Ruach HaKodesh in the church's teaching were shattered when a new controversy arose in the second half of the fourth century. This time, the movement was led by a bishop from Constantinople named Macedonius (d. after 360). His doctrine became known both as "Macedonianism" and "Pneumatomachi heresy." The adherents of this doctrine were called "fighters against the Spirit," the translation of *Pneumatomachi*. As was the case with previous heresies, the original writings of Macedonius and his followers have been lost. Hence, what is known about them primarily comes from refutations by others.

The difference between Macedonianism and its predecessor, Arianism, is that the adherents of the new heresy accepted the Nicene premise of the equality of Father and Son. Yet, just like Arianism, they repudiated the equal status of the Ruach in the Godhead, denying His deity and understanding Him as the climax of the created order in subordination to the Son.

The Pneumatomachi heresy was officially condemned by the Council of Constantinople in 381. Under the direction of Gregory of Nazianzus (ca. 329-390), the council adopted the following addendum to the original Nicene Creed: "We believe in the Holy Spirit, the Lord, the life-giving, who proceeds from the Father, who is to be glorified with the Father and the

---

[1] Robert Payne, *The Holy Fire: The Story of the Early Centuries of the Christian Church in the Near East* (Crestwood, NY: St. Vladimir's Seminary Press, 1957), p. 77.

Son, and who speaks through the prophets." While the revised creed corrected the heretical teachings of Arianism and Macedonianism, it failed to stipulate that the Holy Spirit is of the same substance as the Father and the Son.

5. Pelagianism

The heresy of Pelagianism is named after the theologian Pelagius, who is thought to have been born on the British Isles and who died in the Holy Land (ca. 354-420). His writings have been lost, and some historians teach that he eventually rejected parts of the doctrine that carried his name. Yet, from the refutations of his opponents (mainly Augustine of Hippo, 354-430), several points of his teachings may be identified. Pelagius denied the biblical teaching that Adam's sin is being passed on to every human being at conception. He claimed that this original sin had no hereditary spiritual effect upon humanity. Thus, every baby is born spiritually pure, without any depravity. Furthermore, every human being has an unadulterated free will. Assisted by God's grace, they are able to do spiritual good apart from the divine enablement of the Holy Spirit. The human will alone enables a person to live a sinless life. This denial of human depravity paired with the idea that man's will is enough to do good has led to the view that human beings can earn salvation by their own efforts.

The Council of Ephesus officially condemned Pelagianism as heresy in the year 431.

6. From the Council of Ephesus to the Time of the Reformation

Summarizing the doctrinal development regarding the Spirit from the first council to the Reformation, the progression went like this:

At the First Council of Nicaea (325), the deity of the Son was established.

At the Council of Constantinople (381), the deity of the Spirit was established. This doctrine was reconfirmed at the Council of Chalcedon, in 451.

Some 140 years later, in the year 589, the Synod of Toledo addressed a disagreement of the western and the eastern churches over the Holy

Spirit. The question was whether the Ruach HaKodesh proceeded only from God the Father or also from God the Son. The western church decided that it was from both, hence adding to her creed a term that to this day is a bone of contention between the Catholic and the Eastern Orthodox churches, the famous *filioque* ("and from the Son"). The eastern church left the addition out of their creed.

Another heresy that popped up in the sixth century was tritheism. The founders of this doctrine were John Ascunages, head of the Sophist school at Antioch, and John Philoponus (ca. 490-570), a commentator on Aristotelian teaching. Other leaders were the bishops Conon of Tarsus and Eugenius of Seleucia. Tritheism is like polytheism, but it limits the number of gods to three. It denies the unity of the Godhead and sees three gods with no unity of essence. This heretical doctrine was soon dismissed by the church at large. However, it was picked up again by the Mormons in the 19th century.

In the following centuries, the church did not add anything else to pneumatology, and the general teaching about the Ruach HaKodesh concentrated on His person. Then came the Reformation (1517). Now, theologians such as Martin Luther also addressed the Spirit's work. In his *Basic Theology*, Charles Ryrie recaps the essentials of the development:

> As far as the Spirit's person was concerned, all the Reformed confessions express the orthodox doctrine of the Spirit in relation to the other persons of the Trinity. As far as His work is concerned, there was renewed emphasis on the necessity of His work in regenerating man because there was a return to the Augustinian emphasis on the total depravity of man.
>
> Another important contribution of the Reformers was their emphasis on the need of illumination by the Spirit. The Roman church taught that only the priest could interpret the Word of God, whereas the Reformers advocated openly the study of the Bible, asserting that all believers could be taught its truths by the teaching ministry of the Holy Spirit.[2]

---

[2] Charles C. Ryrie, *Basic Theology* (Chicago, IL: Moody Press, 1999), p. 449.

7. Socinianism

The Reformation was met with skepticism from various sources. One movement that was especially critical of the Reformers' emphasis on the work of the Ruach HaKodesh is called Socinianism. The doctrine was developed in the 16th century by Faustus Socinus (1539-1604).

Socinus taught among the Polish Brethren of the Minor Reformed Church of Poland. He approached the Scriptures from a rationalistic standpoint that essentially ignored the work of the Spirit. When he revisited the discussion on the essence of the triune God, Socinus claimed that the Ruach HaKodesh is a virtue or energy flowing from God to man. Furthermore, he rejected the Nicene concept of *homoousios*, which declared the Father and the Son to be of the same substance. In turn, he introduced a strict unitarianism, which denied the deity of both the Son and the Spirit.

8. Arminianism

Another movement that was equally critical of the Reformers' ideas about the Spirit's work was Arminianism. The theology itself was born out of the Reformation and received its name from the Dutch theologian Jacobus Arminius (1560-1609). In summary, Arminianism downplays the role of the Holy Spirit in the initial salvation of man, emphasizing instead human effort and free will. Salvation and regeneration are viewed as being the work of man rather than of God.

To settle the controversy over Arminianism, a synod was held in the Dutch city of Dordrecht. The council became known as the Synod of Dort. The first meeting was held on November 13, 1618. One hundred fifty-four meetings later, on May 9, 1619, Arminianism was officially condemned, "emphasizing in the strongest possible way the need of the working and power of the Holy Spirit."[3]

---

[3] Ibid., p. 450.

9. Neo-Orthodoxy

Between the Synod of Dort and the 20th century, one could list a few scholars and movements that swept across Christendom, especially the European continent. However, their teachings about the Ruach HaKodesh were not new. Generally speaking, the time was characterized by an increasing liberalism within the church that focused on the fatherhood of God and the brotherhood of man, neglecting both the Son and the Spirit.

Then came the neo-orthodox movement of the 20th century. Claiming to be a new reformation, it arose out of the theology of Karl Barth (1886-1968) in response to the increasing liberal attitude toward the Scriptures and the moral weakness of the church. Neo-orthodox theologians called the church back to the Word of God and were willing to address topics such as sin and humanity's inability to solve its own problems. Yet, they did not correct their predecessors' lax approach to Bible exegesis and continued to interpret the Word allegorically rather than literally. Most neo-orthodox writers denied the personhood of the Holy Spirit. They considered Him a deity insofar as He represents a divine manifestation of God, yet they saw Him as an activity of God rather than a person in the Godhead.

10. Neoliberalism

Barth's neo-orthodoxy was met by what might best be labeled as "neoliberalism." Some theologians of this school shared much of neo-orthodoxy's criticism of classical liberalism. They, too, believed that liberalism had woefully reduced God to the level of humanity. However, they wondered if Barth and his successors had gone too far in their rejection of this theology. Hence, they neither wanted to return to classical liberalism nor to neo-orthodoxy but introduced a theology that included what they considered to be advancements in philosophy, the social sciences, and the natural sciences, as well as other religions. The result was a doctrine that attributed to Messiah a special role in the economy of salvation while at the same time allowing other religions into the teaching of the church.

To summarize the neoliberalism of the 20th century, the doctrine denied the Trinity and saw the Holy Spirit as a "function of God without possessing any distinct quality of personality."[4]

11. Pentecostalism

The Pentecostal movement is often traced back to the Azusa Street Revival of 1906, a meeting that took place in Los Angeles, California. Those who attended the meeting claimed to have become witnesses of unique spiritual experiences, such as physical healings and the "speaking in tongues." Yet, Pentecostals believe that their movement started in Acts 2, when the Holy Spirit fell on the believers in Jerusalem and thus birthed the church. They see the Montanists of the 2nd century as people who tried to carry on the legacy, albeit in a legalistic way. They also consider John Wesley, the 18th century founder of the Methodist Church, as one of their own—and maybe rightly so. In a journal entry for August 15, 1750, Wesley wrote:

> By reflecting on an odd book which I had read in this journey, 'The general delusion of Christians with regard to prophecy,' I was fully convinced of what I had long suspected; 1. That the *Montanists*, in the second and third centuries, were real scriptural Christians; and 2. That the grand reason why the miraculous gifts were so soon withdrawn, was, not only that faith and holiness were well-nigh lost, but that dry, formal, orthodox men, began even then to ridicule whatever gifts they had not themselves, and to decry them all, as either madness or imposture.[5]

Ryrie builds on Wesley's observations when he concludes that "modern Pentecostalism is a reaction to the sterility that began to characterize the established churches in the modern era."[6]

---

[4] Ryrie, *Basic Theology*, p. 452.

[5] John Whitehead, *The Life of the REV. John Wesley, M.A. to Which Is Prefixed, Some Account of His Ancestors and Relation. to Which Is Subjoined an Appendix, 2 Vols* (Dublin, Ireland: John Jones, 1906) Vol. 2, p. 256.

[6] Ryrie, *Basic Theology*, p. 452.

The Pentecostal movement of the 20th century grew rapidly and led to the Charismatic revival of the 1960s and 1970s. In summary, Pentecostalism holds to the view that there are three works of grace: The new birth is the first work of grace. It is followed by sanctification, the second work of grace. The third work of grace is Spirit baptism, which enables the believer to live a Spirit-filled life. The empowerment by the Spirit manifests itself in spiritual gifts, such as the "speaking in tongues" and divine healing. Pentecostalism emphasizes these experiential gifts of the Ruach HaKodesh.

C. Questions and Study Suggestions

Question 1: After studying the false views on the Ruach HaKodesh, discuss the struggles of the early church in light of what you have read in this chapter. Has the study of heresies changed your view of the importance of studying historic developments?

Question 2: On page 5, we mentioned modalism. What is the best way of avoiding modalism?

Question 3: On page 9, we briefly discussed the *filioque* controversy. More will be said about it in a later chapter. From the information that was given so far, what is the controversy about and why is it relevant?

Study Suggestion: Complete the list on the next page.

Views of the Trinity	
Modalism	Founder: Later proponents: Content: God is
Arianism	Represented by: Content: God is
Tritheism	Founders: Content: God is

Chapter II

The Person of the Ruach HaKodesh

The condensed history of pneumatology in the previous chapter shows that the church struggled with two key factors regarding the Holy Spirit: His true and proper deity and His personality (or personhood).

One of the difficulties the church faced is how to determine if the Ruach HaKodesh is distinct from God the Father because the Father Himself is רוּחַ (*ruach*), meaning "spirit." This Hebrew term may be translated as "breath," "wind," "spirit," and "breeze." The Greek equivalent of the word is *pneuma*. Within the Hebrew Scriptures, the term "Ruach HaKodesh" is employed only eleven times. The word "ruach," however, is found 387 times. This shows the importance of looking at each verse carefully to see who or what is meant when the term is used. Only then is it possible to develop a clearer understanding of the deity and personality of the Holy Spirit.

After studying the names and titles of the Ruach HaKodesh, this chapter presents several Scriptures that prove His distinct personality.

A. Names and Titles

The Ruach HaKodesh has several names and titles in the Scriptures. Some designations relate Him to the Father, others to the Son, and again others are used in relation to the Spirit Himself. The following is a list of these titles and names and the verses where they may be found.

1. Names and Titles in Relation to the Father

- The Spirit of God (*Ruach Elohim* in Gen. 1:2; *Pneuma Theou* in Mt. 3:16; Rom. 8:9, 14; I Cor. 3:16; I Pet. 4:14)
- The Spirit of Jehovah (*Ruach Yahweh* in Jdg. 3:10; Isa. 11:2; 63:14)
- The Spirit of the Lord (*Pneuma Kyriou* in Lk. 4:18; Acts 5:9; 8:39)
- My Spirit (Gen. 6:3; Zech. 4:6)
- His Spirit (Num. 11:29, Isa. 48:16)
- Your Spirit (Ps. 139:7)
- The Spirit of the Lord Jehovah (*Ruach Adonai Yahweh* in Isa. 61:1)
- His Holy Spirit (Isa. 63:10-11)
- The Spirit of your Father (Mt. 10:20)
- The Spirit of Him (Rom. 8:11)
- The Spirit of our God (I Cor. 6:11)
- The Spirit of the Living God (II Cor. 3:3)

2. Names and Titles in Relation to the Son

- The Spirit of Messiah (Rom. 8:9, I Pet. 1:11)
- The Spirit of Yeshua (Acts 16:6-7)
- The Spirit of His Son (Gal. 4:6)
- The Spirit of Yeshua the Messiah (Phil. 1:19)

3. Names and Titles in Relation to the Ruach Himself

- The Spirit (I Cor. 2:10)
- Holy Spirit (Ps. 51:11; Mt. 1:20; Mk. 13:11; Lk. 11:13; 12:12; Jn. 14:26; Acts 1:5; 13:4)
- The Spirit of truth (Jn. 14:17; 15:26; 16:13; I Jn. 4:6; 5:7)
- The Comforter (Jn. 14:16, 26; 15:26; 16:7)
- The Spirit of promise (Acts 1:4-5; 2:33; Eph. 1:13)
- The Spirit of wisdom (Ex. 31:3; Eph. 1:17)
- The Spirit of justice (Isa. 4:4)

- ✡ The Spirit of burning (Isa. 4:4)
- ✡ The Spirit of wisdom and understanding (Isa. 11:2)
- ✡ The Spirit of counsel and might (Isa. 11:2)
- ✡ The Spirit of knowledge and of the fear of the Lord (Isa. 11:2)
- ✡ The Spirit of grace and of supplication (Zech. 12:10)
- ✡ The Spirit of holiness (Rom. 1:4)
- ✡ The Spirit of life (Rom. 8:2)
- ✡ The Spirit of adoption (Rom. 8:15)
- ✡ The Lord the Spirit (II Cor. 3:18)
- ✡ The Spirit of faith (II Cor. 4:13)
- ✡ One Spirit (Eph. 4:4)
- ✡ Eternal Spirit (Heb. 9:14)
- ✡ The Spirit of grace (Heb. 10:29)
- ✡ The Spirit of glory (I Pet. 4:14)
- ✡ The Holy One (I Jn. 2:20)
- ✡ Seven Spirits (Rev. 1:4; 3:1)

B. The Personality of the Ruach HaKodesh

There are many references to the Ruach HaKodesh both in the Hebrew Scriptures and in the New Testament, some of which were included in the list above. However, not everyone interprets these references as proof that the Spirit is a person who is distinct from the Father and the Son. They rather view Him as an energy or power or mode of God. It is true that the Hebrew Scriptures often present the Ruach as impersonal wind, breath, or fire. Some of the names and symbols of the Spirit are themselves impersonal. This can even be seen in the New Testament, in verses such as John 20:22, where He is a breath; in John 3:5-8, where He is a wind; in Acts 1:8, where He is a power; in Acts 2:1-4, where He is a fire; and in John 7:38-39, where He is described as water. Furthermore, the Ruach HaKodesh is not always associated with the Father and the Son, as can be seen in I Thessalonians 3:11. Lastly, grammatically, the word most often used in the Greek language in association with the Spirit, *pneuma*, is a neuter noun.

All these points may explain why some do not believe that the Ruach HaKodesh is a person. Yet, a Scripture-based pneumatology proves that He indeed has all characteristics and attributes that define personhood. He is a person in the same sense that the Father is a person and the Son is a person, and He has the same deity as they do. Such a biblical view is essential to the teaching of the Trinity. It is also essential to the believer's life. Hence, in order to develop a correct pneumatology, it is important to study the personality of the Ruach HaKodesh.

1. The Ruach Possesses the Characteristics of a Person

The historical overview of the false views of pneumatology at the beginning of this work shows that the church at large has failed to properly define the personality of the Ruach HaKodesh. Both ancient and contemporary scholars have wrestled with either the divinity or the personhood of the Holy Spirit or with both. A biblical pneumatology rests on the belief that the Holy Spirit is neither a presence nor a power, but a person of the triune Godhead.

Personality (or personhood) is defined as the quality or state of being a person. A person, in turn, is characterized by possessing intellect, emotion, and will. The following paragraphs show that, according to the Scriptures, the Ruach HaKodesh possesses all three of these attributes.

a. Intellect

Isaiah 11:2 declares that the Ruach HaKodesh has knowledge and wisdom and provides counsel and understanding. John 14:26 says that He teaches the believers and brings to remembrance all that Yeshua has said. In John 15:26 and Romans 8:16, the Spirit bears witness of the Messiah. Romans 8:27 speaks of His mind. According to I Corinthians 2:10-13, the Ruach knows the thoughts of God and teaches truth. And finally, in Ephesians 1:17, it is the Spirit who gives wisdom and revelation in the knowledge of God.

All seven verses clearly show that the Spirit of God possesses intellect, the first mark of personality.

b. Emotion

Isaiah 63:10 shows that the Holy Spirit of God has the ability to grieve. Romans 15:30 says that He can love. Ephesians 4:30 repeats that He experiences grief, and I Thessalonians 5:19 says that He can be quenched.

These three verses clearly show that the Ruach HaKodesh possesses emotions, the second mark of personhood.

c. Will

Throughout the book of Acts, the Ruach HaKodesh is portrayed as actively guiding Paul and the apostles, sometimes in rather dramatic ways. Acts 16:6-10 is one example of this leading. Paul and his companions were traveling through Asia Minor (modern-day Turkey) because the Spirit had forbidden them to preach the word in the province of Asia. When they tried to enter Bithynia, the Spirit again stopped them. Hence, the passage shows that the Ruach can forbid things. In I Corinthians 12:11, He also distributes the gifts as He wills.

These two passages clearly show that the Ruach HaKodesh possesses will, the third mark of personhood.

2. The Ruach HaKodesh Performs the Works of a Person

Personality, or personhood, is not only defined by certain attributes, but also by the ability to perform works and actions. As will be seen, the Scriptures give multiple examples of actions performed by the Holy Spirit of God, thus providing perceptible and conclusive evidence for His personality.

a. He Creates

According to Genesis 1:2, the Spirit of God participated in creation as He *moved upon the face of the waters*. It is noteworthy that the second verse of the Hebrew Scriptures introduced the Rauch HaKodesh. Yet, in rabbinic theology, the expression is interpreted as referring to the spirit of King

Messiah.[7] Psalm 33:6-9 confirms the Spirit's involvement in the creation of the heavens and earth.

The fact that the Ruach HaKodesh is able to create proves that He is a person.

b. He Restrains Sin

According to Genesis 6:3, God's Holy Spirit strives against sin. The verse declares God's judgment of the intermarriage between the fallen angels and women. With the words *And Jehovah said*, the oracle of judgment is introduced. The verse goes on to say, *My spirit shall not strive with man for ever*. The Hebrew word for "strive" is *yadon*, which is a *hapax-legomenon*, a word that appears only once in the entire Bible. If the meaning is "to strive," from the Hebrew root *din*, then it means "striving" in the sense of restraining sin; the Spirit was striving in the sense of restraining sin through the preaching of Enoch and Noah. However, if the meaning of *yadon* is "to remain," from the Hebrew root *danan*, then it means the spirit of life, which God breathed into man, will not remain in man forever. The use of the Hebrew word *olam*, translated here as "forever," means that God will not allow the race to continue forever.

In either case, the message of Genesis 6:3 in relation to pneumatology is that the Ruach HaKodesh strives against sin. This action proves His personality.

c. He Empowers

In Zechariah 4:6, God declares that He accomplishes His purposes and goals not by human might or power, but by His Spirit. In the context of Zechariah 4, He promises that the Ruach would enable or empower Zerubbabel to rebuild the Temple.

In relation to pneumatology, the verse shows the active involvement and work of the Ruach. This action proves that He is a person.

---

[7] For a thorough analysis of this verse, please see the author's *Ariel's Bible Commentary: The Book of Genesis* (San Antonio, TX: Ariel Ministries, 2010).

d. He Teaches

Two verses portray the Holy Spirit as a teacher. The first verse is Nehemiah 9:20, according to which God the Father gave His people His "good Spirit" to instruct them. In the second verse, John 14:26,[8] Yeshua promises His disciples that the Father would send the Holy Spirit, that He may teach them all things and remind them of everything Yeshua has said to them.

e. He Comforts

According to John 14:26, the Father will send His Ruach not only for the purpose of teaching His people, but also for the purpose of comforting them. This can be seen in the word translated by the ASV as "Comforter." The Greek word here is *Parakletos*, which may also be rendered as "Advocate," "Intercessor," and "Helper." Literally, it means "called to one's aid." The action of comforting shows that the Ruach HaKodesh is a person.

f. He Guides and Leads

Two verses speak of the Spirit's work of guiding or leading God's people. The first verse is John 16:13. Here, Yeshua promises that the Spirit of truth will come to guide the disciples into all truth. The second verse is Romans 8:14, which states that only the children of God are being led by the Spirit.

g. He Convicts

In John 16:7-8, Yeshua comforts His disciples, who are filled with sorrow over His words. Having told them that He would go to the Father, He responds to their grief by stating that He must leave in order for the Spirit to come. This Spirit is needed to *convict the world in respect of sin, and of righteousness, and of judgment.* The work of conviction confirms that the Ruach HaKodesh is a person.

---

[8] The material cited from John 14-16 comes from the Upper Room Discourse, which is addressed to Messiah's apostles. So, some items are limited to the apostles, while others are applicable to all believers. Context alone determines which is applicable to whom.

h. He Testifies and Witnesses

Three verses speak of the Holy Spirit's work of testifying or witnessing to people. The first verse to consider is John 15:26. God's Spirit, called here *Pneuma tes aletheias,* "the Spirit of truth," will testify about the Messiah. The second verse is Acts 20:23. Here, Paul says that the Ruach testifies unto him in every city, warning that imprisonment and afflictions are awaiting him. The third verse is Romans 8:16, in which Paul speaks the following comforting words: *The Spirit himself bears witness with our spirit, that we are children of God.*

Bearing witness and testifying are actions that clearly prove the personhood of the Ruach HaKodesh.

i. He Issues Orders

Again, three verses speak of the Spirit's action of giving commands. According to Acts 8:29, the Ruach ordered Philip to approach the chariot of the Ethiopian. In Acts 13:2, He commanded the church of Antioch to set apart for Him Barnabas and Paul for the work to which He has called them. Finally, in Acts 16:7, He forbade Paul and his companions to enter Bithynia.

The last verse especially shows not only the Spirit's will, but also His action of issuing orders. Both will and action prove that He is a person.

j. He Performs Miracles

The book of Acts portrays the Ruach HaKodesh as performing miracles. In Acts 8, He ordered Philip to share the gospel with a man from Ethiopia who, while riding in his chariot, was reading from Isaiah. After the man had become a believer and was baptized, the Spirit removed Philip and carried him away (Acts 8:39).

k. He Sends

Acts 13:4 states: *So they, being sent forth by the Holy Spirit, went down to Seleucia; and from thence they sailed to Cyprus.* The action of sending someone proves the Spirit's personality.

l. He Speaks

There are four verses that report on the Spirit's action of speaking. Two verses record words He said to specific people. The first verse is the aforementioned Acts 13:2, in which the Ruach commands the church of Antioch to set apart for Him Barnabas and Paul. The second verse is Acts 21:11, where Paul quotes the Spirit as saying, *So shall the Jews at Jerusalem bind the man that owns this girdle, and shall deliver him into the hands of the Gentiles.* The two other verses show a different kind of speaking. In Galatians 4:6, the Spirit prays to the Father on behalf of the believers. The verse states: *And because ye are sons, God sent forth the Spirit of his Son into our hearts, crying, Abba, Father.* First Timothy 4:1 makes a more general statement about the Spirit's ability to speak, declaring, *But the Spirit says expressly, that in later times some shall fall away from the faith, giving heed to seducing spirits and doctrines of demons.*

The ability to utter words is a clear indication that the Spirit has the attributes of a person.

m. He Prays and Intercedes

Romans 8:26 reiterates the fact that the Spirit prays on behalf of God's people. It states: *And in like manner the Spirit also helps our infirmity: for we know not how to pray as we ought; but the Spirit himself makes intercession for us with groanings which cannot be uttered.*

Praying and interceding on behalf of believers shows an independence in action that goes beyond being a power or a presence. It proves that the Spirit of God is more than a power. He is a person.

3. The Ruach HaKodesh as Personal Object of Faith

Believers who view the Godhead as a trinity regard the Ruach HaKodesh as an object of their faith. From the Scriptures, they know that it is possible for them to sin against the Holy Spirit (Isa. 63:10, Mt. 12:32). They can blaspheme Him (Mt. 12:31), lie to Him (Acts 5:3), resist Him (Acts 7:51), grieve Him (Eph. 4:30), and disrespect Him (Heb. 10:29). But they can also revere Him (Ps. 51:11), obey Him (Acts 10:19-21), and love Him (Rom. 15:30). Understanding that they can respond to the Ruach HaKodesh in these ways makes the believers ascribe certain attributes to the Spirit that are, in fact, based on His personality.

4. Unusual Grammar in Relation to the Ruach HaKodesh

As previously mentioned, the Greek word most often used in the New Testament for the Holy Spirit, *pneuma*, is of the neuter gender. The rules of grammar would require neuter pronouns in connection with this noun. The Spirit would be referred to as an "it." However, in several instances, the masculine pronouns are found, not only in most English translations, but also in the original Greek text.

For example, John 15:26 says: *But when the Comforter is come, whom I will send unto you from the Father, even the Spirit [pneuma] of truth, which proceeds from the Father, he [ekeinos] shall bear witness of me.* The neuter *pneuma* is followed by the masculine demonstrative personal pronoun *ekeinos*, meaning "that one" or "he." The same masculine personal pronoun is also found in John 16:8, 13, and 14, and every time it refers to the neuter *pneuma*.

In Ephesians 1:14, the masculine relative pronoun *ho*, meaning "who," is used, again referring back to *pneuma*, found in Ephesians 1:13.

Occasionally, the Scriptures replace *pneuma* with *parakletos*, meaning "advocate" or "helper." Unlike the neuter *pneuma*, *parakletos* is of the masculine gender (Jn. 14:16, 26).

Lastly, a word on how the Spirit refers to Himself. In Acts 13:2, He is quoted as saying, *Separate **me** Barnabas and Saul for the work whereunto I have called them.* In the Greek text, the "me" is *moi* (also transliterated as *moy*). The "I" is included in the Greek verb *proskeklēmai*. The use of personal pronouns indicates self-consciousness, another criterion for personhood.

In summary, the nouns and pronouns in the masculine gender as well as the fact that the Ruach HaKodesh speaks of Himself in the first person mark His separate and personal distinctness.

5. Distinction Between the Spirit's Power and His Person

The following five verses distinguish between the Spirit's power and His person:

1. Luke 1:35: *And the angel answered and said unto her, The Holy Spirit shall come upon you, and the power of the Most High shall overshadow you: wherefore also the holy thing which is begotten shall be called the Son of God.* The person in this verse is the Holy Spirit and the Most High God. The power is seen in His overshadowing the woman in order to generate her egg and to produce the sinless Messiah.

2. Luke 4:14a: *And Yeshua returned in the power of the Spirit into Galilee.* The person here is the Messiah. The power comes from the Ruach HaKodesh. In Greek, the word translated as "power" is *dunamis*, a term that implies the miraculous. It is the Holy Spirit who empowers Yeshua to perform signs and wonders.

3. Acts 10:38b: *God anointed [Yeshua] with the Holy Spirit and with power.* This verse clearly distinguishes between the person of the Ruach HaKodesh and His power. God anointed Yeshua both with the person of the Holy Spirit and with power.

4. Romans 15:13: *Now the God of hope fill you with all joy and peace in believing, that ye may abound in hope, in the power of the Holy Spirit.* In this verse, the person is God. The power mentioned is that of the Holy Spirit.

5. I Corinthians 2:4: *And my speech and my preaching were not in persuasive words of wisdom, but in demonstration of the Spirit and of power.* The verse distinguishes between the Spirit and His power. Paul's message and preaching were not accompanied by clever, wise words, but by a display of the person of the Holy Spirit and of His power.

C. Questions and Study Suggestions

Question: The Ruach HaKodesh has all characteristics and attributes that define personhood. Why is this fact important?

Study Suggestion 1: On a piece of paper, list from memory some of the proofs of the Spirit's personhood.

Study Suggestion 2: Now complete the list by going through the teaching in this chapter. Which of the proofs is the most convincing argument for you personally that the Ruach HaKodesh is indeed a person in the same sense that the Father is a person and the Son is a person?

Chapter III
The Deity of the Ruach HaKodesh

In the previous chapter, the personality of the Ruach HaKodesh has been established. But what sort of person is He? Is He finite or infinite? Is He man or God? In this chapter, we will confirm that He is God.

Historically, the Spirit's deity has been a principal doctrine of the church since the Arian controversy was settled by the Council of Nicaea, in the year 325. The Scriptures provide ample proof for this doctrine by ascribing to the Spirit divine titles, attributes, and works, and by associating Him with other members of the Trinity.

A. Divine Titles

Rather than attributing proper names to the Ruach HaKodesh, the authors of the Bible used a combination of descriptive titles and a wide variety of symbols relating to the Spirit. Of these titles and symbols, there are four appellations that show His deity.

1. Holy Spirit

The title "Holy Spirit" describes both the deity and the personality of the Ruach HaKodesh.

The adjective "holy" distinguishes Him from all other spirits, who, unlike Him, are created beings. It therefore emphasizes His deity.

The word "Spirit" declares His special manner and order of existence. Sometimes, He is just called "Spirit." Other times, qualifiers are added to the word "Spirit," such as "of God," "of Yeshua," or "of truth." The additions express His properties or His relationships to other persons. Therefore, the word "Spirit" denotes His person and describes His essence: He is of a pure, immaterial nature.

2. God

Several times, the Scriptures call the Holy Spirit "God." One example is Acts 5:3-4, which states:

> *³ But Peter said, Ananias, why has Satan filled your heart to lie to the Holy Spirit, and to keep back part of the price of the land? ⁴ While it remained, did it not remain your own? and after it was sold, was it not in your power? How is it that you have conceived this thing in your heart? You have not lied unto men, but unto God.*

Peter rebuked Ananias for lying not unto men, but unto God the Holy Spirit. Ephesians 2:22 is another example of passages where the Spirit is called God.

3. Lord

In II Corinthians 3:18, Paul refers to the Spirit as *kurios*, Greek for "Lord": *But we all . . . are transformed into the same image from glory to glory, even as from the Lord the Spirit.* Paul usually speaks of Yeshua as *kurios* (e.g. I Cor. 1:3). Sometimes, in quotations from the Hebrew Scriptures, he also calls the Father *kurios* (e.g. I Cor. 3:20). Here, now, he refers to the Holy Spirit as *kurios*, thus making Him equal in deity.

4. Another Comforter

In John 14:16, Yeshua promises His disciples: *I will pray the Father, and he shall give you another Comforter, that he may be with you for ever.* The title "another comforter" is unique in that it does not involve the word "spirit." It is also unique because the Greek adjective *allon*, translated as "another," means "another of the same kind." The Greek word for "comforter" is *parakletos*, which means "helper," "assistant," and "aider." In other words, Yeshua promised His disciples to send another helper of the same kind as He was. If the Messiah is God, then the Spirit is also God. This divine comforter was supposed to take Yeshua's place with the apostles and be with them forever.

B. Divine Attributes

The Scriptures ascribe many properties to God that are taken to be part of His nature. He is described as being almighty, omniscient, omnipresent, good, eternal, and so forth. The following survey will show that the Ruach HaKodesh possesses at least seven attributes that only God has.

1. Omnipotence

The term "omnipotence" refers to God's quality of having unlimited power. The Holy Spirit's omnipotence is seen in His work of creation (e.g., Job 33:4; Ps. 104:30). It is also seen in Zechariah 4:6, where the Spirit's power is contrasted with man's limitations.

2. Omnipresence

The term "omnipresence" refers to God's ability to be everywhere at all times. In Psalm 139:7-10, David asks a rhetoric question:

> [7] *Whither shall I go from your Spirit?*
> *Or whither shall I flee from your presence?*
> [8] *If I ascend up into heaven, you are there:*
> *If I make my bed in Sheol, behold, you are there.*
> [9] *If I take the wings of the morning,*
> *And dwell in the uttermost parts of the sea;*
> [10] *Even there shall your hand lead me,*
> *And your right hand shall hold me.*

David's words state positively that there is no spot nor point from which the Ruach HaKodesh is excluded. This omnipresence proves His deity.

3. Omniscience

The term "omniscience" refers to the state of having total knowledge of everything, an attribute that only God possesses.

Isaiah 40:13 asks: *Who has directed the Spirit of Jehovah, or being his counsellor has taught him?* The obvious answer is "no one." The Holy Spirit is omniscient. This makes Him God.

In I Corinthians 2:6-12, Paul speaks of a mystery that *eye saw not, and ear heard not, and which entered not into the heart of man* (v. 9), things that God revealed to those who love Him *through the Spirit: for the Spirit searches all things, yea, the deep things of God* (v. 10). The Spirit knows the mysteries only God knows. His knowledge and God's knowledge are the same. Like God, He is omniscient. Hence, He must be God.

4. Holiness

The Spirit's holiness is seen in the Parable of the Persistent Friend (Lk. 11:5-13). The parable teaches two lessons using a Jewish method of reasoning called *kal v'chomer*, which means "from the lesser to the greater." The first lesson is that if an unwilling person finally concedes because of persistence, how much more is it true of God, who is willing to give? Second, if an evil father gives good gifts, how much more will God the Father, who is the epitome of good, give? The application is: *If ye then, being evil, know how to give good gifts unto your children, how much more shall <your> heavenly Father give the Holy Spirit to them that ask him?* (Lk. 11:13). The promise to the apostles was that a believer who truly wished to be indwelled by the Spirit could seek God in prayer, and God would honor that prayer by giving him the Holy Spirit.[9]

In the context of this study, it is important to note that Yeshua spoke distinctively of the Holy Spirit (v. 13). By assigning to the Spirit the attribute of holiness, Yeshua acknowledged Him as God.

---

[9] This prayer was valid for believers before Acts 2, when not all were necessarily indwelled by the Spirit. Since the events of Acts 2, however, the moment a person believes, he is automatically indwelled by the Holy Spirit. Therefore, the prayer that the Father would send the Spirit is obsolete. Persistent prayer, on the other hand, is still relevant.

5. Eternity

There are two major theological understandings of eternity. The first view is that God exists endlessly outside of time. The second view is that His existence extends infinitely backwards and forwards through every moment of time. Both views agree that God has always and will always exist. They disagree about whether that existence is in time or outside of time. In either case, the attribute of eternality can only apply to God.

The writer of Hebrews asks in 9:13-14:

> [13] *For if the blood of goats and bulls, and the ashes of a heifer sprinkling them that have been defiled, sanctify unto the cleanness of the flesh:* [14] *how much more shall the blood of Messiah, who through the eternal Spirit offered himself without blemish unto God, cleanse your conscience from dead works to serve the living God?*

Here, the Ruach HaKodesh is called *Pneumatos aioniou*, "eternal Spirit." Since only God is eternal, the Spirit must be God.

6. Life

Life in any form (be it spiritual or physical) originates from God. Eternal life can only be given by one who Himself is eternal. Life, therefore, reveals a divine attribute.

Romans 8:2 states: *For the law of the Spirit of life in Messiah Yeshua made me free from the law of sin and of death.* In this verse, Paul contrasts three things: the law of the Spirit in opposition to the law of sin, life in opposition to death, and freedom in opposition to captivity. Paul then specifies who the Spirit is by calling Him in Greek *Pneumatos tes zoes*, meaning "Spirit of life." The Spirit possesses *zoe*, "life." As the Spirit of life, He can share His gift of life with creation. He bestows eternal life in Messiah Yeshua and makes man a partaker in the divine life. Because the Spirit has eternal life, He is God.

7. Truth

Titus 1:2 mentions that God is *apseudes*, "free of falsehood." This means God cannot lie. It goes against His nature, which possesses no falsehood.

His essence is sheer truth. He is truth. Both the Son and the Spirit also hold the divine attribute of truth. In John 14:6, Yeshua called Himself *the truth*. As to the Spirit, the Scriptures call Him *Pneuma tes aletheias*, or the "Spirit of truth," in John 14:17, 16:13, and I John 4:6. In I John 5:6, it says that *to Pneuma estin he aletheia*, "the Spirit is the truth."[10] Hence, He is God.

C. Divine Works

Another piece of evidence of the Spirit's deity is that He accomplishes works only God can perform. There are six works of God to be considered.

1. Creation

Creation is a work that only God can do. Yet, it is stated in Genesis 1:2 that the Spirit participated in the work of creation: *And the earth was waste and void; and darkness was upon the face of the deep: and the Spirit of God moved upon the face of the waters.*

Job 26:13a specifies what the Spirit's participation in creation looked like: *By his Spirit the heavens are garnished.*

In Job 27:3, Job attributes life-creating power to the Spirit, stating, *For my life is yet whole in me, And the spirit of God is in my nostrils.*

Elihu confirms Job's words in more direct terms when he says in Job 33:4, *The Spirit of God has made me, And the breath of the Almighty gives me life.*

The psalmist says in Psalm 33:6, *By the word of Jehovah were the heavens made, And all the host of them by the breath* [ruach] *of his mouth.*

The final verse to consider is Psalm 104:30: *You send forth your Spirit* [ruach]*, they are created; And you renew the face of the ground.*

These verses prove that the Spirit does the work of creation, which means that He is God.

---

[10] Some translations (such as the ASV, the NASB, and the ESV) add this phrase to verse 7, instead of verse 6.

2. He Generated Messiah

According to Luke 1:35, the Ruach HaKodesh generated the Messiah:

> *And the angel answered and said unto her, The Holy Spirit shall come upon thee, and the power of the Most High shall overshadow thee: wherefore also the holy thing which is begotten shall be called the Son of God.*

This work of generating the Messiah was a creative act performed by the Spirit. He who overshadowed Miriam (Mary) was the same as He who brooded over the waters generating life in Genesis 1:2.

Because of what is said in Luke 1:35, a common misconception has arisen which must be dispelled. Some teach that the virgin birth was necessary to keep the Messiah from inheriting the sin nature. This teaching is based upon the false assumption that the sin nature is transmitted only through the father. However, the sin nature is transmitted through both the father and the mother, and nowhere in the Bible does it ever say that the sin nature is transmitted through the male seed. So, what protected the Messiah from inheriting the sin nature of Miriam? The overshadowing work of the Holy Spirit. By choosing to generate the Messiah this way, God would fulfill His prophecies in the Hebrew Bible—hinted at in Genesis 3:15 and clearly stated in Isaiah 7:14: The Messiah would be conceived in the womb of a virgin, and His birth would provide Him with a unique credential.

Another false teaching is that Miriam's egg was not produced by her ovaries but implanted by the Holy Spirit. This would have made her a surrogate mother and is not the teaching of the text or the Bible as a whole. There had to be a biological connection between Adam, Abraham, Isaac, Jacob, Judah, David, and Yeshua for Him to be truly "the seed" prophesied by the Hebrew Scriptures. So, Miriam's egg was generated by the Holy Spirit and what protected the conceived seed was the Spirit's overshadowing work.

The Greek verb which is translated into English as "shall overshadow" is *episkiasei*. It is used in the New Testament of God's overshadowing presence, which always brings His plan to pass. The word is used in those passages that describe Yeshua's transfiguration (Mt. 17:5; Mk. 9:7; Lk.

9:34). In Luke 1:35, it describes the creative power of the Ruach HaKodesh, which will overshadow Miriam in order for her to conceive a child.

The angel went on to explain that because of the overshadowing work of the Holy Spirit, He who was conceived would be holy—that is, sinless. Furthermore, He would be called *the Son of God* (Lk. 1:35). This Messianic title is based on Psalm 2:7-12 and Proverbs 30:4.

In the context of pneumatology, Luke 1:35 teaches that the Holy Spirit generated the Messiah. This proves His deity.

3. Inspiration

According to II Peter 1:21, the Holy Spirit inspired men to write the Scriptures. The context of the verse, which is II Peter 1:19-21, reveals some important information:

> [19] *And we have the word of prophecy made more sure; whereunto ye do well that ye take heed, as unto a lamp shining in a dark place, until the day dawn, and the day-star arise in your hearts:* [20] *knowing this first, that no prophecy of scripture is of private interpretation.* [21] *For no prophecy ever came by the will of man: but men spoke from God, being moved by the Holy Spirit.*

In verse 19, Peter states that the Hebrew Scriptures are *the word of prophecy made more sure*. They are a surer confirmation of God's truth than any experience. Although Peter did have a great and remarkable experience when he witnessed the transfiguration, the written Word of God is still a more valid source of authority than anybody's experience.

Having addressed the sure word of prophecy, the written Word of God, in verses 20-21, Peter deals with the source of such prophecy. He presents it both negatively and positively. Negatively, verse 20 states that no prophecy *is of private interpretation*. This does not mean that individual believers do not have the ability or authority to interpret Scripture. The word used here does not mean "interpretation" in the sense of interpreting Scripture; rather, it means "disclosure." The point is that no prophecy is of "private disclosure." Peter is dealing with the source of prophecy to man and not with the interpretation of the Scriptures by man. Negatively, the source of prophecy is not of a man's private disclosure. It did not have its source in man.

Positively, verse 21 says that prophecy has its source in God because *no prophecy ever came by the will of man*. Prophecy originated with God; it did not originate with man: *men spoke from God, being moved by the Holy Spirit*. Literally, the Greek word used here for "moved," *pheromenoi*, means to be "borne along." The same Greek word is used of a ship that is being blown along by the wind. The prophets who recorded Scripture were blown by the wind of the Holy Spirit. Scriptures are the revelation of God through men by the compelling urge of the Holy Spirit.

It is true that it was men who recorded Scripture, but these Scriptures were not disclosed from within the prophets; they were the disclosure of the Holy Spirit. The Holy Spirit is the source of inspiration. The Holy Spirit is the source of revelation. Therefore, using the personalities of the prophets, their own writing styles, and their own languages, the Holy Spirit, by "bearing them along," had them write exactly what is written—word for word. The fact that He was the source of inspiration makes Him God.

4. Regeneration

Regeneration is an act of God by which He imparts to men a form of life, which by nature they cannot have because it is not inherent within them. Since the fall, the human soul is dead in sin from the moment of conception. When God regenerates men, He brings to life the souls of dead sinners. He changes the disposition of their soul by bringing it to life and making it holy. "Regeneration" is the theological term for what Yeshua referred to as "new birth" (Jn. 3:3, 8).

According to I Peter 1:3, God the Father is the source of spiritual life: *Blessed be the God and Father of our Lord Yeshua Messiah, who according to his great mercy begat us again unto a living hope by the resurrection of Yeshua Messiah from the dead*. In this verse, Peter declares that the future aspect regarding the character of a believer's salvation concerns *a living hope*—the hope of heaven. This is a product of God the Father. The means by which these believers have come into the living hope is through the experience of being born again (regeneration). The Greek word for "begat" is *anagennēsas*. It means "to cause to be born." This word is not found in Classical Greek or in the Septuagint and seems to be unique to the New Testament. It occurs twice: here and again in I Peter 1:23. Although the word itself does not appear elsewhere, the concept is found in John 3:1-8, James 1:18, and I John 5:1-4. The basis of the living hope is mercy. In accordance with His compassionate character, God acted with mercy by causing the believers to be born again. All this was made possible by the resurrection of the Messiah from the dead. The life God imparts to the believer is everlasting. John 14:6 explains that Yeshua is the life, meaning He is the expression of this new life. John 3:6, finally, points out the role of the Spirit: *That which is born of the flesh is flesh; and that which is born of the Spirit is spirit*. To be born of the Spirit means to have received from God a new spiritual life. The Holy Spirit gives the new life. He is the imparter of the new life.

Titus 3:5 states: *not by works* done *in righteousness, which we did ourselves, but according to his mercy he saved us, through the washing of regeneration and renewing of the Holy Spirit*. Again, the Holy Spirit is viewed as active participant in the regeneration of the believer. New life is not imparted to men on the basis of works, but according to God's mercy through the renewing of the Holy Spirit. This means that when we are born again by grace through faith, we are washed of sin by the Spirit.

The work of the Spirit in regeneration is another proof of His deity.

6. Impartation of Life

Closely related to regeneration is another divine work: the impartation of life. Regeneration is the impartation of spiritual life and of a new nature to those who are spiritually dead through their trespasses and sins (Eph. 2:1). It is the Holy Spirit who imparts this life, using the Word as an instrument (I Pet. 1:23; Jam. 1:18). In John 6:63, Yeshua says: *It is the spirit that gives life; the flesh profits nothing: the words that I have spoken unto you are spirit, and are life*. His words were hard to understand and accept, and yet to understand and believe is what produces eternal life.

In Romans 8:11, Paul states: *But if the Spirit of him that raised up Yeshua from the dead dwells in you, he that raised up Messiah Yeshua from the dead shall give life also to your mortal bodies through his Spirit that dwells in you*. The Spirit of God the Father raised up the Messiah from the dead. This same Spirit is to give life to our mortal bodies and will raise us up from the dead as He did Yeshua.

The fact that the Spirit has the power to impart life proves His deity.

5. Sanctification

According to II Thessalonians 2:13, the Ruach HaKodesh is involved in the sanctification of the believer. The verse states: *But we are bound to give thanks to God always for you, brethren beloved of the Lord, for that God chose you from the beginning unto salvation in sanctification of the Spirit and belief of the truth.* The term "sanctification" refers to the process of making holy. It is the continued transformation of the believer so that his life eventually mirrors the position he already has in God's eyes.

All three persons of the Trinity play a role in the process of sanctification. According to Ephesians 1:4, the Father elected the believer from before the foundation of the world in order that he would be holy: *even as he chose us in him before the foundation of the world, that we should be holy and without blemish before him in love.*

First Thessalonians 5:23-24 promises that the Father will not fail in bringing about the believer's full sanctification: *And the God of peace himself sanctify you wholly; and may your spirit and soul and body be preserved entire, without blame at the coming of our Lord Yeshua Messiah. Faithful is he that calls you, who will also do it.*

According to Ephesians 5:26, the Son is equally dedicated to effect the believer's purity and holiness: *that he might sanctify it* [the church], *having cleansed it by the washing of water with the word.*

However, it is the Holy Spirit who is especially active in the area of sanctification (II Thess. 2:13), and as this study will show in subsequent chapters, nearly His entire ministry to the believer is related to the believer's sanctification in some way or another. Only God can make the sinner holy. Hence, the Spirit must be God.

D. Equal Associations

Sixteen times the Scriptures relate the Ruach HaKodesh by name with other members of the Trinity. The references may be grouped in the following categories: names that relate the Spirit with Jehovah, names that relate Him with God, names that relate Him with the Son, and names that relate Him with both the Father and the Son.

1. With *YHVH* or *YHWH* (Jehovah)

Two New Testament passages identify the Holy Spirit as Jehovah of the Hebrew Scriptures. The first passage is Acts 28:25-28, and the second passage is Hebrews 10:15-17.

In Acts 28, Paul presented several messages to a body of Jewish leaders in Rome, trying to persuade them concerning the Messiahship of Yeshua. While some believed, others did not. As the Jewish leaders were leaving, Paul responded to their disagreement by giving them one last word, in verses 25b-28, quoting from Isaiah 6:9-10:

> [25b] *Well spoke the Holy Spirit through Isaiah the prophet unto your fathers,* [26] *saying, Go you unto this people, and say, By hearing ye shall hear, and shall in no wise understand; And seeing ye shall see, and shall in no wise perceive:* [27] *For this people's heart is waxed gross, And their ears are dull of hearing, And their eyes they have closed; Lest, haply they should perceive with their eyes, And hear with their ears, And understand with their heart, And should turn again, And I should heal them.* [28] *Be it known therefore unto you, that this salvation of God is sent unto the Gentiles: they will also hear.*

Paul said that it was the Holy Spirit who was behind the words spoken by prophets such as Isaiah, emphasizing the dual authorship of the Bible. The apostle stated that Isaiah's message was originally for Isaiah's generation, but now Paul applied it to his own generation, a nation that disbelieved Yeshua and the apostles. Paul showed that the Gentiles were going to receive Isaiah's message. The salvation by grace through faith in the Messiahship of Yeshua, *this salvation of God*, was now passed on to the

Gentiles. Important for the context of this chapter is that the passage identifies the Holy Spirit of the book of Acts as the Spirit of Jehovah in Isaiah.

The writer of Hebrews does the same in 10:15-17:

> [15] And the Holy Spirit also bears witness to us; for after he has said, [16] This is the covenant that I will make with them After those days, says the Lord: I will put my laws on their heart, And upon their mind also will I write them; then says he, [17] And their sins and their iniquities will I remember no more.

Hebrews 10:16 is a quotation of Jeremiah 31:31-34, and again the New Testament author relates the Holy Spirit to Jehovah of the Hebrew Scriptures.

The two passages show that the authors of the New Testament considered the Holy Spirit to be God.

2. With God

Several passages clearly identify the Holy Spirit as God. In previous chapters, we already looked at two of these passages, Genesis 1:2 and Acts 5:1-4. There are three other sections that need to be considered here: II Samuel 23:2-3, I Corinthians 3:16-17, and I Corinthians 6:19-20.

a. II Samuel 23:2-3

Second Samuel 23:1-7 is commonly referred to as "David's Last Words," a title taken from the opening words of the passage. In verses 2-3, the king equates the Spirit of Jehovah to the God of Israel:

> [2] The Spirit of Jehovah spoke by me, And his word was upon my tongue.
> [3] The God of Israel said, The Rock of Israel spoke to me: One that rules over men righteously, That rules in the fear of God,

b. I Corinthians 3:16-17

This passage shows that the Holy Spirit indwells the church at large, the local church (in this case the one of Corinth), and the individual believer:

> [16] *Know ye not that ye are a temple of God, and that the Spirit of God dwells in you?* [17] *If any man destroys the temple of God, him shall God destroy; for the temple of God is holy, and such are ye.*

The church is a temple of God, and the Spirit of God dwells in the church. The verses clearly identify the Holy Spirit as God.

c. I Corinthians 6:19-20

While in the previous verses Paul spoke to the Corinthian church, in I Corinthians 6:19-20, he speaks to individuals:

> [19] *Or know ye not that your body is a temple of the Holy Spirit which is in you, which ye have from God? and ye are not your own;* [20] *for ye were bought with a price: glorify God therefore in your body.*

Believers are a temple of God in three senses: First, in the sense of being part of the universal church, which the Holy Spirit indwells (Eph. 2:21-22); second, in the sense of being part of a local church which the Holy Spirit indwells (I Cor. 3:16-17); third, the Holy Spirit indwells every individual believer, making him a temple of God as well (I Cor. 6:19-20).

The indwelling and the work of making the believer a temple of God relates the Holy Spirit to God's name, thus proving that He is God.

3. With the Son

Four New Testament passages relate the Ruach HaKodesh with God the Son.

a. Luke 4:18-19

Luke 4:18-19 quotes Isaiah 61:1-2a, which is speaking of the nature and style of the Messiah's ministry at His first coming:

> [1] *The Spirit of the Lord Jehovah is upon me; because Jehovah has anointed me to preach good tidings unto the meek; he has sent me to bind up the broken-hearted, to proclaim liberty to the captives, and the opening of the prison to them that are bound;* [2a] *to proclaim the year of Jehovah's favor,*

In verse 1, Isaiah mentioned three individuals: the *Spirit*, the *Lord Jehovah*, and the pronoun *me*. The "me" refers to the speaker, who is the

Servant of Jehovah, the Messiah, God the Son (Isa. 42:1). The word "Spirit" refers to the Holy Spirit. In the book of Isaiah, the Holy Spirit plays a special role in conjunction with the Messiah. In Isaiah 11:2, He is involved with Messiah's incarnation. In Isaiah 42:1, He anoints the Messiah, a reference to the baptism of Yeshua, when He was anointed by the Holy Spirit. In Isaiah 61:1, the Holy Spirit is also connected with the public ministry of the Messiah.

b. Romans 8:9-10

In Romans 8:9-10, Paul also relates God the Son with the Holy Spirit, stating:

> *⁹ But ye are not in the flesh but in the Spirit, if so be that the Spirit of God dwells in you. But if any man has not the Spirit of Messiah, he is none of his. ¹⁰ And if Messiah is in you, the body is dead because of sin; but the spirit is life because of righteousness.*

c. II Corinthians 3:17-18

Paul again connects the Spirit with the Son in II Corinthians 3:17-18:

> *¹⁷ Now the Lord is the Spirit: and where the Spirit of the Lord is, there is liberty. ¹⁸ But we all, with unveiled face beholding as in a mirror the glory of the Lord, are transformed into the same image from glory to glory, even as from the Lord the Spirit.*

d. Philippians 1:19

In Philippians 1:19, Paul writes: *For I know that this shall turn out to my salvation, through your supplication and the supply of the Spirit of Yeshua Messiah.* Paul clearly relates the Ruach HaKodesh by name with the other members of the Trinity, and in the verses above, especially with God the Son.

4. With the Father and the Son

a. Matthew 3:16-17

At the baptism of Yeshua, the Triune God made His appearance, both visibly and audibly. Matthew described this appearance with the following words:

> *3:16 And Yeshua when he was baptized, went up straightway from the water: and lo, the heavens were opened unto him, and he saw the Spirit of God descending as a dove, and coming upon him; 17 and lo, a voice out of the heavens, saying, This is my beloved Son, in whom I am well pleased.*

God the Son was present in the person of Yeshua, as He visibly *went up straightway from the water*.

The second member of the Trinity, the Holy Spirit, was physically present, appearing in the form of a dove and came upon Yeshua. That this was not an actual dove, nor some ghostly form, is seen in Luke's Gospel, where it says that He *descended in a bodily form, as a dove* (Lk. 3:22).

The final member of the Trinity, God the Father, made His presence known audibly: *Lo, a voice out of heaven, saying, This is my beloved Son, in whom I am well pleased* (Mt. 3:17). The account of the voice out of heaven has a rabbinic background. In Hebrew, this voice is called the *Bat Kol*, which literally means, "daughter of a voice." In rabbinic theology, the voice of the prophets ceased with Malachi. However, while the prophetic voice ended, the voice of God did not, and periodically God spoke a short sentence out of heaven. This was the Bat Kol. While the *Shechinah* glory is a visible manifestation of God, the Bat Kol is audible. What God the Father spoke audibly out of heaven at the baptism of Yeshua was: *This is my beloved Son, in whom I am well pleased* (Mt. 3:17), thus identifying Yeshua as the son mentioned in Psalm 2:12: *Kiss the son, lest he be angry, and ye perish in the way, For his wrath will soon be kindled. Blessed are all they that take refuge in him.* This son is the Messianic Son, God the Son.

At the baptism, two things happened: First, God the Father verbally identified Yeshua as the Messianic Son; and second, the Holy Spirit anointed Him for service.

b. Matthew 28:19

In Matthew 28:19, Yeshua ordered the apostles to make disciples: *Go ye therefore, and make disciples of all the nations, baptizing them into the name of the Father and of the Son and of the Holy Spirit.* Yeshua presented a formula for baptism, saying that it is to be done in the name of all three members of the Trinity. The specificity of this phrase was necessary because baptism was a common Jewish practice, and there were different kinds of baptisms, such as proselyte baptism, John's baptism, etc. To distinguish believer's baptism from other baptisms, this one had to be done in the name of the Father and of the Son and of the Holy Spirit, emphasizing both the unity and trinity of the Godhead. The word "name" is singular, emphasizing unity, and baptizing in the name of three persons emphasizes trinity.

The verse very clearly relates the Holy Spirit to the other members of the Trinity, God the Father and God the Son.

c. I Corinthians 12:4-6

In I Corinthians 12:4-6, the New Testament again relates the Spirit to the Father and the Son, stating:

> *⁴ Now there are diversities of gifts, but the same Spirit. ⁵ And there are diversities of ministrations, and the same Lord. ⁶ And there are diversities of workings, but the same God, who works all things in all.*

In these verses, Paul urged the Corinthians to recognize the rich diversity of the Spirit's gifts in their midst. He listed three divine sources of gifted service in the church: the Spirit, the Lord (meaning the Son), and God (meaning the Father). He could not have used clearer words to connect the Holy Spirit with the other members of the Trinity.

d. II Corinthians 13:14

The final example of how the Scriptures relate the Ruach HaKodesh to the other members of the Trinity is found in Paul's blessing in II Corinthians 13:14: *The grace of the Lord Yeshua Messiah, and the love of God, and the communion of the Holy Spirit, be with you all.* Paul pronounces on the Corinthians the Son's grace, the Father's love, and the Spirit's communion.

The verses relating the Spirit to the other members of the Trinity prove that He is God.

E. THE PROCESSION OF THE RUACH HAKODESH

In western theology, the doctrine of procession teaches that the Ruach HaKodesh eternally proceeds from the Father and the Son. The position is primarily based on John 15:26, where Yeshua made a promise to His disciples, saying: *But when the Comforter is come, whom I will send unto you from the Father, even the Spirit of truth, who proceeds from the Father, he shall bear witness of me.* The implications of the subordinate clause "whom I will send unto you from the Father" has been largely misunderstood and debated throughout church history: Is the notion that the Son "sends" the Spirit qualitatively different than the Spirit "proceeding" from the Father? What are the broader ramifications of this debate?

Historically, the eastern church split from the western church over the question whether the Holy Spirit proceeds from the Father only or from both the Father and the Son. In the year 589, the Synod of Toledo addressed this controversy, and the western church determined that the Spirit proceeds from *both* the Father and the Son, using John 20:22 as support. In that verse, Yeshua breathed on His disciples and said, *Receive ye the Holy Spirit*, implying that the Spirit also proceeds from the Son. In order to articulate this standpoint, the western church added the Latin term *filioque* (for "and from the Son"), which has become a point of contention between the eastern and the western churches. The eastern church left the addition out of her creed, arguing that a procession of the Spirit from both the Father and the Son would subordinate the Spirit. The church held to a view of the Trinity where the Father is the ultimate origin of divinity and the eternal source of the eternal, co-equal natures of the Son and the Spirit.

Alister McGrath explains how this view clashed with the *filioque* idea of the western church:

[Within the context of Eastern theology], it is unthinkable that the Holy Spirit should proceed from the Father and Son. Why? Because it would totally compromise the principle of the Father as the sole origin and source of all divinity. It would amount to affirming that there were two sources of divinity within the one Godhead, with all the internal contradictions and tensions that this would generate. If the Son were to share in the exclusive ability of the Father to be the source of all divinity, this ability would no longer be exclusive. For this reason, the Greek church regarded the western idea of a "double procession" of the Spirit with something approaching stark disbelief.[11]

The discussion about the true nature of the Trinity may seem difficult and theoretical. However, finding the proper definition of the procession of the Holy Spirit will establish and affirm the eternal relationship between the three Persons of the Trinity.

1. The Fact of Procession

In the Psalms, there are five references to God's Ruach. At least two of these references present Him as an active, creative agent: Psalm 33:6 and Psalm 104:29-30. The first verse refers the creation of the hosts of the heavens to the Holy Spirit. In Psalm 104:29-30, the psalmist revisits the topic of creation and says to Jehovah:

> [29] *You hide your face, they* [referring to all created beings mentioned in previous verses] *are troubled; You take away their breath, they die, And return to their dust.* [30] *You send forth your Spirit* [ruach]*, they are created; And you renew the face of the ground.*

The most basic interpretation of these verses is that every living being depends on God's Spirit and His presence. Verse 30 is generally accepted as proof that the Spirit proceeds from the Father.[12] It does not explain what "procession" really means, but it confirms that God the Father is its

---

[11] Alister E. McGrath, *Christian Theology: An Introduction* (Chichester, UK: John Wiley & Sons, 2017), p. 288.

[12] John F. Walvoord, "Chapter II: The Deity of the Holy Spirit," in *The Holy Spirit: A Comprehensive Study of the Person and Work of the Holy Spirit* (ePub Edition; Grand Rapids, MI: Zondervan, 2010).

source or origin. A spirit that can be sent forth must be distinct from the sender. The fact that God's Spirit can create and renew not only shows personality, it proves deity. If this were not so, the verse should read: "You create and renew the face of the ground by your power." In other words, the Spirit sent forth by the Father must be more than a power exuding from God. He must be a person, and because He has the authority and ability to create, He must be God.

The other verse commonly used as proof for the doctrine of procession is John 15:26, mentioned above. Yeshua Himself declares that the Spirit proceeds from the Father.

2. The Aspect of Eternality

It is noteworthy that both verses used to establish the fact of the procession may also be used to prove that this procession is eternal in nature. Psalm 104:30 shows that the Ruach HaKodesh was already actively present in the Hebrew Scriptures and that "the procession was then a fact."[13]

The Greek verb for "proceed" in John 15:26 is ἐκπορεύομαι (transliterated as *ekporeuomai*). The verb parses as present tense, middle voice, and indicative mood. The present indicative verb form usually simply states a fact. However, if the context allows it, it may also indicate an ongoing action. Yeshua's statement "who proceeds from the Father" is embedded in two other statements: *whom I will send unto you from the Father* and *he shall bear witness of me*. It is noteworthy that Yeshua switched from future active indicative (*I **will** send*) to present indicative (*who **proceeds***) and then back to future (*he **shall** bear witness*). His statement about the Spirit proceeding from the Father appears to have nothing to do with the Spirit's predicted change of residence and seems to show that no matter where the Spirit resides, He is proceeding from the Father. One verb alone may not suffice as a proof text for a whole doctrine, but the verb and its context as well as the progression of the verbs in John 15:26 do support the idea that the Spirit did not proceed from the Father only one time, but that the procession is ongoing and eternal.

---

[13] Ibid.

3. From the Father and the Son

The fact that the Ruach HaKodesh proceeds from God the Father is confirmed in I Corinthians 2:11-12, which states:

> ¹¹ *For who among men knows the things of a man, save the spirit of the man, which is in him? even so the things of God none knows, save the Spirit of God.* ¹² *But we received, not the spirit of the world, but the spirit which is from God; that we might know the things that were freely given to us of God.*

There are at least three verses which seem to indicate that the Spirit also proceeds from the Son. These are Romans 8:9, Galatians 4:6, and John 16:7. While these three verses do not express the concept of procession from the Son with the same concreteness with which John 15:26 expressed the procession from the Father, they do support the argument of the western church that the Spirit also proceeds from the Son, especially when arranged in the following logical, three-step order.

First, in Romans 8:9, Paul equates the Spirit of God with the Spirit of the Son, stating: *But ye are not in the flesh but in the Spirit, if so be that the Spirit of God dwells in you. But if any man has not the Spirit of Messiah, he is none of his.*

Second, Galatians 4:6 says: *And because ye are sons, God sent forth the Spirit of his Son into our hearts, crying, Abba, Father.*

Third, having equated the Spirit of God with the Spirit of the Son, one may consider Yeshua's promise in John 16:7: *Nevertheless I tell you the truth: It is expedient for you that I go away; for if I go not away, the Comforter will not come unto you; but if I go, I will send him unto you.*

So, God's Holy Spirit is also the Spirit of His Son. The Spirit is sent by the Father as much as by the Son (Gal. 4:6; Jn. 16:7), while proceeding from the Father (Jn. 15:26). The theologian John Walvoord explains why this doctrine is so important:

> [The doctrine] has a vital bearing upon the work of the Holy Spirit as revealed in the Scriptures. In the case of Messiah, His eternal generation involved the work of the Son which was accomplished in time, fulfilling the purpose of redemption. As Messiah became an obedient Son in doing the Father's will, so the Holy Spirit in procession became

obedient to the Father and the Son. This subordination without detracting from the eternal glory and divine attributes which characterized all three Persons is taught specifically in the Scriptures (John 14:16, 26; 15:26; 16:7). The ministry of the Third Person is performed in His own power and gives testimony to His eternal deity and glory, but it is accomplished on behalf of the Father and the Son. Hence, the Spirit is sent into the world to reveal truth on behalf of Messiah (John 16:13-15), with the special mission of making the things of Messiah known and magnifying the Father and the Son. He is not seeking His own glory any more than the Son sought His own glory while in the period of humiliation.

In the work of both the Son and the Spirit, an illustration of the respective doctrines of eternal generation and procession can be seen. While the Father sends the Son and the Spirit, the Son never sends the Father, but does send the Spirit. The Spirit neither sends the Father nor the Son but is subordinate to Their will. This will is His own will at all times and accomplishes His work in the earth. While the nature of procession is largely inscrutable, it is an expression in human words based on the scriptural revelation of the relationship of the persons of the Trinity to each other.[14]

F. Questions and Study Suggestions

Question 1: Having studied the personality and the deity of the Ruach HaKodesh, let's revisit the doctrines of modalism and tritheism. What is the best way of avoiding these heresies?

Question 2: Which of the divine titles means the most to you? Why?

Question 3: In 2013, American singer Pharrell Williams wrote and produced "Happy," a song that won many awards and stayed on the top of international music charts for months. In the song, Williams wrote: "Happiness is the truth." While happiness is certainly wonderful, biblically, the

---

[14] Ibid.

phrase is incorrect. Who is the truth? And what does this mean for you and your position in Messiah?

Question 4: Explain in your own words in what way the Ruach HaKodesh generated the Messiah. What does "overshadowing" mean?

Question 5: We learned in this chapter that the Ruach HaKodesh is actively involved in the sanctification of the believer. What do theologians mean by this statement, and what does it mean to you personally?

Ruach HaKodesh – God the Holy Spirit

Chapter IV

The Ruach HaKodesh in Typology

This chapter deals with the typology of the Ruach HaKodesh. In theology, the term "typology" refers to a theory or doctrine concerning the relationship of one part of the Bible to another. Events or persons in the Hebrew Scriptures are viewed as types for events or persons in the New Testament. For example, Romans 5:14 says that Adam was *a figure of him that was to come*. The Greek term translated here as "figure" is *typos*, from which the English language got the word "type." Hence, Adam was to be a type of Messiah.

Generally speaking, Old Testament types need to be treated like other figures of speech, namely, according to the literal, grammatical, historical methodology. David L. Cooper's "Golden Rule of Interpretation" sums up this methodology:

> When the plain sense of Scripture makes common sense, seek no other sense; therefore, take every word at its primary, ordinary, usual, literal meaning unless the facts of the immediate context, studied in light of related passages and axiomatic and fundamental truths, indicate clearly otherwise.[15]

Equipped with this rule of Bible interpretation, we will look at the types, representations, symbols, emblems, and illustrations the Scriptures use in connection with the Holy Spirit.

---

[15] David L. Cooper, *The World's Greatest Library Graphically Illustrated* (Los Angeles, CA: Biblical Research Society, 1970), p. 11.

A. Oil

The oil the Jewish people used in the Scriptures always came from the olive tree. According to Deuteronomy 8:8, Israel was the land of olive trees. The oil was not only used for cooking, but for anointing kings (I Sam. 16:1), for sanctifying priests (Ex. 29:7, 40:9), as part of the offerings (Lev. 2:1-10), and for lighting lamps (Ex. 27:20; Lev. 24:2).

Zechariah 4:1-14 illustrates the significance of oil as a type. In this passage, the prophet saw a vision, parts of which he understood because of previous revelation; but there was one key element he did not understand (Zech. 4:1-10). He saw a seven-branched lampstand, a menorah, standing in the Temple. Over the menorah was a bowl, and on each side of the bowl stood an olive tree. From each olive tree, a pipe emptied oil into the bowl. From the bowl, seven smaller ducts fed oil to each of the seven lamps, totaling 49 ducts. Zechariah's vision showed Israel as a saved nation, filled with the Holy Spirit, and fulfilling its original calling to be the light to the Gentiles. The olive oil is the single unifying element of the whole vision. It is in the trees, which are its source, as well as the two pipes, the bowl, the 49 ducts, and the seven lamps. Oil is a common symbol of the Holy Spirit, and this passage identifies it as such: *Not by might, nor by power, but by my Spirit, said Jehovah of hosts* (Zech. 4:6). The two olive trees are the source of the oil, or of the Spirit.

When used symbolically in the Scriptures, oil has reference to several ministries of the Ruach HaKodesh: the ministry of induction or anointing, the ministry of illumination, and the ministry of sanctification. Eleven additional passages connect the Ruach HaKodesh with oil.

1. Exodus 27:20-21

[20] *And you shall command the children of Israel, that they bring unto you pure olive oil beaten for the light, to cause a lamp to burn continually.* [21] *In the tent of meeting, without the veil which is before the testimony, Aaron and his sons shall keep it in order from evening to morning before Jehovah: it shall be a statute for ever throughout their generations on the behalf of the children of Israel.*

Opposite the table of showbread in the holy place of the Tabernacle (and later the Temple), there stood a lampstand made of pure gold (Ex. 25:31-39). It was not built to burn candles, but oil. The base of the lampstand supported a center shaft, from which six branches went out. Each branch and the shaft were topped off with oil lamps, making it a total of seven lights. Although the exact form is unknown, the Jewish menorah is commonly associated with this lampstand. According to Exodus 27:20-21, the lampstand was to give forth light continuously. This command required a continual provision of olive oil by the Israelites.

The seven-branch menorah was the only source of light in the Tabernacle. It stood in the holy place, separated from the Holy of Holies and the Ark of the Covenant by a veil. It lit the place where the priests worshiped God. The Spirit's ministry is to illuminate the truth (Neh. 9:20; I Cor. 2:14-16; Eph. 1:15-18). Just as the burning oil in the seven lamps of the menorah illuminated the place where God was worshiped, the Spirit illuminates the believer's mind. He shows him the beauty of the Messiah and leads him in his worship of God.[16]

2. Exodus 40:9-16

[9] And you shall take the anointing oil, and anoint the tabernacle, and all that is therein, and shall hallow it, and all the furniture thereof: and it shall be holy. [10] And you shall anoint the altar of burnt-offering, and all its vessels, and sanctify the altar: and the altar shall be most holy. [11] And you shall anoint the laver and its base, and sanctify it. [12] And you shall bring Aaron and his sons unto the door of the tent of meeting, and shall wash them with water. [13] And you shall put upon Aaron the holy garments; and you shall anoint him, and sanctify him, that he may minister unto me in the priest's

---

[16] Menorah illustration on this page by Jesse and Josh Gonzales.

office. ¹⁴ And you shall bring his sons, and put coats upon them; ¹⁵ and you shall anoint them, as you did anoint their father, that they may minister unto me in the priest's office: and their anointing shall be to them for an everlasting priesthood throughout their generations. ¹⁶ Thus did Moses: according to all that Jehovah commanded him, so did he.

In this passage, God gives clear directions as to how the Tabernacle and the priests were to be anointed. The oil used for the anointing was of a special composition and could not be used for any other purpose (Ex. 30:22-33). Those anointed could not even mourn the death of a relative as long as they bore the oil (Lev. 10:6-7). This consecrating of people and items pictures the Spirit's work of anointing those God has appointed for specific ministries or uses (Acts 1:8).

3. Leviticus 8:10-12, 30

¹⁰ And Moses took the anointing oil, and anointed the tabernacle and all that was therein, and sanctified them. ¹¹ And he sprinkled thereof upon the altar seven times, and anointed the altar and all its vessels, and the laver and its base, to sanctify them. ¹² And he poured of the anointing oil upon Aaron's head, and anointed him, to sanctify him.

³⁰ And Moses took of the anointing oil, and of the blood which was upon the altar, and sprinkled it upon Aaron, upon his garments, and upon his sons, and upon his sons' garments with him, and sanctified Aaron, his garments, and his sons, and his sons' garments with him.

These verses again speak of the anointing of priests with oil. In order to come into the presence of God on behalf of others, they were to be purified by the washing with water (Lev. 8:6); they had to be prepared by putting on specific clothes (Lev. 8:7-9); they were to be sanctified by applying the blood (Lev. 8:30); and together with the place of worship and the items therein, they were to be consecrated by the anointing with oil (Lev. 8:10-12, 30).

The purpose of these anointings was to set apart the Tabernacle and the priests as most holy to God. The act of anointing with oil was representative of the special calling and empowerment by the Spirit of God.

4. I Samuel 10:1

Then Samuel took the vial of oil, and poured it upon his head, and kissed him, and said, Is it not that Jehovah has anointed you to be prince over his inheritance?

Not only the priests, but kings, too, had to be set apart for divine service. In this verse, Samuel poured the anointing oil on Saul's head, showing that God had approved of Saul as leader of His people. According to I Samuel 10:6 and 10, the consecration went hand in hand with the Holy Spirit coming upon the new king.

5. I Samuel 16:13

Then Samuel took the horn of oil, and anointed him in the midst of his brethren: and the Spirit of Jehovah came mightily upon David from that day forward. So Samuel rose up, and went to Ramah.

King Saul was a rebellious king who haughtily rejected God's word (I Sam. 15:23). As a result, God rejected Saul and ordered Samuel to go to Bethlehem and select one of Jesse's sons to be king (I Sam. 16:1-3). After ruling out Jesse's older sons, the Lord chose David, and Samuel anointed him. When he did, the Spirit of the Lord came upon David in a mighty way and stayed with him from that day forward (I Sam. 16:13). The presence of the Ruach enabled the new king to become the leader God wanted him to be.

6. I Kings 1:39

And Zadok the priest took the horn of oil out of the Tent, and anointed Solomon. And they blew the trumpet; and all the people said, Long *live king* Solomon.

Solomon was anointed king by Zadok the priest. The procedure was the same as with Saul and David, and again the anointing signified that God had approved of this leader. His Holy Spirit would be with Solomon. The oil connected the Spirit's work with the responsibilities of the royal office and symbolized the presence and power of God.

7. Psalm 23:5

You prepare a table before me in the presence of mine enemies: You have anointed my head with oil; My cup runs over.

In Psalm 23, David reflected on God's mercy toward him, using images of a shepherd and a gracious host. Verses 1-4 speak of the Lord's leading as a shepherd leads his flock. David recounts four blessings that arise from this guidance: spiritual nourishment (v. 2a), spiritual restoration (v. 2b-3a), leading in the right direction (v. 3b), and protection (v. 4). In verse 5, the imagery changes to a dinner invitation where the host blesses the guest with refreshments. He anoints his head with oil and brings his cup to overflowing. In Jewish culture, oil was used in the welcoming of guests (Lk. 7:46). The anointing of the head released tension and refreshed the weary. Just so, the Holy Spirit brings spiritual refreshment and renewal.

8. Isaiah 61:1-2a and Luke 4:16-21

[1] *The Spirit of the Lord Jehovah is upon me; because Jehovah has anointed me to preach good tidings unto the meek; he has sent me to bind up the broken-hearted, to proclaim liberty to the captives, and the opening of the prison to them that are bound;* [2] *to proclaim the year of Jehovah's favor*

These verses of Isaiah deal with the first coming of the Messiah. This is very clear from Yeshua's reading of the passage, described in Luke 4:16-21:

[16] *And he came to Nazareth, where he had been brought up; and as was his custom, he entered the synagogue on the Sabbath, and stood up to read.* [17] *And the book of the prophet Isaiah was handed to him. And he opened the book, and found the place where it was written,* [18] *"The Spirit of the Lord is upon me, because he anointed me to preach the gospel to the poor. He has sent me to proclaim release to the captives, and recovery of sight to the blind, to set free those who are downtrodden,* [19] *to proclaim the favorable year of the Lord."* [20] *And he closed the book, and gave it back to the attendant, and sat down; and the eyes of all in the synagogue were fixed upon him.* [21] *And he began to say to them, "Today this Scripture has been fulfilled in your hearing."*

Yeshua read verses 1 and 2a of Isaiah 61 and then stopped because these words were now fulfilled. According to verse 1, Messiah would be anointed with the Holy Spirit for His mission and His task. This anointing took place in the life of Yeshua at His baptism (Mt. 3:16). It was at this point that He began His public ministry and openly proclaimed Himself to be Messiah.

9. Acts 10:38

even Yeshua of Nazareth, how God anointed him with the Holy Spirit and with power: who went about doing good, and healing all that were oppressed of the devil; for God was with him.

Acts 10:38 confirms the prophecy of Isaiah 61: Messiah was anointed by God the Father with the Holy Spirit. The context of the verse reveals that Peter was describing the life and work of Yeshua. By way of identification, he told his audience that he was talking about *Yeshua of Nazareth*. More literally, the Greek says, "Yeshua, the One from Nazareth." There must be no mistake as to whom Peter was referring. God *anointed* this One. The Greek word for "anointing" is the same root as the Greek word for "Messiah." God "messiahed" Him *with the Holy Spirit*. Indeed, when John baptized Him, Yeshua received a special anointing of the Holy Spirit in fulfillment of Isaiah 61:1-2a. Because of this anointing by the Holy Spirit, He had *power* to do His work. So, He *went about doing good, and healing all that were oppressed of the devil*, meaning diseases which were caused by demons. The reason He was able to do all this is because *God was with Him*. Peter thus spelled out some of the basic facts about Yeshua of Nazareth and the role of the Holy Spirit in His life.

10. II Corinthians 1:21-22

[21] Now he that establishes us with you in Messiah, and anointed us, is God; [22] who also sealed us, and gave us the earnest of the Spirit in our hearts.

Just like priests, kings, and Yeshua were set apart for their service to God by anointing, the believer in Messiah Yeshua is also consecrated for the ministry God has for him. When God commissions the believer for his tasks, He anoints him. The anointing relates to the believer's position of being "in Messiah." The agent of anointing is God, and the means is the Holy Spirit.

11. I John 2:20

And ye have an anointing from the Holy One, and ye know all things.

Having received the anointing, the believer knows all things. In this context, the expression "all things" refers to all things that relate to salvation, as John 16:13-15 points out:

[13] Howbeit when he, the Spirit of truth, is come, he shall guide you into all the truth: for he shall not speak from himself; but what things soever he shall hear, these shall he speak: and he shall declare unto you the things that are to come. [14] He shall glorify me: for he shall take of mine, and shall declare it unto you. [15] All things whatsoever the Father has are mine: therefore said I, that he takes of mine, and shall declare it unto you.

12. Significance

Summarizing the significance of oil in the study of typology, we note that when used symbolically in the Scriptures, oil has reference to several ministries of the Ruach HaKodesh: the ministry of induction or anointing, the ministry of illumination, and the ministry of sanctification. The Messiah was inducted into His ministry by the Holy Spirit, who anointed Him. Furthermore, the Spirit provides light, illuminating the believer's mind to understand and worship God. Lastly, it is God the Spirit who sets apart a person for a certain position, be it a priest or a king, or for ministry. He sanctifies the believer and empowers him to fulfill his calling.

B. WATER

Water has always been a crucial commodity for the existence of life on this planet. Seventy-one percent of the earth is covered with water. It is no surprise, then, that God would use the figure of water in its various forms as a central type in the Scriptures, representing things such as provision, judgment, blessing, and danger.

God controls water (Job 38:16, 22-34; Ps. 29:3, 10). He oversees its placement and boundaries (Gen. 1:9-10; Ps. 104:6-12; Jer. 5:22). In the Hebrew Scriptures, there are many references to the positive attributes of water. Lot, for example, chose for himself *all the Plain of the Jordan* because he saw *that it was well watered every where* (Gen. 13:10). Good news from distant lands are likened to the refreshment of cold water for a weary person (Prov. 25:25). However, there are also many references to the negative side of water. God uses water for judgment (Gen. 6-9; Amos 5:8). He parts the Red Sea to allow His people safe passage; but after they passed through it, He used the water to judge the Egyptians (Ex. 14:21-31, 15:4-12; Ps. 78:13).

Hence, when used symbolically in the Scriptures, water represents several things. It represents judgment. It also represents trials and tribulation (Ps. 69:2, 14), and in the form of rivers, it stands for invading armies (Isa. 8:6-7). Water also symbolizes the Word of God (Jn. 3:5; Eph. 5:26) and even God Himself (Jer. 2:13; Isa. 55:1).

In the context of pneumatology, water is used as a symbol of the Holy Spirit and His ministry, as the following two passages will show.

1. John 4:14

but whosoever drinks of the water that I shall give him shall never thirst; but the water that I shall give him shall become in him a well of water springing up unto eternal life.

As Yeshua passed through Samaria, He came to Sychar, a town south of Shechem, located between the two mountains of Ebal and Gerizim. He sent His disciples into town to purchase food. In the meantime, He was sitting by the well of Sychar when a Samaritan woman came to draw water. Yeshua asked her to give Him some water. The Samaritan woman was obviously taken aback by Yeshua's request and responded by asking Him why He, being a Jew, would ask her, a Samaritan, to draw Him some water. He responded to her question with an answer meant to further pique her curiosity and to create in her a thirst for eternal life: *If you knew the gift of God, and who it is that says to you, Give me to drink; you would have asked of him, and he would have given you living water* (Jn. 4:10). What was this living water? Normally, living water is running water—

water that is active, moving, and the opposite of stagnant. However, it will soon become apparent that this is not what Yeshua was offering her. The woman's response in John 4:11-12 shows that this statement puzzled her: *Sir, you have nothing to draw with, and the well is deep: from where then have you that living water? Are you greater than our father Jacob, who gave us the well, and drank thereof himself, and his sons, and his cattle?* The woman questioned Yeshua's ability to produce this water, but she also revealed some things about Samaritan theology. According to that theology, Jacob himself had provided this well for them. Was Yeshua claiming to be able to provide better water than Jacob?

Yeshua then began to move from the physical to the spiritual, pointing out to her that anyone who drank of the water from Jacob's well would eventually thirst again. That was a simple fact of human life. Then He continued, *whosoever drinks of the water that I shall give him shall never thirst; but the water that I shall give him shall become in him a well of water springing up unto eternal life* (Jn. 4:14). The water Yeshua offered would permanently quench one's thirst—not physically, but spiritually. The gift of this inner well of living water brought eternal life.

The next passage will reveal that the *water springing up unto eternal life* is related to the Holy Spirit.

2. John 7:37-39

[37] Now on the last day, the great <day> of the feast, Yeshua stood and cried, saying, If any man thirst, let him come unto me and drink. [38] He that believes on me, as the scripture has said, from within him shall flow rivers of living water. [39] But this spoke he of the Spirit, which they that believed on him were to receive: for the Spirit was not yet <given>; because Yeshua was not yet glorified.

This passage begins with the words, *Now on the last day, the great <day> of the feast* (Jn. 7:37a). Of the seven days of the Feast of Tabernacles, the seventh was by far the most important. During the first six days, the priests circled the altar only once; but on the last day, they circled the altar seven times and continued to recite Psalm 118:25: *Hoshanah Rabbah, save us in the highest.* Furthermore, they held an additional willow branch during their circuits around the altar, and water was especially emphasized. In response to this ceremony, Yeshua declared: *If any man thirst, let him come unto me and drink. He that believes on me, as the scripture has said, from within him shall flow rivers of living water* (Jn. 7:37b-38). John interpreted this to refer specifically to the Holy Spirit, saying that *this spoke he of the Spirit* (Jn. 7:39a). By saying if anyone believes, *from within him shall flow rivers of living water*, Yeshua applied the ceremony to the individual. Those who accept His Messiahship will be indwelled by the Holy Spirit, and *rivers of living water* will flow from within.

At this point, many people already believed in Yeshua, but had not yet received the indwelling of the Holy Spirit *because Yeshua was not yet glorified* (Jn. 7:39b). The permanent and universal indwelling of the Spirit among all believers would only occur after His ascension. Old Testament saints experienced the regenerating work of the Holy Spirit, which was different than His indwelling work. Only some of them, especially the prophets, were indwelled by the Holy Spirit, but not on a permanent basis. David's prayer "take not your holy Spirit from me" (Ps. 51:11) was valid in Old Testament times. However, it is not a valid New Testament prayer because now the Holy Spirit indwells all believers forever.

3. Significance

Combining John 4:14 and John 7:37-39 shows that eternal life springs from the Ruach HaKodesh. It springs up from that which is barren and therefore symbolizes the Spirit's ministry of regeneration.

The eternal life which follows the regeneration is an abundant life, full of power through the Spirit. The blessing of living water is received by having been baptized into Messiah.

Because the believer has been given this abundant life, out of him shall flow rivers of living water. He has all he needs for his service to the Lord. It is now his responsibility to allow the Spirit to use him and to make his heart the origin of this outflow of continuous spiritual blessing.

C. Fire

The figure of fire is used in several different ways in the Scriptures. In Leviticus 10:2, it stands for God's judgment (see also Num. 11:1; II Kgs. 1:10, 12. In Jeremiah 5:14 and 20:9, it symbolizes God's Word. It expresses God's presence (Ex. 3:2; Heb. 12:29; Num. 9:15-16; Ezek. 1:4), His power (Jdg. 13:20), His protection (Ex. 13:21; Zech. 2:5), and His approval (e.g., I Kgs. 18:38). Fire provides light in Exodus 13:21-22. In several verses, such as Malachi 3:3 and Hebrews 12:29, it represents God's testing and discipline. Finally, in Isaiah 6:1-7, fire symbolizes sanctification and cleansing.

Fire was also important for the sacrificial system of the Hebrew Scriptures. Leviticus 9:24 says that the fire that consumed the burnt offering on the altar came from God Himself. Hence, it was His gift. The priests had to keep the fire going (Lev. 6:13) and could not use fire from any other source (Lev. 10:1-2).

In the New Testament, fire is used as a powerful picture of the work of the Ruach HaKodesh, as the following verses will show.

1. Acts 2:1-4

In Acts 1:4-5, Yeshua gave His apostles a final commission. They were to remain in Jerusalem until the coming of the Holy Spirit. When the Spirit arrived, three things would occur. First, *the promise of the Father* would be fulfilled (Lk. 24:49a). During the Upper Room Discourse, the Father, through the Son, promised to send them another Comforter—the Holy Spirit. Second, they would receive divine power, or *power from on high* (Lk. 24:49b), to fulfill their commission (Acts 1:8). Third, a new ministry of the Spirit would begin, the work of Spirit baptism (Acts 1:5). While the Spirit had many ministries in the Hebrew Bible, He never baptized anyone. The result of Spirit baptism is membership in the body of the Messiah: *For in one Spirit were we all baptized into one body, whether Jews or Greeks, whether bond or free; and were all made to drink of one Spirit* (I Cor. 12:13). Spirit baptism caused the birth of the body, the church (Col. 1:18), and according to Acts 11:15-16, it began in Acts 2:1-4:

> [1] *And when the day of Pentecost was now come, they were all together in one place.* [2] *And suddenly there came from heaven a sound as of the rushing*

of a mighty wind, and it filled all the house where they were sitting. ³ *And there appeared unto them tongues parting asunder, like as of fire; and it sat upon each one of them.* ⁴ *And they were all filled with the Holy Spirit, and began to speak with other tongues, as the Spirit gave them utterance.*

When the Ruach HaKodesh began His ministry of baptism and indwelling the believer, He appeared as cloven tongues of fire. He filled the people who were gathered there in Jerusalem and allowed them to speak in other languages. Their bodies became temples of the living God (II Cor. 6:16).

While the Scriptures do not elaborate on the usage of fire in Acts, the symbolic meaning can be interpreted along the lines of its Old Testament usage. God was present. He approved of this event. He offered His protection and would cleanse and sanctify His people. Just like He set apart the kings and priests and the Tabernacle and all of its furnishings in the Hebrew Scriptures, He also set apart the believers for the ministry to which He had called them, for upon receiving this power, the apostles were to preach the gospel in four stages, proceeding from Jerusalem to Judea, Samaria, and then to the Gentile world (Lk. 24:47; Acts 1:8).

2. Revelation 4:5

And out of the throne proceed lightnings and voices and thunders. And there were seven lamps of fire burning before the throne, which are the seven Spirits of God;

These seven Spirits of God are representative of seven attributes of the Holy Spirit described in Isaiah 11:2: *And the Spirit of Jehovah shall rest upon him, the spirit of wisdom and understanding, the spirit of counsel and might, the spirit of knowledge and of the fear of Jehovah.* The One on whom the Spirit of Jehovah will rest is Yeshua, the Messiah. He will have the sevenfold fullness of the Spirit. In Scripture, the number seven signifies perfection and completeness. The sevenfold fullness of the Spirit is seen in His name: He has the sacred name of God. He can be called by this sacred name because He is God. The fullness is also seen in His wisdom, His understanding, the counsel He gives, the strength He possesses, the insight He has, and the fear of the Lord that is His.

The New Testament teaches that all who believe in Yeshua as Messiah are given a measure of the Holy Spirit. Because each believer only has a measure of the Spirit, each one has different gifts and ministries (I Cor. 12:12-31). No one ever has all of the gifts because God has ordained that the members of the church be mutually dependent. Yeshua, however, was given the Spirit without measure (Jn. 3:34). The sevenfold nature of the Spirit in Isaiah 11:2 is therefore synonymous with the measureless fullness in John 3:34.

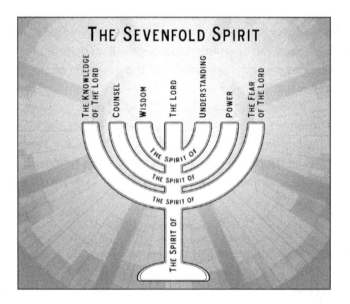

3. Significance

To summarize how fire is used symbolically of the Holy Spirit, five points will be made. First, fire is used to illustrate the Spirit's ministry of indwelling, which shows that God is present with His people. Second, fire represents the Spirit's ministry of illumination as it gives forth light. Third, fire is used to emphasize the Spirit's ministry of cleansing, which is used in the sanctification process of the believer. Fourth, the first baptism with the Spirit reminded those who experienced it of tongues of fire. Fifth, the believer receives a measure of the Spirit for his service to the Lord. Only one person had the fullness of the Spirit, and that was the Messiah Himself. The fullness is compared to a Jewish menorah with its seven lamps.

D. Wind

In the Hebrew Scriptures, the word *ruach* means "air in motion," "wind," "breath," or "spirit." When it refers to a "spirit," it could be any spirit or entity apart from a body. However, in roughly one hundred Old Testament passages, it refers to the Spirit of God. Hence, the very word used for the Holy Spirit in the Hebrew Scriptures relates Him to wind, a type that is frequently found in reference to Him. The Greek equivalent for *ruach* is *pneuma*. This word rarely carries the meaning of "wind." Yet, its verbal form, *pneō*, means "to blow." The implication, therefore, remains the same: When used symbolically, wind makes for a comprehensive picture or type of the Holy Spirit.

There are many passages in the Scriptures where wind is nothing but the natural phenomenon all human beings experience at times. The earliest example of this usage is Genesis 8:1, which states: *And God remembered Noah, and all the beasts, and all the cattle that were with him in the ark: and God made a wind to pass over the earth, and the waters assuaged.*

Some verses speak of east, west, and south winds that were sent by God (Ex. 10:13, 19; Ps. 78:26; Jonah 4:8; Acts 27:13-15). Others simply speak of wind driving along ships (Acts 27:15). The last example in the Scriptures is Revelation 7:1: *After this I saw four angels standing at the four corners of the earth, holding the four winds of the earth, that no wind should blow on the earth, or on the sea, or upon any tree.*

These and other verses show that God is in control of the wind, just as He is in control of the water. In fact, Amos 4:13 says that God creates the wind:

> *For, lo, he that forms the mountains, and creates the wind, and declares unto man what is his thought; that makes the morning darkness, and treads upon the high places of the Earth—Jehovah, the God of hosts, is his name.*

As human beings, we do not see the source of wind, but experience it nonetheless as an invisible force. Sometimes, the effects of this force are soothing and refreshing, other times they are violent. Hot winds may ruin crops. Typhoons and hurricanes may devastate whole regions, uprooting huge trees and toppling over buildings. This is what makes wind a good type of the Holy Spirit. Man cannot comprehend the power of the Holy Spirit. He cannot grasp the Spirit's creative and sovereign will, nor His immaterial, invisible nature.

Three passages give some insight into the Spirit's working symbolized as wind.

1. John 3:8

The wind blows where it will, and you hear the voice thereof, but know not whence it comes, and whither it goes: so is every one that is born of the Spirit.

The Gospel of John records seven of Yeshua's discourses, John 3:1-21 being the first one, the discourse on the new birth. Among the many who heard what Yeshua proclaimed and saw what He did was *a man of the Pharisees named Nicodemus* (Jn. 3:1). The fact that Nicodemus was a Pharisee reveals his fundamental beliefs. There were certain tenets to which a Pharisee held that distinguished him from a Sadducee, an Essene, a Zealot, or one of the other branches within the Judaism of that day. An important tenet of Pharisaic Judaism was the belief that all Israel has a share in the age to come. This meant that anyone born a Jew automatically had the right to enter the kingdom of God by virtue of God's election of Israel as a nation. When writing about physical birth, the rabbis often used the phrase "to be born of water." This was derived from passages such as Proverbs 5:15-23, where semen is symbolized as water. The expression simply meant that anyone who was born physically was born of water, and to be born physically as a Jew was enough to enter the kingdom of God.

It was a man with this theological frame of reference who came to Yeshua. He came because of what he had heard and what he had seen during the Passover in Jerusalem. Before the conversation got very far, Yeshua declared, *Except one be born anew, he cannot see the kingdom of God* (Jn. 3:3). Unless Nicodemus experienced the new birth, he would not see the kingdom of God. Nicodemus was stumped: *How can a man be born when he is old? Can he enter a second time into his mother's womb, and be born?* (Jn. 3:4). When Yeshua responded to the question Nicodemus posed, He used a very common Jewish method of teaching—going from the known to the unknown. The known factor was the term "born again." As a Pharisee, Nicodemus knew the six ways a man could be born again according to Judaism.[17] The unknown factor was its spiritual ramifications, because in Pharisaism, the term had nothing but a physical connotation. So Yeshua moved from the known to the unknown, from the physical to the spiritual, and said: *Verily, verily, I say unto you, Except one be born of water and the Spirit, he cannot enter the kingdom of God!* (Jn. 3:5). When Yeshua declared that one must be born of both water and Spirit, He rejected the Pharisaic fundamental teaching that all Israel automatically have a share in the age to come. Merely being born of water was insufficient. One had to be born of both water **and** the Spirit. One must have two kinds of birth, a physical birth and a spiritual birth, to qualify for the kingdom.

John 3:5 is an example of a rather typical Greek construction where a sentence has two parts and each part is then elaborated upon separately. After stating that every person must have two kinds of birth, Yeshua defined the differences. To be born of water was to be born of the flesh: *That which is born of the flesh is flesh* (Jn. 3:6). However, this kind of birth alone is insufficient for entrance into the kingdom, and all human beings also must undergo a spiritual birth because only *that which is born of the Spirit is spirit* (Jn. 3:6). To be born of the Spirit means the Holy Spirit regenerates the dead human spirit to become alive to God. That is the kind of new birth which is essential for entry into the kingdom. Until Nicodemus experienced this kind of new birth, he would neither see nor enter God's kingdom.

Then Yeshua said: *Marvel not that I said unto you, Ye must be born anew. The wind blows where it will* (Jn. 3:7-8a). Using the type of wind, Yeshua declared that the Spirit blows as He wills. This points both to the Spirit's sovereignty and the fact that His work in the new birth cannot be seen by men.

---

[17] For details about the six ways, please see the author's book series titled *Yeshua – The Life of Messiah from a Messianic Jewish Perspective*, published by Ariel Ministries.

2. Acts 2:1-4

¹ And when the day of Pentecost was now come, they were all together in one place. ² And suddenly there came from heaven a sound as of the rushing of a mighty wind, and it filled all the house where they were sitting. ³ And there appeared unto them tongues parting asunder, like as of fire; and it sat upon each one of them. ⁴ And they were all filled with the Holy Spirit, and began to speak with other tongues, as the Spirit gave them utterance.

Acts 2:1-4 describes the birth of the church. The passage has been studied in previous chapters. What is important here is that Luke compared the arrival of the Spirit to a sound that came from heaven. This sound resembled *the rushing of a mighty wind*. Notice that it does not say the wind *was* the Spirit. Yet, the events that accompanied the sound (*the tongues parting asunder, like as of fire* and the sudden knowledge of other languages) indicate that the Spirit was at work here. Just as the meeting place where the believers were gathered together in Jerusalem was filled with the sound of a mighty wind, the believers themselves were *all filled with the Holy Spirit* (Acts 2:4). Hence, the implication is that the work of the Spirit is symbolized by wind. This wind is not just a mild breeze, but a *mighty wind*. The Holy Spirit's power is mighty. His work is sovereign.

3. II Peter 1:21

For no prophecy ever came by the will of man: but men spoke from God, being moved by the Holy Spirit.

The Greek verb translated as "being moved" is *pheromenoi*, which comes from the verb *pheró*, meaning "to bear, carry, bring forth." The verb implies the idea of a ship being moved across the sea by the wind. Just so, the Spirit of God bore men along as they wrote the Scriptures. He watched over them, making sure they would not write any error.

Second Timothy 3:16 declares that all Scripture is *theopneustos*, meaning "God-breathed" or "inspired." God superintended the human beings who, with their own individual personalities and styles, authored His Word. They composed and recorded without error God's message to man. Hebrews 1:1 states that when God revealed His words to *the fathers*, it was *in the prophets*. The term "fathers" does not only pertain to the patriarchs Abraham, Isaac, and Jacob; the term covers the whole span of Old Testament revelation.[18] Those who received direct revelation from God were the prophets. They were indwelled by the Holy Spirit and became the means of divine revelation. They spoke as they were moved by the Holy Spirit. That is why the Scriptures are God-breathed. The prophets spoke exactly what God wanted them to speak down to the very words, a fact Yeshua confirmed in Matthew 5:18.

4. Significance

The verses show that wind is an appropriate symbol of the Holy Spirit. Just like wind, the Ruach HaKodesh is immaterial and invisible. He performs His ministries of regeneration, illumination, and inspiration sovereignly and with infinite power.

E. DOVE

1. Scriptures

All four Gospels use the type of a dove when speaking of the Holy Spirit. In all four instances, the passages speak of Yeshua's baptism.

Matthew 3:13-17	Mark 1:9-11	Luke 3:21-22
[13] Then comes Yeshua from Galilee to the Jordan unto John, to be baptized of him. [14] But John would have hindered him, saying, I have need to be baptized of you, and come you to me? [15] But Yeshua	[9] And it came to pass in those days, that Yeshua came from Natzereth of Galilee, and was baptized of John in the Jordan.	[21] Now it came to pass, when all the people were baptized,

---

[18] In John 6:31, 49, and 58, the term is used of the Exodus and wilderness generation. In John 7:22, it is used of the patriarchs.

answering said unto him, Suffer <it> now: for thus it becomes us to fulfil all righteousness. Then he suffered him.		
¹⁶ *And Yeshua when he was baptized, went up straightway from the water:*	¹⁰ *And straightway coming up out of the water,*	*that, Yeshua also having been baptized,*
and lo, the heavens were opened unto him, and he saw the Spirit of God descending as a dove, and coming upon him;	*he saw the heavens rent asunder, and the Spirit as a dove descending upon him:*	*and praying, the heaven was opened,* ²² *and the Holy Spirit descended in a bodily form, as a dove, upon him,*
¹⁷ *and lo, a voice out of the heavens, saying, This is my beloved Son, in whom I am well pleased.*	¹¹ *And a voice came out of the heavens, You are my beloved Son, in you I am well pleased.*	*and a voice came out of heaven, You are my beloved Son; in you I am well pleased.*

John 1:32-34

³² *And John bore witness, saying, I have beheld the Spirit descending as a dove out of heaven; and it abode upon him.* ³³ *And I knew him not: but he that sent me to baptize in water, he said unto me, Upon whomsoever you shall see the Spirit descending, and abiding upon him, the same is he that baptizes in the Holy Spirit.* ³⁴ *And I have seen, and have borne witness that this is the Son of God.*

All four Gospel passages pertain to the baptism of Yeshua, during which the Triune God made His appearance, both visibly and audibly. God the Son was present in the person of Yeshua, as He visibly *went up straightway from the water*. God the Father made His presence known audibly: *Lo, a voice out of heaven, saying, This is my beloved Son, in whom I am well pleased* (Mt. 3:17). The account of the *voice out of heaven* has a rabbinic background. In Hebrew, this voice is called the *Bat Kol*. The term literally means "daughter of a voice," and in rabbinic writings, it is defined as follows:

> BATH ḲOL (Lit., 'daughter of a voice'); (*a*) a reverberating sound; (*b*) a voice descending from heaven (cf. Dan. IV, 28) to offer guidance in human affairs, and regarded as a lower grade of prophecy.[19]

God the Spirit appeared in the form of a dove that came upon Yeshua. Luke specified that He *descended in a bodily form, as a dove* (Lk. 3:22), thus making it clear that this was not merely a ghostly form.

In all the various ways the Holy Spirit could have made His appearance, why did He choose a bird? And why specifically a dove? The first time the Holy Spirit appeared in the Scriptures was in Genesis 1:2, where it says that He *moved upon the face of the waters*. The Hebrew verb for "moved" is *merachephet*, a word used of a mother bird hovering over her eggs just before they hatch. Thus, the Hebrew wording of Genesis 1:2 relates this appearance of the Holy Spirit to the actions of a mother bird: He was brooding over the waters like a mother bird, just before the hatching of dry land. The Midrash Rabbah tells the story of Rabbi Simeon b. Zoma, who at one point was contemplating the creation and came to the conclusion "that between the upper and the nether waters there is but two or three fingerbreadths, . . . For it is not written here, AND THE SPIRIT OF GOD blew, but HOVERED, like a bird flying and flapping with its wings, its wings barely touching [the nest over which it hovers]."[20] So, the rabbis specified

---

[19] Isidore Epstein, ed., *The Babylonian Talmud*, 18 vols., (London: Soncino Press, 1961), *b. Niddah*, Glossary, p. 514. In rabbinic theology, the voice of the prophets ceased with Malachi, and the next prophet would be Elijah, who would return to announce the coming of the Messiah. However, while the prophetic voice ended, the voice of God did not, and periodically God spoke a short sentence out of heaven. This was the Bat Kol. While the Shechinah glory is a visible manifestation of God, the Bat Kol is audible. What God the Father spoke audibly out of Heaven at the baptism of Yeshua was: *This is my beloved Son, in whom I am well pleased* (Mt. 3:17), thus identifying Yeshua as the son mentioned in Psalm 2:12: *Kiss the son, lest he be angry, and ye perish in the way, For his wrath will soon be kindled. Blessed are all they that take refuge in him*. This son is the Messianic Son, God the Son. There were three times during Yeshua's public ministry when God the Father spoke audibly out of heaven. This was the first of those three times.

[20] *Midrash Rabbah*: Genesis II.4.

the bird of Genesis 1:2 to be a dove, and this was still the mindset of the Jewish community of Yeshua's day. To communicate this clearly in the passages that describe His baptism, the Holy Spirit came down in the bodily form of a dove.

At the baptism, God the Father audibly identified Yeshua as the Messianic Son, and the Holy Spirit anointed Him for service.

2. Significance

The use of the dove as a type for the Holy Spirit shines light on a different side of the Holy Spirit. Unlike wind that can be violent, a dove is generally seen as a gentle and peaceful bird. In Matthew 10:16, Yeshua reminds His disciples to be *harmless as doves*. The Greek word used here is *akeraioi*, which means "unmixed" in the sense of "simple," "sincere," and "blameless." It also means "pure," and it is that purity of heavenly origin the type of the dove emphasizes.

F. Earnest

There are three passages in the New Testament that relate the Holy Spirit to an earnest someone pays in advance as a security that the whole amount will be paid in the future.

1. II Corinthians 1:21-22

> [21] Now he that establishes us with you in Messiah, and anointed us, is God;
> [22] who also sealed us, and gave us the earnest of the Spirit in our hearts.

The Greek word translated here as "earnest" is *arrabōna*. The word is used for a deposit or down payment which guarantees the balance will be paid later. In the context of II Corinthians 1:21-22, the earnest of the Spirit is connected with His work of sealing the believer. God the Father is the agent who does the sealing by means of the Holy Spirit. The Spirit Himself is the earnest. As Walvoord puts it, "He is the token and pledge that all the Father has promised while not ours now as to actual enjoyment is nevertheless our possession and will be ours to enjoy later."[21]

2. II Corinthians 5:5

Now he that wrought us for this very thing is God, who gave unto us the earnest of the Spirit.

This verse reiterates the fact that the giving of the Spirit as an earnest is the work of God. In context, Paul explains the reasons for the full and confident hope believers have. The sealing made them safe in their position as believers, and the earnest guarantees to them the ultimate realization of the hope they have in Messiah. Being of the same nature as the full price, it is a pledge that future glories await the believer in heaven.

3. Ephesians 1:13b-14

[13b] ye were sealed with the Holy Spirit of promise, [14] which [better: who] is an earnest of our inheritance, unto the redemption of God's own possession, unto the praise of his glory.

In Greek, the antecedent of "which" is "the Holy Spirit," and the relative pronoun used here, *ho*, may also be translated as "who." Then, the verse more clearly states that the believer is sealed with the Holy Spirit, who is an earnest of his inheritance. Again, Paul connects the sealing with the earnest, but this time, the earnest is God's assurance of the believer's eternal *inheritance*. The Greek word is *klēronomia*, which is often used for a share of things to come or for something that is given to one as a present or future possession.

4. Significance

Summarizing the verses, the Holy Spirit is viewed as an earnest because He is God's guarantee to the believer that he will receive all the promised future blessings of salvation. The type implies that God is bound to full

---

[21] Walvoord, "Chapter III: The Typology of the Holy Spirit," in *The Holy Spirit: A Comprehensive Study of the Person and Work of the Holy Spirit*.

salvation. He has put Himself under the obligation to complete the believer's salvation and pledges to the believer the eternal security of the final redemption.

G. Seal

The next symbol to be considered is the seal. The previous type of the earnest already alluded to this picture, and II Corinthians 1:22 and Ephesians 1:13b-14 clearly connected the sealing with the earnest of the Spirit. In fact, the verses made clear that the Ruach Himself is the seal, while the Father does the sealing.

One other verse connects the Holy Spirit with the work of sealing, and that is Ephesians 4:30: *And grieve not the Holy Spirit of God, in whom ye were sealed unto the day of redemption.* In this passage, the Holy Spirit is the agent of sealing. He is the guarantor of final redemption. Because believers have been sealed by the Spirit, they are not to grieve the Holy Spirit.

Summarizing the significance of the three passages that speak of the sealing by the Holy Spirit, the type signifies ownership. The believer belongs to God, which is proven by the seal that only God can break. God alone has authority over that which He owns. Being owned by God, the believer enjoys eternal security. The seal is the realization of all promised blessings on the day of the believer's final redemption.

H. Clothing

The last type to consider in this study portrays the Holy Spirit as clothing. In Luke 24:49, Yeshua said: *And behold, I send forth the promise of my Father upon you: but tarry ye in the city, until ye be clothed with power from on high.* In this verse, Yeshua gave His apostles the third and final commission. They were to remain in Jerusalem until the coming of the Holy Spirit (Acts 1:4-5). When the Spirit arrived, three things would occur. First, *the promise of the Father* would be fulfilled (Lk. 24:49a). During the Upper Room Discourse, the Father, through the Son, promised to send them another Comforter—the Holy Spirit. Second, they would receive divine power, or *power from on high* (Lk. 24:49b), to fulfill their commission (Acts 1:8). Third, a new ministry of the Spirit would begin, the work of Spirit baptism (Acts 1:5).

When Yeshua said that His disciples would be clothed with power from on high, He basically said they would be clothed with the Holy Spirit. This clothing with the Holy Spirit guaranteed protection and the power they needed to fulfill their calling. The agent is God.

In Ephesians 4:24, Paul also used the figure of clothing, saying: *put on the new man, that after God has been created in righteousness and holiness of truth*. Here, the believer is encouraged to be the agent and to put on spiritual garments. Just like one puts on physical clothes, the believer is to put on the new man. However, the one who creates this new man is God, and the new man is created after the likeness of God in true righteousness and holiness.

I. QUESTIONS AND STUDY SUGGESTIONS

Study Suggestion 1: In the image below, add the missing words from Isaiah 11:2 that express the sevenfold nature of the Ruach HaKodesh.

Study Suggestion 2: List all symbols the Scriptures use for the Ruach HaKodesh.

Question 1: Of these symbols, which one means the most to you?

Question 2: Name the first occurrence of the Ruach HaKodesh as a dove in the Hebrew Scriptures. Name the first occurrence in the New Testament. Why did the Spirit decide to descend upon Yeshua in the form of a dove?

Chapter V

The Works of the Ruach HaKodesh

The works of the Ruach HaKodesh can also be referred to as His ministries. This chapter will deal with these works in five areas: first, in relation to the recording of Scripture; second, His works in the Hebrew Scriptures; third, in relation to the natural world, i.e., how the Spirit ministers to the unsaved; fourth, in relation to believers; and fifth, in relation to the future.

A. THE WORKS IN RELATION TO SCRIPTURE

There are three areas in which and by which and through which the Holy Spirit works in relation to Scripture: revelation, inspiration, and illumination.

1. The Ministry of Revelation

What is meant by "revelation" is the unveiling or revealing of truth. Revelation is the unveiling of something that had not been known before. The source of divine revelation, the One who unveils the truth, is the Holy Spirit. In the Hebrew Scriptures, this is taught in II Samuel 23:2-3; Ezekiel 2:2; 8:3; 11:1, 24; and Micah 3:8. In the New Testament, it is taught in John 16:12-15, I Corinthians 2:9-10, and II Peter 1:21.

So, the first area of the Holy Spirit's work in relation to Scripture is revelation, as He is the One who unveils the truth. Revelation also concerns the receiving of the truth from God.

2. The Ministry of Inspiration

The second ministry in relation to Scripture is the work of inspiration. Inspiration concerns the recording of truth. When men recorded what was revealed to them, they were able to record it totally free of error by virtue of this ministry of the Holy Spirit. While revelation simply means that the truth has been revealed to a person directly from God, inspiration involves the actual recording of the newly revealed truth.

Not everything that was revealed was necessarily recorded. For example, in Revelation 10:3-4, the Apostle John heard something which the *seven thunders uttered*. When he began to write down what was uttered by the seven thunders, he was immediately told to seal up what they had said. This is an example of revelation without inspiration, for something was revealed to John, but he was not allowed to record what the seven thunders had said.

Whatever was revealed by the Holy Spirit and recorded at the time of the revelation was inspired by the Holy Spirit. The Holy Spirit is the source of inspiration. In the Hebrew Scriptures, this is taught in Isaiah 59:21. In the New Testament, it is taught in Matthew 22:43-44; Mark 12:36-37; and Acts 1:16, 4:25-26, and 28:25-28. By far, the most famous passage is II Timothy 3:16: *Every scripture inspired of God [is] also profitable for teaching, for reproof, for correction, for instruction which is in righteousness.*

3. The Ministry of Illumination

The third ministry of the Holy Spirit in relation to Scripture is the work of illumination. When the Holy Spirit did the work of revelation, He revealed a truth to a prophet. When the Holy Spirit did the work of inspiration, He caused that prophet to write down, free from error, the truth which was revealed. Illumination is a ministry that relates to the believer. The Ruach HaKodesh helps believers to understand that which the prophets wrote. He does this in two ways: by illuminating the believer's mind during personal Bible study, and by means of giving the gift of teaching to certain believers who, in turn, help other believers to understand the Word. When a believer understands spiritual truth, he understands it because of the Spirit's ministry of illumination.

In the Hebrew Scriptures, this is taught in Nehemiah 9:20. In the New Testament, it is taught in I Corinthians 2:14-16 and Ephesians 1:15-18.

B. The Works in the Hebrew Scriptures

The ministries of the Holy Spirit in the Hebrew Scriptures can be divided into three categories: those in relation to creation, those in relation to the world, and those in relation to man.

1. The Ministry of the Holy Spirit in Relation to Creation

All three persons of the Triune God were involved in the work of creation. As to the Holy Spirit, Genesis 1:2 explains that the Spirit of God, the *Ruach Elohim,* hovered or brooded over the deep to bring order out of chaos. In Job 26:13, God's Spirit gave the adornment to the universe at the time of its creation. In Job 33:4, the Spirit of God is credited with the creation of life in man. In Psalm 33:6, the *breath of his mouth*, the Ruach, is responsible for the creation of the material universe. In Psalm 104:29-30, the Holy Spirit is responsible for the creation and preservation of life. In Isaiah 40:12-14, the Spirit of Jehovah brought design to creation.

These verses show that one of the major ministries of the Holy Spirit in the Hebrew Scriptures was His work in creation.

2. The Ministry of the Holy Spirit in Relation to the World

The ministry of the Holy Spirit in relation to the world specifically covers His work of striving, to which there is also an element of restraining. This is found in Genesis 6. In Genesis 3:15, it is predicted that the Messiah would come from the seed of the woman, and that He would have continuous conflict with the serpent: *I will put enmity between you and the woman, and between your seed and her seed.* There was going to be enmity between Satan and human womanhood, and the enmity would continue between Satan and that which the "seed of the woman" would produce: the Messianic Person. We see this enmity already at work in the first two verses of Genesis 6, where Satan had some of his fallen angels take on human form and intermarry with human women. This was to corrupt the seed of the woman and prevent the fulfillment of the prophecy of Genesis 3:15. Satan's enmity is well displayed against womanhood in this chapter. The result of the union between women and fallen angels was a grotesque race, the *Nephilim*, and this corruption of the human race would eventually bring on the Flood.[22]

Then, in Genesis 6:3, God said: *My Spirit shall not strive with man for ever, for that he also is flesh: yet shall his days be a hundred and twenty years.* Thus, in His relationship to the world, the Holy Spirit did the work of striving. Once the Spirit ceased to strive, judgment would follow. At the end of the 120 years, the Flood came and destroyed all but one family.

According to II Peter 2:4, the demons who had intermarried with human women were restrained in hell (Greek, *Tartarus*, a section of *Sheol* or *Hades*).[23] After the Flood, the Spirit continued to do His work of striving with man as mankind began to multiply, and this work of striving was augmented by His work of restraining evil.

In relation to the world in general, the Holy Spirit's work in the Hebrew Scriptures was to strive and to restrain evil.

3. The Ministries of the Holy Spirit in Relation to Humanity

There were three specific ministries of the Holy Spirit among humanity in the Hebrew Scriptures. The first ministry was that of indwelling. The Holy Spirit was *in* some people. He did not indwell all believers, but He indwelt some, such as Joshua (Num. 27:18), Daniel (Dan. 6:3), and the prophets (I Pet. 1:10-11):

> [10] *Concerning which salvation the prophets sought and searched diligently, who prophesied of the grace that [should come] unto you:* [11] *searching what [time] or what manner of time the Spirit of Messiah which was in them did point unto, when it testified beforehand the sufferings of Messiah, and the glories that should follow them.* [12] *To whom it was revealed, that not unto themselves, but unto you, did they minister these things, which now have*

---

[22] For more details on this subject, see the author's commentary on Genesis titled *The Book of Genesis* and published by Ariel Ministries.

[23] Further details on this specific subject will appear in a following volume of this series that will deal with demonology.

been announced unto you through them that preached the gospel unto you by the Holy Spirit sent forth from heaven; which things angels desire to look into.

The second ministry was that the Holy Spirit came upon some people. He indwelt some, He came *upon* others. For example, He came upon Othniel (Judg. 3:9-10), Gideon (Judg. 6:34), Jephthah (Judg. 11:29), Samson (Judg. 13:24-25; 14:6, 19; 15:14), Saul (I Sam. 10:9-10), and David (I Sam. 16:13).

The third ministry was that of *filling*. Examples of the Holy Spirit's ministry of filling people are Exodus 28:3, 31:3, and 35:30-31. The differences between filling and indwelling will be studied in a later chapter.

There is a key distinction between the Holy Spirit's work in the New Testament and His work in the Hebrew Scriptures, which is brought out in John 7:37-39:

[37] Now on the last day, the great day of the feast, Yeshua stood and cried, saying, If any man thirst, let him come unto me and drink. [38] He that believes on me, as the scripture has said, from within him shall flow rivers of living water. [39] But this spoke he of the Spirit, which they that believed on him were to receive: for the Spirit was not yet given; because Yeshua was not yet glorified.

This passage records the promise that someday the Ruach HaKodesh would be in all believers, but Yeshua pointed out that the Spirit had not yet been given. This does not mean the Spirit had not been active, because He was active throughout the time of the Hebrew Scriptures and in the Gospels. Yet, at that time, the Holy Spirit was not doing something which He would do in the New Testament believer after the Messiah's ascension.

What Yeshua meant in John 7:37-39 is explained in John 14:16-17:

[16] And I will pray the Father, and he shall give you another Comforter, that he may be with you for ever, [17] even the Spirit of truth: whom the world cannot receive; for it beholds him not, neither knows him: ye know him; for he abides with you, and shall be in you.

When Yeshua spoke these words, the Holy Spirit was *with* the believer. Later, He would be *in* the believer. That is the key distinction between the Holy Spirit's work during Old Testament times and New Testament times.

As of Acts 2, the Holy Spirit indwells all believers. He did not indwell all believers prior to Acts 2, though He did indwell some, as can be seen from II Kings 2:9-12 (see also Num. 11:17, 25; 27:18). Those who did have the indwelling of the Holy Spirit did not necessarily have it permanently. For example, in I Samuel 16:14, the Holy Spirit departed from Saul. In Psalm 51:11, King David prayed: *take not your holy Spirit from me*. The Holy Spirit did indwell David, but his prayer shows that the Holy Spirit could also leave David. David's prayer was therefore a valid prayer at that time, but it is not a valid prayer for believers now. It should be noted (and will be discussed later in this chapter) that this type of indwelling was not relevant to salvation. Unlike indwelling, salvation is directly related to the Spirit's work of regeneration.

In summarizing the work of the Holy Spirit among humanity in the Hebrew Scriptures, five ramifications should be pointed out:

1. The work of the Holy Spirit, as recorded in the Hebrew Scriptures, was connected to special service. Those who were called to a special service were the ones who received the special works of the Holy Spirit.
2. The work of the Holy Spirit was a provision of divine enablement. In order to enable someone to accomplish a special task, the Holy Spirit did a special work.
3. The work of the Holy Spirit often meant a provision of divine wisdom. This was especially true in the case of Daniel, who received unique wisdom from God through the work of the Holy Spirit.
4. The Holy Spirit provided special skills. The two men who oversaw the work on the Tabernacle, Bezalel and Oholiab, received this ministry of the Holy Spirit (Ex. 31:1-6). They were filled *with the Spirit of God, in wisdom, and in understanding, and in knowledge, and in all manner of workmanship* (Ex. 31:3) to do the special work required for the construction of the Tabernacle, its furnishings, and the priestly garments.
5. The work of the Holy Spirit sometimes meant the provision of physical strength. One example of a person who was empowered by the Spirit to do great things is Samson (Judg. 13:25; 14:6, 19; 15:14).

C. The Works in the Life of Messiah

In the Gospels, the Holy Spirit followed the pattern of the Hebrew Scriptures. He continued His work of coming *upon* specific people and *filling* them for certain purposes. These people were John the Baptist in Luke 1:15, Elizabeth in Luke 1:41, and Zacharias in Luke 1:67. In Luke 2:25 and 4:17-21, we learn that the Holy Spirit was also upon Simeon and that He came upon the Messiah Himself. In Luke 11:13, Yeshua promised His disciples that the heavenly Father would give the Holy Spirit to them that ask Him. Later, in John 20:22, He breathed the Holy Spirit on them. These events show that the Spirit's work was neither limited to the Messiah, nor to only a few people, but was extended to the disciples as well.

Before delving into the Spirit's works in the life of Yeshua, it needs to be noted that much of His work in the Hebrew Scriptures related to revealing truths about the Messiah. Two passages serve as examples for this point. In Isaiah 42:1-4, God said:

> *¹ Behold, my servant, whom I uphold; my chosen, in whom my soul delights: I have put my Spirit upon him; he will bring forth justice to the Gentiles. ² He will not cry, nor lift up his voice, nor cause it to be heard in the street. ³ A bruised reed will he not break, and a dimly burning wick will he not quench: he will bring forth justice in truth. ⁴ He will not fail nor be discouraged, till he have set justice in the earth; and the isles shall wait for his law.*

Of importance for the topic at hand is verse 1, which makes four points: First, Messiah is the Servant of Jehovah. Second, He is God's Chosen One, in whom Jehovah will greatly delight. Third, He is anointed with the Spirit. Fourth, He will benefit the Gentile nations.

The second example is Isaiah 61:1-2:

> *¹ The Spirit of the Lord Jehovah is upon me; because Jehovah has anointed me to preach good tidings unto the meek; he has sent me to bind up the broken-hearted, to proclaim liberty to the captives, and the opening of the prison to them that are bound; ² to proclaim the year of Jehovah's favor, and the day of vengeance of our God; to comfort all that mourn;*

Verse 1 reaffirms Isaiah 11:2 and 42:1. Messiah will be anointed with the Holy Spirit for His mission and His task.

These two examples show that the work of the Ruach HaKodesh in the Hebrew Scriptures was inseparably related to the Messiah and God's Messianic program. The following sections will illustrate how His prophecies came true in the life of Yeshua.

1. The Agent of Conception

The Gospels bear a clear testimony to the work of the Holy Spirit that resulted in the virgin birth. Two passages need to be considered in this context. The first passage is Matthew 1:18-21:

[18] Now the birth of Yeshua the Messiah was on this wise: When his mother Miriam had been betrothed to Joseph, before they came together she was found with child of the Holy Spirit. [19] And Joseph her husband, being a righteous man, and not willing to make her a public example, was minded to put her away privately. [20] But when he thought on these things, behold, an angel of the Lord appeared unto him in a dream, saying, Joseph, you son of David, fear not to take unto you Miriam your wife: for that which is conceived in her is of the Holy Spirit. [21] And she shall bring forth a son; and you shall call his name YESHUA; for it is he that shall save his people from their sins.

The emphasis of this section is clearly on the virgin birth. Matthew wrote the account from Joseph's perspective and stated in verse 18: *before they came together she was found with child of the Holy Spirit.* This verse makes it very clear that Miriam was pregnant before there had been any sexual relations between her and Joseph. Even after the wedding ceremony, they had no sexual relations whatsoever until after the birth of Yeshua. Conversely, the very word "before" points out that after the Messiah was born, they did have sexual relations and Miriam had at least six more children: four sons and at least two daughters (Mt. 13:55-56).

Verse 19 states that Joseph had privately begun to write out a bill of divorcement, concluding that in light of her pregnancy, she had been unfaithful. As a righteous man, he could not marry a woman he assumed was immoral. However, he chose to keep it private because he was not willing to make her a public example and shame her.

It was at this point that an angel appeared to Joseph with a message containing three essential elements (Mt. 1:20-21). First, he was to fulfill the marriage vow; although Miriam was pregnant, he was to proceed with the wedding ceremony. Second, the child was conceived of the Holy Spirit, not through an immoral relationship. Third, it was pointed out to Joseph that everything was happening according to plan and that this pregnancy was the fulfillment of the divine prophecy of Isaiah 7:14, which states, *Therefore the Lord himself will give you a sign: behold, a virgin shall conceive, and bear a son, and shall call his name Immanuel.* In verse 21, the angel instructed Joseph to call the baby to be born Yeshua. The reason was because *it is he that shall save his people from their sins*. The angel was speaking in Hebrew and used a Hebrew wordplay: "You shall call his name *Yeshua* for it is he that shall *yoshia* his people from their sins."

The second verse that has important information regarding the Holy Spirit's role in the conception of Yeshua is Luke 1:35: *And the angel answered and said unto her, The Holy Spirit shall come upon you, and the power of the Most High shall overshadow you: wherefore also the holy thing which is begotten shall be called the Son of God.* In Luke 1:34, Miriam had raised a question: *How shall this be, seeing I know not a man?* The angel Gabriel answered her by explaining the Holy Spirit's role in the conception. Because of what he said, some teach that the virgin birth was necessary to keep the Messiah from inheriting the sin nature. This teaching is based upon the false assumption that the sin nature is transmitted only through the father. However, the sin nature is transmitted through both the father and the mother. So, what protected the Messiah from inheriting the sin nature of Miriam? The overshadowing work of the Holy Spirit. God's omnipotence would have allowed Him to produce an absolutely sinless being by normal human conception, using both male sperm and a female egg. However, He chose to do it another way, thus fulfilling His prophecies in the Hebrew Bible—hinted at in Genesis 3:15 and clearly stated in Isaiah 7:14: The Messiah would be conceived in the womb of a virgin, and His birth would provide Him with a unique credential.

Another false teaching is that Miriam's egg was not produced by her ovaries but implanted by the Holy Spirit. As previously mentioned, this would have made her a surrogate mother and is not the teaching of the text or the Bible as a whole. There had to be a biological connection between Adam, Abraham, Isaac, Jacob, Judah, David, and Yeshua for Him to be truly "the seed." So, Miriam's egg was generated by the Holy Spirit and what protected the conceived seed was the Spirit's overshadowing work.

The Greek verb which is translated into English as "shall overshadow" is *episkiasei*. It is used in the New Testament of God's overshadowing presence, which always brings His plan to pass. The word is also used in passages describing Yeshua's transfiguration (Mt. 17:5; Mk. 9:7; Lk. 9:34). It means "to surround," "to encompass," or, in a metaphorical sense, "to influence." In Luke 1:35, it describes the Spirit's creative influence which will overshadow Miriam in order for her to conceive a child. The angel went on to explain that because of the overshadowing work of the Holy Spirit, He who was conceived would be holy—that is, sinless. Furthermore, He would be called the Son of God (Lk. 1:35). This Messianic title is based on Psalm 2:7-12 and Proverbs 30:4.

2. Other Activities in the Life of Messiah

There are five events or indications which prove that the Ruach HaKodesh was actively involved in the life of the Messiah.

a. Anointing

There are five passages that speak of the Ruach HaKodesh anointing the Messiah. The first passage is John 1:29-34, which reports that the anointing occurred at Yeshua's baptism:

> [29] *On the morrow he sees Yeshua coming unto him, and says, Behold, the Lamb of God, that takes away the sin of the world!* [30] *This is he of whom I said, After me comes a man who is become before me: for he was before me.* [31] *And I knew him not; but that he should be made manifest to Israel, for this cause came I baptizing in water.* [32] *And John bore witness, saying, I have beheld the Spirit descending as a dove out of heaven; and it abode upon him.* [33] *And I knew him not: but he that sent me to baptize in water, he said unto me, Upon whomsoever you shall see the Spirit descending, and abiding upon him, the same is he that baptizes in the Holy Spirit.* [34] *And I have seen, and have borne witness that this is the Son of God.*

The day of Yeshua's baptism was ordained by God the Father for the Messiah to be publicly identified by His herald, John the Baptizer. There are various ways that John could have identified Yeshua, but he simply said, *Behold, the Lamb of God, that takes away the sin of the world!* (Jn. 1:29) By calling Him Lamb of God, John identified Yeshua with two Old Testament concepts: the paschal lamb of Exodus 12 and the Messianic Lamb of Isaiah 53. In verse 32, the Baptizer went on to show how he could be certain that this was the Messianic Person. Initially, he *knew him not* (Jn. 1:33). However, it had been revealed to him that upon whomever he would see *the Spirit descending, and abiding upon him, the same is he that baptizes in the Holy Spirit*. So then, at the baptism, when the Spirit descended in the form of a dove upon Yeshua, this certified once and for all to John that He was the Messianic King.

The second passage is Luke 4:17-21. Because the verses were discussed previously, a short summary is enough to note that the passage speaks of the Messiah's induction by the Spirit into His prophetic office. Isaiah, who is quoted in these verses by Luke, predicted that the Spirit would anoint the Messiah in preparation for His preaching ministry, and this prophecy now came true. Yeshua was anointed with the Holy Spirit for His mission and His task. As mentioned above, this anointing took place i at His baptism (see also Mt. 3:16). It was at this point in Yeshua's life that He began His public ministry and openly proclaimed Himself to be Messiah.

The third passage is Acts 4:23-28, which confirms that the Holy Spirit anointed Yeshua as the Messianic Person.

The fourth passage is Acts 10:38, which connects the Spirit's ministry of anointing the Messiah with Yeshua's ministry of doing good: *even Yeshua of Nazareth, how God anointed him with the Holy Spirit and with power: who went about doing good, and healing all that were oppressed of the devil; for God was with him*.

The fifth and final passage is Hebrews 1:9, which again speaks of the anointing of the Messianic Person: *You have loved righteousness, and hated iniquity; Therefore God, your God, has anointed you with the oil of gladness above your fellows*.

b. Being Upon the Messiah

Three passages in Isaiah speak of the Ruach HaKodesh as being *upon* the Messiah. These passages are Isaiah 11:2-3, 42:1, and 61:1-2; all three have been discussed previously in this book. Because the Holy Spirit anointed the Messiah and was upon Him, Yeshua was able to preach good tidings, release captives, recover the sight of the blind, and set at liberty them that were bruised. The Spirit's power allowed Him to prophesy and preach, and it allowed Him to perform miracles.

c. Filling

According to Luke 4:1 and John 3:34, Yeshua was *filled* with the Spirit. The context of the first verse is Yeshua's temptation. All three Gospel accounts make the point that this event was very much part of the divine plan, as it was the Holy Spirit who played the active role. Matthew stated, *Then was Yeshua led up of the Spirit* (Mt. 4:1). Mark added urgency to the same event: *And straightway the Spirit drives him forth* (Mk. 1:12). And Luke mentioned the work of the Spirit twice: *And Yeshua, full of the Holy Spirit, returned from the Jordan, and was led in the Spirit* (Lk. 4:1). All this shows that the temptation was very much part of God's plan. It also shows that the Ruach HaKodesh ministered to the Messiah by filling Him.

John 3:34 adds some important information to the same truth: *For he whom God has sent speaks the words of God: for he gives not the Spirit by measure*. As prophesied in Isaiah 11:1-5, the Messiah did not receive the Spirit by measure but received the Spirit's sevenfold fullness.

d. Sealing

In John 6:27, Messiah declared that the Father had *sealed* Him: *Work not for the food which perishes, but for the food which abides unto eternal life, which the Son of man shall give unto you: for him the Father, even God, has sealed*. The verse does not directly indicate that it was the Spirit who did the sealing. Yet, of importance here is that the act of sealing was accomplished entirely by God. It marked the Messiah's heavenly origin and proved His divine Sonship.

e. Leading

According to Matthew 4:1 and Luke 4:1, Yeshua was *led* by the Spirit. The context is Yeshua's temptation, and the verses prove that the Holy Spirit played the active role in this event. Matthew stated, *Then was Yeshua led up of the Spirit.* Luke confirmed this by saying, *And Yeshua . . . was led in the Spirit.*

3. Messiah's Response to the Ruach HaKodesh

Having been anointed, filled, and sealed by the Ruach HaKodesh, the Messiah responded by rejoicing in the Spirit and by being empowered by the Spirit.

a. Rejoicing

Luke 10:21 states:

> *In that same hour he [Yeshua] rejoiced in the Holy Spirit, and said, I thank you, O Father, Lord of heaven and earth, that you did hide these things from the wise and understanding, and did reveal them unto babes: yea, Father; for so it was well-pleasing in your sight.*

The Greek verb translated here as "rejoiced" is *ēgalliasato*, which carries the meaning of "exulting" and "being full of joy." It is a verb that would be used to describe someone who jumps for joy. Yeshua rejoiced in—or by—the Spirit.

b. Empowered

In the context of the Holy Spirit's work in the life of the Messiah, it is important to note that Yeshua was empowered by the Ruach HaKodesh in several ways, four of which will be discussed here.

(1) For Prophetic Ministry

Luke 4:14a states that the Holy Spirit empowered the Messiah to return to Galilee, stating: *And Yeshua returned in the power of the Spirit into Galilee.* Yeshua's departure from Judea was part of the divine plan. The Spirit led the Messiah to Galilee, and He prompted Him to pass through Samaria (Jn. 4:4). This route was necessary because the Messiah had a divine appointment with the Samaritan woman. Furthermore, the Spirit wanted Yeshua to perform His second miracle in Cana.

Matthew 12:17-21 speaks of this empowerment in the context of Yeshua's prophetic ministry, and the passage has been discussed before. It quotes Isaiah 42:1-4, which is a prophecy of the nature of Messiah's ministry during His first coming.

Luke 4:17-19 mentions that Yeshua read the prophetic portion of the synagogue service, and it happened to be a quotation from Isaiah 61. The complete prophecy is Isaiah 61:1-3, and it is an example of a type of Messianic prophecy where aspects of the first and second comings are blended into one picture, there being no indication in the text itself that there is a gap of time between the events, or that the prophecy actually refers to two comings. The passage quoted by Yeshua is an amalgam of Isaiah 61:1-2 and 58:6:

Isaiah 58:6b & 61:1-2a	Luke 4:18-19
⁶¹:¹ The Spirit of the Lord Jehovah is upon me; because Jehovah has anointed me to preach good tidings unto the meek; he has sent me to bind up the brokenhearted, to proclaim liberty to the captives, and the opening of the prison to them that are bound; ⁵⁸:⁶ᵇ to undo the bands of the yoke, and to let the oppressed go free, and that ye break every yoke? ⁶¹:²ᵃ to proclaim the year of Jehovah's favor,	¹⁸ The Spirit of the Lord is upon me, Because he anointed me to preach good tidings to the poor: He has sent me to proclaim release to the captives, And recovering of sight to the blind, To set at liberty them that are bruised, ¹⁹ To proclaim the acceptable year of the Lord.

Yeshua Himself provides the proper interpretation of this prophecy. After reading verse 1 of Isaiah 61 and one clause of verse 2, He stopped and said, *Today has this scripture been fulfilled in your ears* (Lk. 4:21). That day, Isaiah 61:1-2a had been fulfilled. The rest of verse 2 and all of verse 3 will be fulfilled in conjunction with the second coming. The purpose of Messiah's first coming was to bring the good news, to proclaim the gospel in all of its various facets. It is at His second coming that He will *proclaim the day of vengeance of our God*. At a normal first-century Sabbath service, seven men were selected to read the Torah portion. The seventh reader, the *maftir*, would read a shorter part, but he had to read at least three verses and then read from the Prophets. The rule was that this last reader, when reading from the Prophets, must not read less than 21 verses. This may mean that Yeshua read the short Torah portion, and then He was to read the appropriate passage from Isaiah 61, but He did not. He stopped in the middle of verse 2 (Lk. 4:18-19), *closed the book,* or, more correctly, the scroll, *and gave it back to the attendant* (the *chazzan*). Then He *sat down* (Lk. 4:20a) for the purpose of expounding upon the text, because a rabbi would teach in a sitting position. By cutting the reading short, He did something that went contrary to Jewish tradition. In the context of the Messiah's empowerment by the Holy Spirit, it is important to note that He acted because *the Spirit of the Lord Jehovah* (Isa. 61:1), or *the Spirit of the Lord* (Lk. 4:18), was upon Him. It is by the power of this Spirit that He was able to prophesy and preach.

(2) *To Cast Out Demons*

Because Yeshua was empowered by the Holy Spirit, He was also able to cast out demons. This can be seen in the events described in Matthew 12 and is especially mentioned in verses 28 and 31. The incident preceding Matthew 12:28 began when Yeshua exorcised a demon that caused the possessed person to be both *blind and dumb*, meaning he could neither see nor speak (Mt. 12:22). The account will be discussed in Chapter VII. At this point, it is only important to note that Yeshua had cast out that demon *by the Spirit of God* (Mt. 12:28a). This showed that the kingdom of God had come upon the people, and the miracle authenticated His declaration of being the Messiah.

Israel rejected Yeshua as their Messiah, claiming that He was only able to perform these unique miracles in the power of Satan himself. As a result, Yeshua spoke a judgment on the generation of Israel that had rejected Him on the grounds of being demon possessed, saying: *Every sin and blasphemy shall be forgiven unto men; but the blasphemy against the Spirit shall not be forgiven* (Mt. 12:31). That generation of Israel was guilty of a very unique sin, which has become known as the unpardonable sin or the blasphemy of the Holy Spirit (see Chapter VII). Because it was unpardonable, a judgment that could never be removed or alleviated was set against *this generation*. That judgment came forty years later, in the year A.D. 70, when Jerusalem and the Temple were destroyed. Matthew 12:31, however, again proves that the Ruach HaKodesh empowered Yeshua to perform unique and mighty miracles.

(3) To Perform Miracles

From the previous two points, it is clear that the Messiah was empowered by the Holy Spirit to perform miracles (Lk. 4:18). However, it should be noted that not all miracles Yeshua performed were due to the Spirit's empowerment. Mark 5:30 and Luke 5:17, 6:19, 8:46 show that He performed some miracles in His own divine power.

4. In Relation to the Death of Messiah

Hebrews 9:14 states: *how much more shall the blood of Messiah, who through the eternal Spirit offered himself without blemish unto God, cleanse your conscience from dead works to serve the living God?* This verse indicates that Yeshua offered Himself unto God in death by the Spirit. The combination of the Greek adjective *aiōniou* ("eternal") and the noun *pneumatos* ("Spirit") must mean that the expression refers to the Holy Spirit. Yet, some have argued that the lack of the definite article before *pneumatos* means that the word may be a reference to Messiah's human spirit. Walvoord settles the debate this way:

> While in the last analysis the Greek would admit either interpretation, the matter must be settled on theological grounds. The question is whether Messiah offered up His whole person as a sacrifice, or whether merely the human nature was the sacrifice . . . To explain the text as if it described the divine nature as priest and the human nature as the sacrifice is inadmissible. The whole person is priest and victim;

for all done by either nature belongs to the Person: He offered Himself, says the apostle.[24]

5. In Relation to the Resurrection of Messiah

There are three passages that seem to speak of the Spirit's work in the resurrection of the Messiah. These verses are generally used to prove the Spirit's involvement in this event. However, it needs to be pointed out that the Scriptures are not clear on the topic. They refer Yeshua's resurrection to the triune Godhead without distinguishing which Person was involved. Acts 2:24 and Ephesians 1:17-20, for example, state that God raised Messiah up from the dead. In John 10:17-18, Yeshua declared that He alone had the power to lay down His life and to take it up again. In John 11:25, He called Himself the resurrection. The three verses that seem to indicate that the Spirit, too, was involved in the resurrection are Romans 1:4, 8:11; and I Peter 3:18.

a. Romans 1:4

who was declared to be the Son of God with power, according to the spirit of holiness, by the resurrection from the dead; even Yeshua Messiah our Lord,

Some translations render the verb "declared" as "designated": Yeshua was designated to be the Son of God by His own resurrection.

The subordinate clause "according to the spirit of holiness" may either refer to the Holy Spirit or to Yeshua's own human spirit. There are two thoughts that support the latter interpretation. First, if the expression refers to Messiah's human spirit, it stands in contrast to the expression "according to the flesh" of the previous verse, Romans 1:3. According to the flesh, Yeshua was a descendant of David. According to His spirit, He was divine. Second, the source of the resurrection is *the dead*. In the Greek, the word is *nekron*, a masculine adjective that is in the plural. Hence, a better translation would be "the resurrection from among the dead

---

[24] Walvoord, "Chapter IX: The Holy Spirit in the Sufferings and Glorification of Messiah," in *The Holy Spirit: A Comprehensive Study of the Person and Work of the Holy Spirit*.

ones." Combining these two thoughts, one can say: Messiah's human spirit was resurrected from the dead. The resurrection proved His deity, and this is what was declared by the Holy Spirit.

b. Romans 8:11

But if the Spirit of him that raised up Yeshua from the dead dwells in you, he that raised up Messiah Yeshua from the dead shall give life also to your mortal bodies through his Spirit that dwells in you.

At first reading, this verse may seem to prove that the Holy Spirit had a part in the resurrection of the Messiah. Yet, a more thorough examination shows that it does not prove this thought. The independent clause of the sentence is "he shall give life also to your mortal bodies." The subordinate clause specifies who the "he" is: "He who raised up Messiah Yeshua from the dead." How will He give life to the mortal bodies of the believers? Through His Spirit that dwells in the believer. That this is God the Father is also proved by the preceding subordinate clause starting with "But if." The "he" of the independent clause is the "him" of the subordinate clause, for it is the "him" who raised up Yeshua from the dead.

Replacing the personal pronouns and separating the parts of the verse by asking a few questions may help understand who is doing what:

- ✡ God shall give life to the mortal bodies of the believers.
- ✡ Who is this God? He is the One who raised up Messiah Yeshua from the dead.
- ✡ How will God do it? Through His Spirit.
- ✡ Who is this Spirit? He is the Spirit of God.
- ✡ Which God? The One who raised up Yeshua from the dead.
- ✡ What does this Spirit do? He indwells the believers.
- ✡ What is the precondition for God to give life to the mortal bodies of the believers? The precondition is that the believers are indwelled by the Spirit.

Hence, the "he" in the independent clause refers to God and not the Holy Spirit. The verse does acknowledge that the Spirit of God indwells the believer, and it is this indwelling of the believer that guarantees the believer's future resurrection. Yet, according to Romans 8:11, it was God the Father who resurrected the Messiah.

c. I Peter 3:18

Because Messiah also suffered for sins once, the righteous for the un-righteous, that he might bring us to God; being put to death in the flesh, but made alive in the spirit;

Yeshua was *put to death in the flesh*. The first part of the phrase ("put to death") indicates that Messiah died a violent death. The second part ("in the flesh") means that Messiah died physically, and the expression emphasizes His humanity. The next statement is that He was *made alive*. The verb could also be translated as "quickened." It is in the aorist participle, which does not express action subsequent to the main verb, but contemporaneous to the main verb. The main verb of the sentence is "suffered." Hence, while Yeshua was suffering on the cross, He was made alive in the spirit. Because the phrase is in the passive voice, it means that God made Him alive again; Yeshua was *made alive* spiritually after experiencing spiritual death. He was resurrected spiritually on the cross before He ever died physically. He died physically, but He was quickened in the human spirit; He was made spiritually alive before He died physically.

Now, the question arises whether the making alive happened *in the spirit*, as the above translation says, or "by the spirit." The first option is locative and would mean that Yeshua was made alive in His own spirit. The second option is instrumental and means that He was made alive by the Spirit of God, who has the attribute of being omnipotent. In the Greek, the word "spirit" has no article, which indicates that it does not refer to the Holy Spirit, but to Yeshua's human spirit. Hence, I Peter 3:18 does not deal with the resurrection of the Messiah, but with the fact that He was made spiritually alive while He was still suffering on the cross.

Having looked at all three verses, the conclusion is that there is no clear and specific proof from the Scriptures that the Ruach HaKodesh was involved in the resurrection of the Messiah. It is declared with certainty that He was involved in the conception and in many of the miracles and so forth. Yet, we cannot say with the same clarity of proof that He was also directly involved in the resurrection of the Messiah.

D. The Works in the Natural World

Looking at the here and now, the Holy Spirit is doing an ongoing work in the natural world. He convicts the unbeliever of the truth. The single best passage describing the work of conviction is John 16:7-11:

> *⁷ Nevertheless I tell you the truth: It is expedient for you that I go away; for if I go not away, the Comforter will not come unto you; but if I go, I will send him unto you. ⁸ And he, when he is come, will convict the world in respect of sin, and of righteousness, and of judgment: ⁹ of sin, because they believe not on me; ¹⁰ of righteousness, because I go to the Father, and ye behold me no more; ¹¹ of judgment, because the prince of this world has been judged.*

In its biblical usage as a work of the Holy Spirit, conviction means to place the truth of a case in such a clear light that it is acknowledged as truth even if it is not accepted. In reference to the gospel, conviction means to clearly state the good news so that the unbeliever understands what the content of the gospel is and acknowledges it as true regardless of whether he accepts it personally.

According to the above passage, the Holy Spirit's work of conviction will be in three areas: sin, righteousness, and judgment. From the way each area is explained, it is possible to determine exactly what kind of sin, what kind of righteousness, and of what kind of judgment the Holy Spirit will be convicting the world. In respect to sin, He convicts the world of the sin of unbelief, or as Yeshua put it: *because they believe not on me*. Man is condemned before God not because he is a sinner, but because he is in a state of sin. He was born into the state of sin, a state of unbelief. Being in a state of sin, he has refused to believe in the Savior.

In respect to righteousness, the Holy Spirit convicts the unbeliever of the righteousness of the Messiah, as was proved by His ascension to the Father. The ascension and reception of Yeshua into heaven vindicated His righteousness. If He were not righteous, He would not have been able to ascend into heaven. Because of the sin of unbelief, the sinner fails to receive the imputed righteousness of the Messiah.

In respect to judgment, the Holy Spirit's work of conviction pertains to the final judgment, called the Great White Throne judgment. Yeshua expressed it this way: *because the prince of this world has been judged*. If the prince of this world has been judged to everlasting flames, so will his subjects be judged. Failure to receive the imputed righteousness of the Messiah will result in the final judgment.

The Holy Spirit's work of conviction, then, follows these three logical steps. He will convict unbelievers of the sin of unbelief. Because of their unbelief, they fail to receive the imputed righteousness of the Messiah. Because they fail to receive the imputed righteousness of the Messiah, they will share in Satan's final judgment in the Lake of Fire.

E. The Works in the Life of the Believer

The Holy Spirit is very active in the life of the believer, and this is an area where there is a great deal of biblical revelation. To better understand this material, it will be studied in two categories. The first is titled "The Ministries of the Holy Spirit in Relation to Salvation." The second is titled "The Ministries of the Holy Spirit in Relation to Spiritual Growth."

1. The Ministries of the Holy Spirit in Relation to Salvation

In relation to salvation, the Holy Spirit has five ministries.

a. The Ministry of Regeneration

The first ministry is the work of regeneration. The word "regeneration" (*paliggenesia*) is found twice in the New Testament. Matthew 19:28 speaks of the regeneration of the material universe, the heavens and the earth, which will occur with the Messianic kingdom:

> And Yeshua said unto them, Verily I say unto you, that ye who have followed me, in the regeneration when the Son of man shall sit on the throne of his glory, ye also shall sit upon twelve thrones, judging the twelve tribes of Israel.

The second passage is Titus 3:5, which speaks of regeneration in relation to humanity:

> *not by works done in righteousness, which we did ourselves, but according to his mercy he saved us, through the washing of regeneration and renewing of the Holy Spirit,*

The basic meaning of regeneration is the concept of a new birth, a reproduction, a renewal, or a recreation. The best definition of what it means to be regenerated is that eternal life has been imparted to the person. It means that he has been born of God, for it is the act of God that imparts eternal life. "New birth" is simply a figure of speech that means the same thing as regeneration. With a new birth, one is born of God and has eternal life imparted to him.

(1) The Means of Regeneration

The means of regeneration is the Holy Spirit. This is shown by the most famous passage on the new birth, John 3:5-6:

> *⁵ Yeshua answered, Verily, verily, I say unto you, Except one be born of water and the Spirit, he cannot enter into the kingdom of God. ⁶ That which is born of the flesh is flesh; and that which is born of the Spirit is spirit.*

According to Yeshua, the means of regeneration is the Holy Spirit, for regeneration is the Spirit's work.

The same truth is taught by Titus 3:5, which uses the term "regeneration" and credits the work to the Holy Spirit: *not by works done in righteousness, which we did ourselves, but according to his mercy he saved us, through the washing of regeneration and renewing of the Holy Spirit.* It is the Holy Spirit who is the means of regeneration. Faith itself is not the means of regeneration. Faith is the human requirement which enables the Holy Spirit to do the work of regeneration. When someone believes and accepts Yeshua as his Messiah, when he accepts Him as his substitutionary sacrifice, he exercises faith. That faith allows the Holy Spirit to do the work of regeneration. In reality, faith and regeneration occur simultaneously, because the instant one believes, he is regenerated or born anew.

The Word of God is not the means of regeneration either, but it provides the content of faith. It tells what one must believe in order to be regenerated by the Holy Spirit.

(2) Faith is the Basis of Regeneration

The basis of regeneration is faith. Faith is not the means, but it is the human requirement that allows the Holy Spirit to do the work of regeneration. This is taught in John 1:12-13:

> *¹² But as many as received him, to them gave he the right to become children of God, even to them that believe on his name: ¹³ who were born, not of blood, nor of the will of the flesh, nor of the will of man, but of God.*

This is also taught by John 3:16: *For God so loved the world, that he gave his only begotten Son, that whosoever believes on him should not perish, but have eternal life.*

(3) The Figures of Speech for Regeneration

There are two figures of speech that are used to describe the concept of regeneration as revealed in the New Testament. The figures are: "being born again" or "new birth," (Jn. 3:3-7) and "spiritual resurrection" (Rom. 6:1-6; Eph. 2:5-6).

(4) Two Aspects of the Work of Regeneration

Regeneration is the work of the Holy Spirit by which eternal life is received. This ministry has two aspects. First, it is non-experiential. An experience might accompany regeneration, but regeneration itself is non-experiential. It is not something that can be felt. It is a work that the Holy Spirit does. The moment people are saved, they may react in different ways: There are those who react very emotionally, others react totally unemotionally, and there are all behaviors in between, but regeneration itself is not experiential.

Second, regeneration is instantaneous; it is not a process. The moment one believes, he is once-and-for-all born again or regenerated and will remain regenerated from that point onward. The Greek aorist tense, which emphasizes an instantaneous type of work, is used in John 1:13; 3:3, 5, and 7. The first of these verses, John 1:13, states: *who were born, not of blood, nor of the will of the flesh, nor of the will of man, but of God.* The Greek perfect tense, which emphasizes an event that was completed in the past but continues unchanged into the present, is used in I John

2:29; 3:9; 4:7; 5:1, 5, and 18. The first of these verses, I John 2:29, states: *If ye know that he is righteous, ye know that every one also that does righteousness is begotten of him.* The Greek perfect tense expresses the fact that one is born again—regenerated—instantaneously and completely in the past, and his regeneration continues to the present day. Hence, regeneration is instantaneous, not a process.

(5) The Results of Regeneration

Once a person is regenerated, four things happen. First, the believer has eternal life (Jn. 3:16). The moment one believes, he has been regenerated, and because he has been regenerated, he now has eternal life.

The second result is that the believer is seen as a new creation. He is looked upon as having been created anew (II Cor. 5:17; Gal. 6:15; Eph. 2:10; 4:24).

The third result of regeneration is eternal security. Philippians 1:6 explains: *being confident of this very thing, that he who began a good work in you will perfect it until the day of Yeshua Messiah.* The work of regeneration cannot be undone. Once a person is born into this world he cannot be "unborn"; he cannot return into his mother's womb. The work of physical birth cannot be undone once it has occurred. The same is true of spiritual birth. The work of regeneration cannot be undone. Once a person has been born into God's family, he can never go back again into any kind of "spiritual womb." Furthermore, the regenerated person has eternal life. If this life could be lost, it was not eternal to begin with, but only temporary life.

The fourth result is a new life and a new nature. The first epistle of John describes what this new life and new nature are all about. First John 2:29 describes a life that practices righteousness. First John 3:9 proclaims: *Whosoever is begotten of God does no sin, because his seed abides in him: and he cannot sin, because he is begotten of God.* What is true of Yeshua the Messiah is true of us because of our union with Him. As Paul teaches in the book of Romans chapter 6, grace gives us the desire and power to live a holy life; we never have to sin again. We may, but we don't have to. First John 4:7 and 5:1 set forth a life that expresses itself in love. In I John 5:4, believers overcome the world by faith. First John 5:18 describes the believer in his new nature; he does not sin and keeps himself in the truth.

If he fails (and all believers do), this is not in keeping with his new nature or new man, but in keeping with his old nature or old man. The new nature cannot sin, but the old nature does sin.

b. The Ministry of Indwelling

The second work of the Holy Spirit in relation to salvation is the ministry of indwelling. While regeneration puts the Messiah into the life of the believer, indwelling puts the Holy Spirit within the believer.

(1) *Scriptures Concerning the Ministry of Indwelling*

The fact that the Holy Spirit indwells believers is taught by a number of Scriptures. In John 7:37-39, the indwelling was anticipatory in that it was still future. The Holy Spirit had not yet begun His work of indwelling all believers, but the promise was made. At this point, *the Spirit was not yet given; because Yeshua was not yet glorified*. The glorification of the Son occurred when He ascended into heaven. Ten days later, the Holy Spirit came and began His work of indwelling all believers.

In John 14:16-17, Yeshua promised to send *another Comforter*, the Holy Spirit, who would indwell the believer *for ever*—not temporarily, not until they committed their next sin, not until they fell out of fellowship, but forever.

In Acts 11:17, Peter called the indwelling of the Holy Spirit a gift from God.

In Romans 5:5, Paul taught that the indwelling of the Holy Spirit is a product of *the love of God*.

In Romans 8:11, Paul said the indwelling of the Holy Spirit guarantees future resurrection of the believer's mortal body.

In I Corinthians 6:19-20, Paul asked the Corinthians, *know ye not your body is a temple of the Holy Spirit?* because the Holy Spirit indwelt them.

Galatians 4:6 states the Holy Spirit is in the believer's heart, praying for him.

In I John 3:24 and 4:13, John referred to the Holy Spirit abiding in the believer.

The consistent teaching of the New Testament is that the Holy Spirit now indwells all believers as a result of the death, burial, resurrection, ascension, and glorification of the Messiah. In the Hebrew Scriptures, the Holy Spirit indwelt only some believers. Now He indwells all believers.

(2) The Means of Indwelling

The means of indwelling is faith. The moment faith is exercised, the Holy Spirit indwells the believer. In Galatians 3:2, Paul expressed this truth in the form of a question: *This only would I learn from you, Received ye the Spirit by the works of the law, or by the hearing of faith?*

Acts 5:32 adds another aspect to the means of indwelling. Peter had been brought before the Sanhedrin for preaching Yeshua at the Temple. When urged not to continue to do so, he told the high priest that it was impossible because he and the other apostles were *witnesses of these things; and so is the Holy Spirit, whom God has given to them that obey him.* We learn here that an unbeliever must obey something to receive the indwelling of the Holy Spirit. The only command one must obey to receive the Holy Spirit is the command to believe on the Lord Yeshua (Jn. 6:28-29: Acts 16:31). The unbeliever must have faith, and faith is not a work (Acts 6:7; Rom. 1:5, 16:26). The obedience of faith is the means by which one receives the indwelling of the Holy Spirit.

(3) The Universality of Indwelling

The indwelling of the Ruach HaKodesh is universal among all believers. In the Hebrew Scriptures, only some believers were indwelt. As of Acts 2, all believers are indwelt. This is evident in three ways. First, Romans 8:9 states: *But ye are not in the flesh but in the Spirit, if so be that the Spirit of God dwells in you. But if any man has not the Spirit of Messiah, he is none of his.* The verse teaches that the absence of the indwelling Holy Spirit is proof of an unsaved state. A person who does not have the indwelling Spirit is not a believer to begin with: *he is none of his*.

Another passage that teaches the very same thing is Jude 18b-19, which states:

> [18b] *In the last time there shall be mockers, walking after their own ungodly lusts.* [19] *These are they who make separations, sensual, having not the Spirit.*

The "these" in verse 19 refers to the mockers, the unbelievers, of verse 18. Jude said they do not have the Holy Spirit indwelling them.

The second piece of evidence that the indwelling of the Holy Spirit is universal is the fact that the Ruach even indwells sinning believers. The best example of this truth is the Corinthian church, by far the worst church in the biblical record. Divisions, party factions, and immorality were tolerated in this church; believers were taking other believers to court; they were getting drunk at the Lord's Supper; and they misused their spiritual gifts. Yet, in spite of the fact that the Corinthian believers were guilty of all these carnal sins, Paul wrote in I Corinthians 6:19-20:

> [19] *Or know ye not that your body is a temple of the Holy Spirit which is in you, which ye have from God? and ye are not your own;* [20] *for ye were bought with a price: glorify God therefore in your body.*

Despite their terrible spiritual state, the Corinthians had the Holy Spirit indwelling them because they were true believers. This indwelling is the basis for living a spiritual life, and Paul encouraged the Corinthians to pursue such a life. Thus, even carnal, sinning believers have the Spirit, and this truth proves that the indwelling is universal among all believers.

The third proof is that the indwelling of the Holy Spirit is a gift. Gifts are not based upon merit (Jn. 7:37-39; Acts 11:17; Rom. 5:5; I Cor. 2:12).

Hence, there is no doubt that the indwelling work of the Spirit is universal among believers; He indwells all believers.

(4) *The Permanence of Indwelling*

The indwelling of the Holy Spirit is permanent. This is taught by John 14:16: *And I will pray the Father, and he shall give you another Comforter, that he may be with you for ever.* If the Ruach HaKodesh could be taken away, then He was not indwelling the believer forever. "Forever" means just that; otherwise, it would be only temporary. Indwelling is not only universal among all believers, it is also permanent.

(5) *The Results of Indwelling*

There are two results of indwelling. First, the Spirit's indwelling is an earnest or down payment of many more blessings to come. This is taught by

Paul in II Corinthians 1:21-22 and 5:5. Furthermore, in Ephesians 1:13b-14, he wrote:

> [1b3] *ye were sealed with the Holy Spirit of promise,* [14] *which is an earnest of our inheritance, unto the redemption of God's own possession, unto the praise of his glory.*

The second result of indwelling is that the believer becomes a temple of God in three senses: first, in the sense of being part of the universal church, which the Holy Spirit indwells (Eph. 2:21-22); second, in the sense of being part of a local church, which the Holy Spirit indwells (I Cor. 3:16-17); third, in the sense of being an individual believer, whom the Holy Spirit indwells (I Cor. 6:19-20).

c. The Ministry of Spirit Baptism

A third ministry of the Holy Spirit in relation to salvation is the ministry of baptism. There is much confusion, debate, and error regarding this ministry today. The Scriptures themselves are quite clear on this issue, but because people frequently interpret the Word by their own experiences rather than by what the text states, there has been a great deal of error.

(1) Several Reasons for the Confusion Regarding Spirit Baptism

There are at least five reasons why so many believers are confused about Spirit baptism. The first reason is that many do not understand the distinctiveness of the church in this age. Baptism was not a ministry which the Spirit ever performed in the Hebrew Scriptures. He did regenerate all believers, and He did indwell some believers, but He never baptized anyone in the Hebrew Scriptures. A failure to realize that Spirit baptism is a unique ministry for this age only and for the church only has resulted in faulty conclusions.

A second reason for confusion concerning the correct meaning of Spirit baptism is an over-emphasis on water baptism. This author is a firm believer in water baptism; sometime after one believes, he should undergo water baptism, but the over-emphasis on water baptism has led to an improper understanding of Spirit baptism. As a result, passages that speak of Spirit baptism, such as Romans 6:1-4, have been misapplied to water baptism.

A third reason for the confusion is that Spirit baptism has been associated with the gift of speaking in tongues. As will be shown later, there is a distinction made between speaking in tongues and being baptized by the Holy Spirit. Confusion has resulted because the two works of the Ruach HaKodesh have been inappropriately associated together by those who teach that when one is baptized by the Holy Spirit, he speaks in tongues, and if one does not speak in tongues, he has not been baptized by the Holy Spirit.

A fourth reason for confusion about the true nature of Spirit baptism is that the same Greek word for the prepositions "in," "on," "at," "by," and "with" (ἐν, *en*) has been translated into English in more than one way in some versions of the Bible. For example, in the King James Version, Acts 1:5 reads: *baptized **with** the Holy Ghost*; but I Corinthians 12:13 reads: *For **by** one Spirit are we all baptized* [emphasis added]. One might assume from the text of the King James Bible that there is a difference between being baptized with the Holy Spirit and being baptized by the Holy Spirit. Based upon this translation, some groups teach that while all believers are baptized by the Spirit, only some—those who speak in tongues—are baptized with the Spirit or vice versa. The trouble with this theology is that "with" and "by" are the same word in the Greek text of the verses listed above. Therefore, no such distinction is valid. People have misunderstood what the baptism of the Spirit is because they are basing their theology on the English translations.

The fifth reason for confusion is that people often do not understand the difference between the Spirit's work of baptizing as compared to His work of filling. Spirit baptism is a work of the Spirit in relation to salvation. Spirit-filling is a work of the Spirit in relation to spiritual growth. In a later chapter, the ministry of Spirit-filling will be studied in depth. Because people have confused Spirit baptism with Spirit-filling, this, too, has led to error.

(2) Scriptures Concerning the Ministry of Spirit Baptism

Spirit baptism is mentioned only in the New Testament. In the four Gospels, it is always mentioned as something still future (Mt. 3:11; Mk. 1:8; Lk. 3:16; Jn. 1:33). In these verses, John the Baptist predicted that when Messiah came, He would baptize by the Holy Spirit. John, on the other hand, only baptized by water, and he consistently distinguished his baptism from the Messiah's work, baptism by the Holy Spirit. There is no record of Spirit baptism occurring in the Gospels.

In Acts 1:5, Spirit baptism was mentioned again, this time by Yeshua Himself. Yet, here again Spirit baptism was still future. As of Acts 1, it had not yet occurred.

In Acts 11:15-16, Spirit baptism is mentioned again, this time by Peter:

> [15] *And as I began to speak, the Holy Spirit fell on them, even as on us at the beginning.* [16] *And I remembered the word of the Lord, how he said, John indeed baptized with water; but ye shall be baptized in the Holy Spirit.*

The verses include a quotation of Acts 1:5 and state that Spirit baptism began *at the beginning*, meaning at Pentecost in Acts 2. Although Acts 2 does not mention Spirit baptism, in Acts 11:16 Peter states that that was the time when Spirit baptism began.

In Romans 6:3-5, Spirit baptism identifies the believer with the death and resurrection of the Messiah.

According to I Corinthians 12:13, *all* believers are baptized by the Ruach HaKodesh into one body—*all*, not some.

Galatians 3:27 teaches that believers have been *baptized into Messiah*.

Ephesians 4:4-6 speaks of *one baptism*. The reason why this baptism refers to the ministry of the Spirit and not to water baptism is because it relates to other things in the verse which are clearly in the spiritual and not the physical realm.

In Colossians 2:12, Spirit baptism again connects believers with the burial and resurrection of the Messiah.

These are all of the passages in the New Testament where Spirit baptism is mentioned by name. It is from these passages that the teachings and doctrines about Spirit baptism must be derived. We must be careful to not confuse this ministry with other ministries of the Spirit. In studying these passages, it should be noted that regardless of how many different English constructions there may be, the Greek construction is always the same. Baptism is always *by* the Holy Spirit. Believers are baptized *by* the Holy Spirit. Believers are baptized *into* the body of the Messiah. The word "by" emphasizes the instrumentality: Believers are baptized *by* the instrumentality of the Holy Spirit. The word "in" emphasizes sphere: Believers are always baptized *into* the sphere of the body of the Messiah. No distinction may be made between being baptized *by* the Spirit and being baptized *with* the Spirit. The Greek construction is always the same, and in every case, the believers are being baptized *by* the Spirit *into* the body of the Messiah.

(3) *The Beginning of Spirit Baptism*

As previously mentioned, Spirit baptism is a unique ministry for this age, the dispensation of grace, the church age. It is a distinctive, unique ministry in that it is something that the Spirit never did in the Hebrew Scriptures. It is recorded that He regenerated people and He indwelled some, but He never baptized anyone during that time or during the time of the Gospels. Hence, the Spirit's work of baptism is a ministry unique to the church age. This becomes clear by comparing four passages of Scripture, some of which were mentioned in the previous point. However, because they are so important for a proper understanding of Spirit baptism, the verses will be studied again in depth here.

The first passage is Colossians 1:18, which teaches that the church is the body of the Messiah: *And he is the head of the body, the church: who is the beginning, the firstborn from the dead; that in all things he might have the preeminence.*

The second passage is I Corinthians 12:13, which teaches that entrance into this body is by means of Spirit baptism: *For in one Spirit were we all baptized into one body, whether Jews or Greeks, whether bond or free; and were all made to drink of one Spirit.* The church is the body of the Messiah. Entering into this body can only happen by Spirit baptism.

The third passage is Acts 1:5, which teaches that at that time Spirit baptism was still future: *for John indeed baptized with water; but ye shall be baptized in the Holy Spirit not many days hence.*

The fourth passage, which quotes Acts 1:5 and teaches that Spirit baptism began at Pentecost in Acts 2, is Acts 11:15-17:

> [15] *And as I began to speak, the Holy Spirit fell on them, even as on us at the beginning.* [16] *And I remembered the word of the Lord, how he said, John indeed baptized with water; but ye shall be baptized in the Holy Spirit.* [17] *If*

then God gave unto them the like gift as he did also unto us, when we believed on the Lord Yeshua Messiah, who was I, that I could withstand God?

In summary, the church is the body of the Messiah; entrance into this body is only possible by means of Spirit baptism; as of Acts 1, Spirit baptism was still future; according to Acts 11, Spirit baptism began at Pentecost (Acts 2). Obviously, that is also when the church began. Hence, the Spirit's ministry of baptism is uniquely and only for this age. It is a ministry that the Spirit performs only in relation to the church. Once the church is complete and raptured, the Ruach will no longer be performing the work of Spirit baptism. He did not baptize anyone in the Hebrew Scriptures or in the Gospels; He is baptizing in the church age. Once the church is removed, there will be no more ministry of Spirit baptism. There will be no ministry of Spirit baptism in the tribulation or in the millennial kingdom.

(4) The Agent of Spirit Baptism

There is a primary agent and an indirect agent of Spirit baptism. The primary agent is the Ruach HaKodesh. That is the point of I Corinthians 12:13: *For in one Spirit were we all baptized into one body*. The primary agent of Spirit baptism is the Ruach HaKodesh Himself, for He baptizes the believer. The indirect agent is the Messiah, for He sends the Spirit to do the work of Spirit baptism (Mt. 3:11; Mk. 1:8; Lk. 3:16; Jn. 1:33). The Messiah is the ultimate and indirect agent, and the Holy Spirit is the intermediate and primary agent in the act of Spirit baptism.

(5) The Universality of Spirit Baptism

Another truth concerning Spirit baptism is that it is universal among all believers. Not merely some are baptized by the Spirit, but as of the day of Pentecost in Acts 2, every believer is baptized by the Holy Spirit. This truth is spelled out in I Corinthians 12:13: *For in one Spirit were we all baptized into one body, whether Jews or Greeks, whether bond or free; and were all made to drink of one Spirit*. The clear teaching of this verse is that every believer—without exception—is baptized by the Spirit. The gifts of the Spirit are also part of I Corinthians 12 and will be discussed in later chapters of this book. What we will note here is the following: In verse 13, Paul made clear that every believer is baptized by the Holy Spirit. Yet, in verses 29-31, when listing the gifts of the Spirit, he pointed out that not all speak in tongues. That is why Spirit baptism and speaking in tongues must not be seen as a cause-and-effect relationship. Not all speak in tongues, but all are baptized by the Holy Spirit. It will not do to try to distinguish between being baptized *by* the Holy Spirit and being baptized *with* the Holy Spirit. It is wrong to teach that all are baptized *by* the Spirit and only some are baptized *with* the Spirit because in the Greek text, the original language in which the New Testament was written, there is no difference and the construction is always the same. Furthermore, Ephesians 4:5 clearly teaches that there is only one type of Spirit baptism, saying, *one Lord, one faith, one baptism.* Just as there is only one God, there is only one Spirit baptism, not two or more.

(6) When Spirit Baptism Occurs

The New Testament clearly emphasizes that every believer becomes part of the body of the Messiah at the moment he or she believes (Eph. 2:11-22). Every believer is a part of the body of the Messiah because they have been baptized by the Holy Spirit (I Cor. 12:13). If every believer were not baptized by the Spirit at salvation, it would mean that some believers today are in the body of the Messiah and some believers are outside the body of the Messiah. Yet, that is exactly what the New Testament says is *not* true. Every believer today, without exception, is part of the body of the Messiah, and the only way to get into this body is by means of Spirit baptism. Since every believer is part of the body of the Messiah from the moment he believes, then Spirit baptism obviously occurs at the moment one believes. Spirit baptism occurs at salvation.

(7) The Frequency of Spirit Baptism

How often does Spirit baptism occur? On one hand, it occurs only once; but on the other hand, it is repeated. It occurs only once in the life of a believer because at the moment of salvation, he is baptized into the body of the Messiah by the Spirit. When another person gets saved, Spirit baptism is "repeated." Therefore, each person is baptized only once, but Spirit baptism is repeated every time someone is saved.

(8) The Results of Spirit Baptism

There are three results of Spirit baptism. First, Spirit baptism unites all believers by making them members of the body of the Messiah. Never is it stated that any particular spiritual gift is the result of Spirit baptism. Rather, the result of Spirit baptism is that it unites believers into one body; it makes all believers members of the body of the Messiah (I Cor. 12:13).

The second result is that it unites believers with the Messiah in co-crucifixion, co-burial, and co-resurrection in respect to the sin nature (Rom. 6:3-4; Gal. 3:27; Col. 2:12). Because of our baptism into the body of the Messiah by the Holy Spirit, we are united with Yeshua; regarding our sin nature, we are reckoned as being co-crucified, co-buried, and co-resurrected with the Messiah.

Third, Spirit baptism makes believers "new." They now have a new identification, because they are co-crucified, co-buried, and co-resurrected with the Messiah. They also have a new position, because they are in the body of the Messiah. Furthermore, there is a new union with God and with fellow believers because the Messiah is the head of the church and believers are the body. Finally, there is a new association in that believers are no longer of the world, or as the Scriptures say, "in Adam," but "in Messiah."

(9) Summary of the Spirit's Ministries in Relation to Salvation

So far, this study revealed the following points regarding the ministries of the Holy Spirit in relation to the believer and salvation. First, at the point of salvation, three things happen:

- ✡ The believer is **regenerated** or born again by the Holy Spirit, and Yeshua enters his life. Regeneration puts Yeshua into the believer.
- ✡ The believer is **indwelt** by the Holy Spirit, and the Spirit enters his life as well. Indwelling puts the Spirit into the believer.
- ✡ The believer is **baptized** by the Spirit into the body of Yeshua, so he becomes a member of the body. Baptism by the Spirit puts the believer into the body.

Second, the epistles teach that every believer, without exception, is baptized by the Spirit; every believer is a member of the body of Yeshua. One cannot be a member of the body without having been baptized by the Spirit. Spirit baptism occurs the moment one believes.

(10) The Delay of Spirit Baptism in the Book of Acts

Some of the things stated above seem to present a problem in light of events in the book of Acts. There are places in Acts where Spirit baptism did not occur at the moment of salvation for some believers. This would seem to contradict the doctrine of the epistles according to which every believer is baptized by the Spirit at the instant he or she believes. Furthermore, the "delay" concerned not only Spirit baptism, but also indwelling. While regeneration occurred, indwelling and baptism by the Holy Spirit happened at a later time. Therefore, it is necessary to study each circumstance where this "delay" happened in the book of Acts to discern how the Holy Spirit was working at that time.

The instances are recorded in Acts chapters 2, 8, 10, and 19. What we can discern from a study of these chapters is that Spirit baptism occurred at a later time in these specific instances because God used the coming of the Spirit as an authentication. Something needed to be authenticated to someone. To show this, six questions will be asked. All six questions will be applied to each of the four chapters where it is recorded that the Spirit came upon believers after their salvation occurred. The first question is, "Who specifically received the baptism?" Second, "Who were they, meaning what was their background or origin?" Third, "What were the circumstances?" Fourth, "What were the means?" Fifth, "What was the goal of the authentication?" Sixth, "What were the results?"

One final word before we look at the book of Acts. The only Gospel that mentions the *kehilah*, the *ecclesia*, meaning the "church," is Matthew. This Gospel is addressed to the Jewish people. Matthew traces the results of Israel's rejection of the Messiah, one of which is the creation of a new entity: the body of Messiah. In Matthew 16:19, Peter was given *the keys of the kingdom of heaven*. It is important to understand what this means. When the word "key" is used symbolically in the Hebrew Scriptures, it represents authority (Isa. 22:20-24), including the authority to open and close doors. Hence, in the context of Matthew 16, Yeshua was saying that Peter would be given the authority to open the door of the church facet of God's kingdom program, and His statement is a prediction of Peter's special role in the book of Acts.

Another important element for the understanding of Acts is that in Old Testament times, humanity was divided into two groups: Jews and Gentiles. In the Gospel period, there were three groups: Jews, Samaritans, and Gentiles. Peter was going to be responsible for opening the doors of the church facet of the kingdom program for all three groups. Once he opened the door for one group, it stayed open for that group. The church is the body of the Messiah (Col. 1:18), and the means of entering the church is Spirit baptism (I Cor. 12:13). There is an inseparable connection between this baptism and the existence of the church; one cannot exist without the other. Peter, the keys, and Spirit baptism would all come together for each of the three groups in the book of Acts.

In Acts 2, Peter opened the door for the Jews. Once he opened the door for the Jews, it stayed open. From then on, the moment a Jew believed, they were baptized by the Spirit into the body. In Acts 8, Philip went into Samaria and preached the gospel to the Samaritans, and many Samaritans believed. They were regenerated by the Holy Spirit and received salvation. However, the Spirit did not baptize them into the body, because while Philip had the gospel, he did not have the keys. So, the church of Jerusalem sent Peter to Samaria, and by the laying on of hands, the Samaritans were baptized by the Spirit into the body (Acts 8:17). Once Peter had opened the door for the Samaritans, it stayed open. From then on, every time a Samaritan believed, the Spirit baptized them into the body. In Acts 9, Paul was saved, and God commissioned him to be the apostle to the Gentiles. While he was the one called to establish Gentile Christianity, he did not have the keys either. So, before Paul could start his missionary work, God had to send Peter to the house of Cornelius. By his preaching, the Gentiles believed, and the Spirit baptized them into the body (Acts 10:44-48). Once the door was opened for the Gentiles, it stayed open. From then on, every time a Gentile believed, the Spirit baptized him or her into the body.

Once Peter had opened all three doors, I Corinthians 12:13 became the doctrine: *For in one Spirit were we all baptized into one body, whether Jews or Greeks, whether bond or free, and were all made to drink of one Spirit.* Now, all who believe are baptized by the Spirit into the body.

Having considered these introductory notes, we will now look at the four chapters of Acts in more depth, answering each of the six questions mentioned before.

(a) Acts 2

The first question is: "Who specifically received the baptism?" The answer is: the twelve apostles. It was not all *hundred and twenty* on that occasion who received the Spirit, but just *the twelve*, because the nearest antecedent of the words "they" and "all" in Acts 2:1 is "the twelve" of Acts 1:26. The rules of Greek grammar are that a pronoun must refer back to the nearest antecedent. Furthermore, Acts 2:7 describes those upon whom the Spirit came, those speaking, as being only the Galileans, and Acts 2:14 mentions only Peter and the other eleven. Hence the answer to who specifically received Spirit baptism in Acts 2 is the twelve apostles.

The second question is: "Who were they, and what was their background?" The answer is: the apostles (Acts 1:26, 2:14). In Matthew 16:17-19, Peter was given the keys of the kingdom and the authority to bind and loose. The authority to bind and to loose was also given to the rest of the apostles in Matthew 18:18. The coming of the Holy Spirit on the day of Pentecost with the corollary gift of tongues authenticated Peter's message that day and the calling of him and the eleven, that they were all apostles.

The third question is: "What were the circumstances?" According to Acts 1, prior to the day of Pentecost, the apostles had been waiting and praying for the promise of the Father (v. 4), i.e. the baptism of the Holy Spirit. The experience of Acts 2:1-4 was the answer to that prayer (Acts 2:33).

The fourth question is: "What was the means?" The answer is: The Holy Spirit came directly. There was an initial filling of the Holy Spirit (Acts 2:4). Now, they were baptized by the Holy Spirit (Acts 11:15-17) into the body of the Messiah (I Cor. 12:13) and given a spiritual gift. The gift in this case was the speaking in tongues. The Holy Spirit came upon them directly, not by any intermediate way.

The fifth question is: "What was the goal of the authentication?" To the apostles, it authenticated that the promise of the Father had now been fulfilled. To the Jewish audience, it authenticated the message that the apostles were preaching. The coming of the Holy Spirit with the gift of tongues authenticated the apostles' calling and message; they were who they claimed to be.

The sixth question is: "What were the results?" The results were threefold. First, the Jews from the Diaspora were able to hear the gospel in their own language (Acts 2:8-11). Second, they fell under the conviction of the Holy Spirit (Acts 2:37). Third, three thousand of them became believers (Acts 2:41). This group included proselytes, meaning Gentiles who had previously converted to Judaism.

In Acts 2, baptism by the Holy Spirit was not actually "delayed" because it was at that point the Holy Spirit began His ministry of baptism. The events of the day of Pentecost authenticated the apostles' message to the Jewish people. At that point, the Jews for the first time entered into the body of the Messiah. Peter, who had the keys, opened the door to the Jews in Acts 2; from then on, the door stayed open to the Jews.

(b) Acts 8

The first question is: "Who specifically received the baptism?" The answer is: believers in Samaria (Acts 8:14).

The second question is: "Who were they, and what was their background?" The answer is: They were Samaritans (Acts 8:14-17). There was antagonism between Jews and Samaritans. The Samaritans had set up a competing religious system to Judaism. They used a competing Mosaic Law from which any and all references to Jerusalem had been removed. They also had a competing temple on Mount Gerizim to rival the Temple in Jerusalem.

The third question is: "What were the circumstances?" The circumstances were that Philip, one of those chosen by the Jerusalem church to be a deacon (Acts 6:1-7), was sent to Samaria to preach. As he preached, many Samaritans came to a saving knowledge of Yeshua the Messiah. This raised questions on the part of the Jewish believers in Jerusalem who had the above-mentioned antagonism in mind. They were wondering if it was possible for Samaritans to be saved. The Jerusalem church sent

Peter and John to investigate and authenticate the reports that Samaritans had been saved.

The fourth question is: "What was the means of the Samaritans' receiving the Holy Spirit?" While the Samaritans believed and were therefore regenerated by the Holy Spirit, for some reason, the Holy Spirit did not immediately indwell them, nor did He immediately baptize them into the body of Messiah. The means by which they finally received the Spirit was when Peter laid his hands on them (Acts 8:17). In other words, there was the necessity of Peter's presence. In Acts 2, the Spirit came directly upon the apostles. Here, in Acts 8, Peter laid hands upon the Samaritan believers, and then they received the Holy Spirit. The means by which the Samaritans received the Holy Spirit was the laying on of hands by Peter. At that point, the Samaritans entered into the body of the Messiah. Peter had opened the door for the Samaritans; from then on, the door stayed open for the Samaritans. From then on, every time a Samaritan believed, he was immediately baptized by the Spirit into the body of the Messiah.

The fifth question is: "What was the goal of the authentication?" For the apostles and Jewish believers in Jerusalem, these events authenticated that Samaritans were savable. For the Samaritan believers, the event authenticated the authority of the Jewish apostles who came to them from Jerusalem, their former rival city.

The sixth question is: "What were the results?" The results were two-fold. First, the Samaritans received the Holy Spirit and were baptized into the body of the Messiah (Acts 8:17). Second, they did not set up a rival Samaritan church to compete with the church of Jerusalem, which would have been their tendency. Because they received the Holy Spirit by the laying on of hands by Peter, the Jewish apostle who came to them from Jerusalem, they did not do so.

(c) **Acts 10**

The first question is: "Who specifically received the baptism?" The answer is: Cornelius and his entire household (Acts 10:24, 44).

The second question is: "Who were they, and what was their background?" They were uncircumcised Gentiles (Acts 10:1). So far, the church was opened by Peter only for the Jews and Samaritans, but not as yet for these people.

The third question is: "What were the circumstances?" The circumstances were the preaching of the gospel to these uncircumcised Gentiles by Peter (Acts 10:44, 46). Peter's presence was necessary because he had the keys of the kingdom. In Acts 9, Paul was saved to become the apostle to the Gentiles (v. 15). However, although Paul was the apostle to the Gentiles, he did not have the keys to the kingdom. Therefore, Peter was the one who first preached the gospel to the Gentiles to open the door for them to enter the church. Then, in Acts 13, Paul began to fulfill his commission of preaching the gospel to the Gentiles. Hence, concerning the circumstances in Acts 10, it was Peter who preached to these uncircumcised Gentiles.

The fourth question is: "What was the means?" The Holy Spirit came to the Gentiles directly, as He had done with the Jews. With the Samaritans, the baptism came when Peter laid his hands on them. There was no need to have the laying on of hands with the Gentiles because there was no danger they would set up a Gentile church to rival the church in Jerusalem as was the case with the Samaritans. So, to the uncircumcised Gentiles, the Spirit came directly.

The fifth question is: "What was the goal of the authentication?" For the uncircumcised Gentiles, this experience authenticated the message of Peter. For the Jewish believers, it authenticated that this people group was savable. The Jews who observed this experience (Acts 10:45-46) were amazed that these uncircumcised Gentiles received the Holy Spirit along with the gift of tongues, and it authenticated to them that these people were truly saved. In Acts 11:1-2, 15-18, Peter used this experience as evidence to defend his actions of going to the home of an uncircumcised Gentile. In Acts 15:7-14, this experience of Gentile salvation and Spirit baptism was used again as evidence in the Jerusalem Council to show that uncircumcised Gentiles really were savable.

The sixth question is: "What were the results?" The results were twofold. First, it opened the door of the church for the Gentiles in preparation for Paul's ministry. Peter had to be the one to open the door; from then on, the door stayed open for uncircumcised Gentiles. Every time a Gentile is saved, he is baptized into the body of the Messiah. The second result is that Gentile Christianity was recognized as valid (Acts 10:45-46; 11:18).

(d) Acts 19

The first question is: "Who specifically received the baptism?" The answer is: Jews of the Diaspora who were disciples of John the Baptist (Acts 19:1-3) and who were living in Ephesus.

The second question is: "Who were they, and what was their background?" These were Jews who had become disciples of John the Baptist, were baptized by him in the early part of his ministry, and then left Israel to go back to Ephesus. After they left the country, John identified Yeshua as the Messiah; but these disciples had never heard about Yeshua, so they had not personally believed upon Him. They were members of a distinct Jewish group within the Jewish world. On one hand, they no longer belonged to Pharisaic Judaism; but on the other, they were not Jewish believers in Yeshua, just disciples of John the Baptist. They were at the same stage as Apollos before Aquilla and Priscilla explained to him that Yeshua was the Messiah of whom John spoke (Acts 18:24-28).

The third question is: "What were the circumstances?" The circumstances were that when Paul met these Jewish men, he recognized them as being believers of some sort, but they seemed to have a limited content of faith. They were believers to some degree but had not exercised actual faith in Yeshua. Paul's question shows that he expected them to have received the Spirit when they believed. Paul asked: *Did ye receive the Holy Spirit when ye believed?* (Acts 19:2) The King James Version translated this phrase as "since you believed," but this is incorrect; it should be *when*, and this is the way all other translations have translated it. Paul expected these people to have received the Holy Spirit when they believed on the Messiah. The trouble is that while they believed John's message that the Messiah was coming, they had not yet believed on Yeshua. Because they had not yet believed on Him, they had not yet received the ministry of Spirit baptism.

The fourth question is: "What were the means of their baptism?" The answer is: There were two means. First, they had to be baptized in water again because believer's baptism is different from John's baptism. This action showed that they really did believe that Yeshua was the Messiah of whom John prophesied. Second, there had to be the laying on of hands by the Apostle Paul. This is significant in that unlike the other apostles, Paul had not previously been a disciple of John. So, these were the two means: believer's baptism in contrast to John's baptism and the laying on of hands by the Apostle Paul rather than an apostle like Peter, who previously had been a disciple of John the Baptist.

The fifth question is: "What was the goal of the authentication?" There was a real danger that these believers would set up a competing "John the Baptist church." However, the experience these disciples of John the Baptist now had authenticated to them that it was now believer's baptism that was the proper identification and no longer the baptism of John. From now on, the proper formula of baptism was in the name of the Father, the Son, and the Holy Spirit. It authenticated the fact that only faith in Yeshua was necessary, not faith in both John and Yeshua, for they received the Spirit by the laying on of hands by Paul, who was never baptized by John. It authenticated Paul's message.

The sixth question is: "What were the results?" The results were that the disciples of John became believers in Yeshua the Messiah, and no rival church was set up.

(11) The Transitional Nature of the Book of Acts

The book of Acts marks the transition between the dispensation of law and the dispensation of grace. Part of the transition is a dispensational change in the ministry of the Holy Spirit. Chronologically, the events recorded in Acts chapters 2, 8, and 10 occurred before any of the New Testament epistles were even written. The book of Acts also emphasizes the apostolic authority of Peter and Paul.

A corollary event, which happened at the Spirit baptism mentioned in the above cases, is that the gift of tongues was given in at least three of these events, namely in Acts 2, 10, and 19, and possibly also in Acts 8, although that gift is not specifically mentioned in that chapter. The coming of the gift of tongues occurred only as an "opener" to select people groups: the Jews, the Gentiles, the Samaritans, and the disciples of John the Baptist. There is no record in Acts where the giving of the gift of tongues was repeated with other members of the same group. For example, in Acts 2, the gift of tongues was for those Jews, and there is no record of other Jews receiving the gift of tongues later. Second, the Samaritans in Acts 8 possibly received it, and there is no record of other Samaritans receiving the gift of tongues later. In Acts 10, it is the Gentiles in Cornelius' household who received the gift, but there is no record of other Gentiles receiving it later. In Acts 19, those disciples of John the Baptist received the gift of tongues, and there is no record of other disciples of John receiving it again later.

The biblical norm is that everyone is baptized by the Spirit at the moment he believes. In the book of Acts, Spirit baptism came first upon the Jews, then the Samaritans, then uncircumcised Gentiles, and lastly followers of John the Baptist; each group had to be initiated individually. Once a group was introduced into the body, the door stayed opened for that group. From then on, the norm is in force for all other people of each group, and so it is to this day. In fact, in Acts 19, Paul already expected people to have received the Spirit *when* they believed.

(12) The Danger of Deriving Doctrine from Historical Accounts

The one key purpose of the gift of tongues in the book of Acts was authentication. It is very important to remember that doctrine must not be developed from historical accounts, but from clear, positive, directive statements made in Scripture. The danger of deriving theology from historical accounts is the misconception that because something happened a certain way at a certain point in time, it must always happen the same way. In the case of the gift of tongues, some erroneously teach that the only way to know whether a person has been baptized by the Spirit is when he speaks in tongues. They derived their doctrine from a historical account (the book of Acts) according to which, in some cases, when a person was baptized by the Spirit he spoke in tongues. The positive directive, the doctrinal statement on the gift of tongues, is found in I Corinthians 12. Paul clearly states that all do not speak in tongues, but *all* are baptized by the Spirit. This is a crucial thing to understand. Historical accounts can be used to illustrate doctrine, but they should not be used to formulate doctrine. Doctrine must be derived from clear, positive statements in the Scriptures.

The fallacy of deriving doctrine from historical accounts can also be illustrated by the following account. The book of Exodus contains the story of Moses leading the children of Israel out of the land of Egypt. When they came to the Red Sea, it divided for the Jews, and they crossed over on dry land to the other side. That is the historical account. Would it be correct to teach that every time Jews come to the Red Sea, it will always divide for them? Will that always happen? No, for it was only a one-time event. Jews have come to the Red Sea many times since then, but it never divided again. That was simply a historical event, and doctrine cannot be derived from it; yet, the event can be used to illustrate doctrine. For example, it is a biblical doctrine that God is the keeper of Israel, and He will save and deliver Israel. The crossing of the Red Sea is an illustration of that doctrine and shows one of the ways God has kept and saved Israel. It is another biblical doctrine that God is omnipotent; He is all-powerful; He can do great things. The dividing of the Red Sea is an illustration of the doctrine of the omnipotence of God. The point is that doctrine must be derived from clear statements of Scripture. Historical accounts can only be used to illustrate doctrine. It is exceedingly dangerous to derive doctrine from historical events.

(13) Summary of Spirit Baptism

To summarize the teachings of the epistles concerning the doctrine of the baptism of the Holy Spirit, the following statement will be made: Every person—without exception—is baptized by the Spirit at the moment he believes. The result of Spirit baptism is not one particular gift, but rather membership in the body of the Messiah, the church. Since all believers, without exception, are members of the body of the Messiah, all believers therefore have been baptized by the Holy Spirit. This is the norm throughout the church age.

d. The Ministry of Sealing

The fourth ministry of the Holy Spirit in relation to salvation is the ministry of sealing. Every believer is sealed by the Holy Spirit.

(1) Scriptures

There are three passages that teach about the sealing ministry of the Spirit. The first passage is II Corinthians 1:21-22:

> ²¹ *Now he that establishes us with you in Messiah, and anointed us, is God;* ²² *who also sealed us, and gave us the earnest of the Spirit in our hearts.*

In this passage, the Holy Spirit Himself is the seal. This seal is the *earnest*, the down payment, for and of the believer's final salvation, which is still future.

The second passage is Ephesians 1:13-14:

> ¹³ *in whom ye also, having heard the word of the truth, the gospel of your salvation,—in whom, having also believed, ye were sealed with the Holy Spirit of promise,* ¹⁴ *which is an earnest of our inheritance, unto the redemption of God's own possession, unto the praise of his glory.*

In this passage, the Holy Spirit is the agent as well as the seal. Believers are *sealed with the Holy Spirit of promise* at the time of salvation, for Paul stated that having believed, the believer was sealed. At the time of salvation, one is sealed. The basis of sealing is faith.

The third passage is Ephesians 4:30: *And grieve not the Holy Spirit of God, in whom ye were sealed unto the day of redemption.* Here, the Holy Spirit is the agent of sealing. He is the guarantor of final redemption. Because believers have been sealed by the Spirit, they are not to grieve the Holy Spirit.

(2) *The Ramifications of the Ministry of Spirit-Sealing*

The three passages studied above point out five ramifications of the sealing ministry of the Holy Spirit. First, the Holy Spirit is both the agent and the seal. He is the agent, that is, the One who does the sealing. He is also the seal itself.

Second, the Holy Spirit is the substance of the seal itself, and God is the outside Person who does the sealing. The point is that God the Father is the main cause of sealing, and the Holy Spirit is the intermediate cause of sealing.

Third, sealing is universal among all believers. The only condition for being sealed by the Spirit is faith. Since every believer obviously has believed in Yeshua the Messiah, every believer has been sealed by the Holy Spirit. Sealing is the basis for not grieving the Holy Spirit, which is something only believers can do.

Fourth, the time of sealing is at the point of salvation (Eph. 1:13). Literally, the Greek reads, "In whom having believed, ye were sealed with the Holy Spirit of promise." The cause of sealing is merely hearing and believing. From the moment one believes, he is sealed by the Holy Spirit.

Fifth, the significance of being sealed by the Holy Spirit is eternal security. By Spirit baptism, a believer is placed into the body of the Messiah. By Spirit-sealing, a believer is locked or sealed into the body so that he can never fall out. The key idea of sealing is eternal security, that we have been saved once and forever through the Holy Spirit.

(3) The Concept of the Seal in the Hebrew Scriptures

In the Hebrew Scriptures, the seal on a document was a mark of authority from the owner of the seal (I Kg. 21:7-9; Esth. 3:9-12, 8:7-10). Because believers have been sealed, they have authority from God against the world and against Satan.

Furthermore, in the Hebrew Scriptures, the sealing of a document marked the transaction as being completed (Jer. 32:10-15). For the believer, salvation is a finished work. Having believed, all the benefits of salvation have been applied to the believer, so the seal of the Holy Spirit is the mark of a finished transaction.

When something was secured, it was officially stamped with a seal (Dan. 6:17). This is the main point of the Spirit's sealing ministry in the New Testament: It is a mark of the believer's eternal security.

(4) The Significance of the Ministry of Spirit-Sealing

The significance of the sealing ministry of the Holy Spirit to believers is fivefold. First, it signifies the certainty that a believer has become God's possession. God now owns the believer, and the seal is the mark of God's ownership of the believer.

Second, it signifies the certainty of the promise of salvation. Only God can break His own seal, and He promised not to break it; therefore, the believer's salvation is secured.

Third, the seal signifies the certainty of God's purpose to keep the believer until the day of redemption. The future redemption is the redemption of the believer's body in the resurrection. The seal guarantees that should the believer die, he will be resurrected in the day of redemption.

Fourth, it signifies that the believer has the authority of the Messiah with the right to exercise it. The believer has authority over his own sin nature and over the world, and he has the authority to resist Satan.

Fifth, the seal signifies that the transaction for the believer's salvation is finished, although the full enjoyment of it is to come later.

e. The Ministry of Anointing

The fifth and final work of the Holy Spirit in relation to salvation is the His ministry of anointing. There are three passages that speak of this work.

The first passage is II Corinthians 1:21-22, which states: *Now he that established us with you in Messiah, and anointed us, is God; who also sealed us, and gave us the earnest of the Spirit in our hearts.* Not only has the Spirit sealed the believer, He has also anointed the believer. The agent of anointing is God; the means is the Holy Spirit. Like sealing, anointing relates to the believer's being in Messiah.

The second verse is I John 2:20: *And ye have an anointing from the Holy One, and ye know all things.* In this passage, the agent of anointing is the Holy One. The result is that they know all things. In this context, the expression "all things" relates to salvation.

The third verse is I John 2:27:

> And as for you, the anointing which ye received of him abides in you, and ye need not that any one teach you; but as his anointing teaches you concerning all things, and is true, and is no lie, and even as it taught you, ye abide in him.

Anointing is from the One that abides in the believer, that is, the Lord. The result is that the believer has no need for anyone to teach him the truth of the gospel. The believer has already accepted the truth of the gospel and has been regenerated by the Holy Spirit. The anointing by the Holy Spirit confirmed both the believer's faith and his regeneration forever. Furthermore, the anointing teaches the believer the truth concerning all things. In this context, the expression "all things" relates to the truth of the gospel.

This passage is sometimes used to claim that the believer does not need human teachers because the Holy Spirit is the believer's only teacher. However, such claims contradict other passages of Scripture. One of the gifts of the Holy Spirit is the gift of teaching, and God has given the church gifted teachers so that the saints can learn. In the context of this passage, what the believer does not need to be taught is the truth of the gospel. These truths have already been confirmed because of the believer's faith.

From these three passages, we learn that God does the anointing. Furthermore, anointing is not repeated; a believer is anointed once and for all at the moment he is saved. Having been anointed, Spirit-anointing continually abides.

The significance of anointing is threefold:

1. It is the basis for the firm conviction of the truth of the gospel.
2. It is the basis for learning more spiritual truth.
3. Throughout the Scriptures, people are often anointed for service. Hence, anointing is the basis for service.

f. Summary

These are the five ministries of the Holy Spirit in relation to salvation:

1. **Regeneration**, by which a person is born again, and the Messiah enters into his life.
2. **Indwelling**, by which the Spirit makes His residence in the believer.
3. **Baptism** by the Holy Spirit, not water baptism, by which a believer is placed into the body of Messiah.
4. **Sealing**, by which a believer is locked into the body so as never to fall out.
5. **Anointing**, by which the believer has no need for anyone to teach him the truth of the gospel, for it has been confirmed to him by the experience of salvation. Anointing is also the basis for the believer's ability to continue learning more spiritual truths.

These are five things that happen at the moment one believes. They are instantaneous, all happening at the same time. The sequence of the above five ministries of the Spirit is logical, not chronological.

2. The Ministries of the Ruach HaKodesh in Relation to Spiritual Growth

The second major category of the ministries of the Holy Spirit relates to spiritual growth, and within this category, there are seven works.

a. The Ministry of Spirit-Filling

The first and by far the most important of the ministries of the Holy Spirit in relation to spiritual growth is the ministry of Spirit-filling.

(1) The Greek Words

When speaking of Spirit-filling, the New Testament uses three different Greek words. All three words are translated into English as "to fill" or "to be filled." The first Greek word is *pletho*, a verb. It is used eight times, but only by Luke, both in his Gospel and in the book of Acts. In the Gospel, the author uses *pletho* of John the Baptist (Lk. 1:15), of Elisabeth (Lk. 1:41), and of Zacharias (Lk. 1:67). In the book of Acts, he uses it of the twelve disciples in the upper room (Acts 2:4), of Peter (Acts 4:8), of the apostles (Acts 4:31), and of Paul (Acts 9:17; 13:9).

The second Greek word is *pleres*, an adjective derived from *pletho*. It is used four times, also only by Luke, in his Gospel and in the book of Acts. In Luke 4:1, it speaks of the Messiah being filled. In the book of Acts, it is used of the seven deacons (Acts 6:3), of Stephen (Acts 7:55), and of Barnabas (Acts 11:24).

The third Greek word is again derived from *pletho* and is another verb, *pleroo*. It is used twice concerning being filled by the Spirit. The first time is in Acts 13:52, where Luke speaks of the disciples being filled *with joy and with the Holy Spirit*. It is used the second time by Paul in Ephesians 5:18, where the command is given to *be filled with the Spirit*.

It is from these passages in Luke, Acts, and Ephesians that the biblical teaching about the ministry of filling with the Spirit can be derived.

(2) The Meaning of Spirit-Filling

To be filled means "to be controlled." For example, Ephesians 5:18 states: *And be not drunken with wine, wherein is riot, but be filled with the Spirit.* To be filled with wine means "to be controlled by wine." Hence, to be filled with the Spirit means "to be controlled by the Spirit." It means that the Spirit has possession of that area in the life of a believer, which He has filled.

The ministry of Spirit-filling is accomplished when the believer yields to the indwelling Holy Spirit. The Spirit indwells a believer at the moment he believes, for that is His ministry in relation to salvation. But when a believer submits any part of his life to the control of the indwelling Spirit, then he is filled with the Spirit in that area of his life, and that area of his life is now controlled by the Spirit.

(3) The Nature of Spirit-Filling

There are three things to note about the nature of Spirit-filling, all based on Ephesians 5:18. First, it is commanded. A believer is never commanded to be regenerated, indwelt, baptized, sealed, or anointed by the Holy Spirit. These things happen automatically at the moment one believes, but the believer is commanded: *be filled with the Spirit.* This is the point of Ephesians 5:18, and to be filled with the Spirit is an imperative.

Second, the ministry of Spirit-filling can be repeated. All the ministries of the Holy Spirit in relation to salvation are not repeatable; they are once-and-for-all, instantaneous actions which occur at the moment one believes. The ministries in relation to spiritual growth are repeatable, as is the case with being filled with the Spirit. In Ephesians 5:18, the verb *pleroo* is in the Greek present tense, which emphasizes a continuous and repeated action. This means that the filling does not happen once; we are to "keep on being filled" with the Spirit. This does not necessarily mean the believer has lost his previous filling, although at times it may mean that. To be filled with the Spirit means to place a new area of one's life under control of the Spirit. In the book of Acts, the apostles were said to be filled with the Spirit at least two different times (Acts 2:4; 4:31). Peter alone is filled again in Acts 4:8. Stephen was said to be filled with the Spirit twice (Acts 6:3-6; 7:55). Paul was filled at least three different times (Acts

9:17; 13:9, 52). Barnabas was said to be *full of the Holy Spirit* in Acts 11:24. In none of these cases was the previous filling lost. In every case, a new area needed to be under the Spirit's control, so in each of those areas, they were filled with the Spirit.

Third, the passive voice in Ephesians 5:18 indicates that someone else is doing the filling. The believer submits himself so that the filling can take place, but the Holy Spirit does the actual filling.

Based on what is commanded in Ephesians 5:18, the following summary may be given: Being filled with the Spirit is an imperative, a command. The Greek verb is in the present tense, indicating the filling is to be repeated and may occur many times. The Greek verb is also in the passive voice, indicating that someone else does the filling. Hence, the Spirit's ministry of filling, which relates to spiritual growth, is ongoing, continuous, repeated.

Filling must be kept distinct from the Spirit's ministries relating to salvation which are once-for-all actions that are instantaneous, occurring at the moment one believes. Once a person has believed, he or she does not need to seek to be regenerated, indwelled, baptized, sealed, or anointed by the Spirit. This is why the Bible never commands us to seek these things or to have them done. We are commanded to believe on the Lord, Yeshua, the Messiah, and then the ministries of the Spirit in relation to salvation happen to us. Then, once we believe, these other ministries of the Spirit take effect, one of which is Spirit-filling.

(4) *The Conditions for Living a Spirit-Filled Life*

There are four conditions which a believer must meet to be filled with the Spirit. The first condition is a dedicated life. Since the Spirit-filled life is a life that is controlled by the Spirit, obviously, the believer's life must be dedicated to God for His use. This is expressed in Romans 12:1-2:

> [1] *I beseech you therefore, brethren, by the mercies of God, to present your bodies a living sacrifice, holy, acceptable to God, which is your spiritual service.* [2] *And be not fashioned according to this world: but be ye transformed by the renewing of your mind, that ye may prove what is the good and acceptable and perfect will of God.*

In verse 1, Paul encourages the believers to present their *bodies a living sacrifice* as an act of an initial dedication. The Greek word translated here as "to present," *parastēsai*, is in the aorist tense, which emphasizes that there must be a one-time presentation of the body. In verse 2, Paul then teaches that the believer should live a continuously separated life, allowing himself to be continuously *transformed*, becoming more like Yeshua and not conformed to the world. The Greek verb for "to be transformed" is *metamorphousthe*. It is in the present tense, which indicates that the believer is to keep on being transformed. The act of dedication of Romans 12:1 is something one does after he becomes a believer. If one has personally received Yeshua as his savior and Messiah but has not at any point in his life personally made this once-and-for-all presentation of his body as a living sacrifice for God's use, then he is not at this point filled with the Spirit, for his body is not under the Spirit's control. The believer needs to make that initial act of dedication (Rom. 12:1) and from then on allow God to work in his life in a continuous way (Rom. 12:2). One can do no better than to meditate upon these two verses and apply their demands to his life.

The second condition to being filled with the Spirit is an undefeated life. Ephesians 4:30 states: *And grieve not the Holy Spirit of God, in whom ye were sealed unto the day of redemption*. Grieving the Holy Spirit is a sin that only believers can commit. The subject of sinning against the Holy Spirit will be discussed in detail in the next chapter. For now, it can be said that when a believer commits a sin in his body, he sins against the indwelling Spirit who has sealed him to the day of redemption, and so the Spirit is grieved. If the believer is grieving the Spirit, he is not being filled by the Spirit. Living a defeated life means grieving the Spirit. Living an undefeated life is the means by which a believer does not grieve the Spirit. This becomes a condition of being filled by the Spirit.

The third condition to being filled by the Spirit is a dependent life. Galatians 5:16 states: *But I say, Walk by the Spirit, and ye shall not fulfil the lust of the flesh*. In this verse, "the Spirit" is most likely the newborn human spirit rather than the Holy Spirit, but the issue does not change. The command in this verse emphasizes that the believer should be living a life dependent upon his new nature. It is the new nature which is under the Spirit's control. The believer should live the dependent life.

The fourth condition to being filled with the Spirit is that of obedience. Obviously, if the believer is disobeying the commandments of the Law of the Messiah, he is not being filled with the Spirit. Yeshua declared in John 14:15: *If ye love me ye will keep my commandments.* The believer shows his love for God by obedience. In I Thessalonians 5:19, Paul commands believers not to *quench the Spirit.* If the believer lives a life of obedience to the commandments of the Law of the Messiah, he is also living a Spirit-filled life.

(5) The Results of Spirit-Filling

There are ten results of the Spirit-filled life. The first result is that the believer becomes more like the Messiah (Gal. 5:22-23). If the believer allows himself to be under the Spirit's control and be filled with the Spirit, he will become more and more conformed to the image of the Son.

The second result is worship and praise. This is mentioned in Ephesians 5:19-20, which follows the command to be filled with the Spirit in verse 18. The same point is made in Philippians 3:3.

The third result is submissiveness. This is found in Ephesians 5:21, in the same context as Ephesians 5:18, where the believer is told to be filled with the Spirit. An attitude of submissiveness to one another and to authority—home, church, or government—is a result of being filled with the Spirit.

The fourth result is service (Jn. 7:37-39; II Cor. 3:6). A Spirit-filled believer will be living a life of service to the Lord. This, too, is a natural outworking of being filled with the Spirit, for if the believer is under the Spirit's control, he is going to want to serve God.

The fifth result is liberation (Rom. 8:2). In living the Spirit-filled life, the believer is freed *from the law of sin and death* and lives in newness of life instead.

The sixth result is spiritual strength (Eph. 3:16). Living a Spirit-filled life will result in the strengthening of the believer's spiritual vitality.

The seventh result is divine empowerment and enablement (Acts 1:8; Rom. 15:13, 19; I Thess. 1:5). The believer will be empowered by the Spirit if he is filled with Him.

The eighth result is witnessing (Acts 4:8-12, 11:23-24). Spirit-filling will spur the believer to witness of his faith. Not all believers will become great evangelists, but by simply living the Spirit-filled life and allowing the Spirit to control him, the believer will naturally begin witnessing to others concerning the claims of Yeshua the Messiah.

The ninth result is fellowship with God and other saints (Phil. 2:1-4). When a believer is not filled with the Spirit, he does not enjoy fellowship with other saints. When he is filled with the Spirit, he seeks out this fellowship; he thirsts after it. This desire for fellowship is a result of being filled with the Spirit.

The tenth result is progressive sanctification. The believer is more and more sanctified or set apart as a special vessel for God, becoming more and more like the Messiah and holy in this life.

(6) Summary of Spirit-Filling

There is an initial filling that takes place at the moment one believes. The Spirit takes control of that part of the believer that concerns his faith and salvation. As the believer grows in the spiritual life, God shows him other areas of his life which need to be filled or controlled by the Spirit. Every time a believer submits a new area of his life to the Spirit's control, he is filled again. That is why a believer can be filled many times in his spiritual growth, and he should be.

b. The Ministry of Teaching

The second ministry of the Holy Spirit in relation to spiritual growth is teaching believers spiritual truth. The main passage that speaks of this ministry is John 16:12-15, where Yeshua declares:

> [12] *I have yet many things to say unto you, but ye cannot bear them now.* [13] *Howbeit when he, the Spirit of truth, is come, he shall guide you into all the truth: for he shall not speak from himself; but what things soever he shall hear, these shall he speak: and he shall declare unto you the things that are to come.* [14] *He shall glorify me: for he shall take of mine, and shall declare it unto you.* [15] *All things whatsoever the Father has are mine: therefore said I, that he takes of mine, and shall declare it unto you.*

In these verses, Yeshua declared that the Holy Spirit has a ministry of teaching the believer as part of his spiritual growth. The content of what the Ruach teaches the believer involves two things: first, biblical truth in general; and second, prophecy in particular. The more the believer understands biblical truth in general and prophecy in particular indicates that the Holy Spirit has been teaching him as a part of his spiritual growth. The result of the teaching ministry of the Holy Spirit in the believer's life is that the Messiah is glorified. The more the believer learns about spiritual truth, the more he acts upon what he learns, the more his life is consistent with what he learns, Yeshua the Messiah is glorified that much more.

There are three methods that the Holy Spirit uses to teach the believer. The first method is the Spirit's ministry of illumination (I Cor. 2:9-16). It is the Holy Spirit who illuminates the believer's mind to help him understand spiritual truth.

The second method is the Spirit's gift of teaching. He uses men who have received this gift to teach other believers (I Cor. 12:29; Eph. 4:11). They are responsible for communicating the teachings of the Word of God to others.

The third method is based on the anointing ministry of the Holy Spirit (I Jn. 2:27), which was discussed earlier. The teaching the believer receives through illumination and through men with the gift of teaching is confirmed by the Holy Spirit. This confirmation is not by some feeling, but by the written Word of God in that what is being taught is in conformity with the written Scriptures.

c. The Ministry of Guiding

The third ministry of the Holy Spirit in relation to spiritual growth is that of leading or guiding. Two verses speak of this work. The first verse is Romans 8:14: *For as many as are led by the Spirit of God, these are sons of God.* All believers are led by the Spirit of God because all believers are sons of God. The more a believer matures in his sonship, the more the leading and guiding of the Spirit will be seen in the believer's life.

The second verse is Galatians 5:18: *But if ye are led by the Spirit, ye are not under the law.* Being led or guided by the Spirit means that the believer is no longer under the Mosaic Law. The believer does not turn to the Law of Moses for guidance, but to the Holy Spirit. The Spirit leads the believer in conformity with the written Word of God.

There are several examples in the book of Acts which illustrate this leading of the saints by the Holy Spirit, and a few will be listed here: Philip is led by the Spirit in Acts 8:29, Peter in Acts 10:19-20 and 11:12, Barnabas and Saul in Acts 13:2-4, Paul in Acts 16:6-7 and 20:22-23, and the elders of Ephesus in Acts 20:28.

d. The Ministry of Assurance

The fourth ministry of the Holy Spirit in relation to spiritual growth is the ministry of assurance. Because of this work of the Ruach, the believer knows that he really is saved and is a child of God. Three verses speak of this ministry. The first verse is Romans 8:16: *The Spirit himself bears witness with our spirit, that we are children of God.* According to this verse, the means of assurance is that the Holy Spirit testifies with the believer's newborn human spirit, his regenerated spirit, that he is indeed a child of God.

The second verse is I John 3:24: *And he that keeps his commandments abides in him, and he in him. And hereby we know that he abides in us, by the Spirit which he gave us.* According to this verse, the believer knows that God now abides in him because of the Spirit given to him. By means of the indwelling Holy Spirit which one receives at the moment he believes, the Holy Spirit testifies that it is God indeed who is indwelling the believer.

The third verse is I John 4:13: *hereby we know that we abide in him and he in us, because he has given us of his Spirit.* In this verse, the believer knows God abides in him, and that he abides in God, because God has given His Spirit to the believer.

e. The Ministry of Praying and Interceding

The fifth ministry of the Holy Spirit in relation to spiritual growth is that of praying and interceding. Three main passages speak of this ministry. The first is Romans 8:26-27:

> [26] And in like manner the Spirit also helps our infirmity: for we know not how to pray as we ought; but the Spirit himself makes intercession for us with groanings which cannot be uttered; [27] and he that searches the hearts knows what is the mind of the Spirit, because he makes intercession for the saints according to the will of God.

The Holy Spirit is praying for the believer. He needs to do this because of the believer's weakness in his prayer life. Being finite, the believer does not always know what his real needs are. The Holy Spirit, on the other hand, always does, and so He prays for the believer. The method He uses for this work is found in the word "helps." The Greek word is *synantilambanetai* and means "to take hold with at the side" or "to take a share in." In other words, the Holy Spirit assists the believer to perform the task of praying. He puts His hands to the work in cooperation with the believer and lends him a hand in his prayer life. Furthermore, the Holy Spirit prays *with groanings which cannot be uttered*. This expression is sometimes misused to teach that the groanings refer to speaking in tongues. But the verse clearly states that these groanings cannot be uttered—period! It does not say, "With groanings which cannot be uttered unless one speaks in tongues." In the context of Romans 8:26-27, Paul is speaking of things that are true of all believers. Hence, the ministry of interceding on behalf of the saints is not only for those who speak in tongues; it is a promise to all believers.

The second verse is Ephesians 6:18: *with all prayer and supplication praying at all seasons in the Spirit, and watching thereunto in all perseverance and supplication for all the saints.* This verse speaks about praying in the Spirit for two things: the perseverance of the saints and the supplication for all the saints. Prayers should be said on all occasions and persistently, in the power of the Ruach HaKodesh, for all believers, since all are targets of the evil one.

The third passage is Jude 20-21:

> [20] But ye, beloved, building up yourselves on your most holy faith, praying in the Holy Spirit. [21] keep yourselves in the love of God, looking for the mercy of our Lord Yeshua Messiah unto eternal life.

In verse 21, Jude gives a command, saying, "Keep yourselves in the love of God." To obey this command, the believer is to build on the truth of

God (v. 20), pray in the Holy Spirit (v. 20), and look with an eternal perspective for the mercy of the Messiah (v. 21). Praying in the Holy Spirit means being guided by Him.

f. The Ministry of the Witness of the Spirit

The sixth ministry of the Holy Spirit in relation to spiritual growth is His witness. The Spirit indwells believers at the moment of salvation. Therefore, the witness of the Spirit is internal.

Several passages describe this ministry and what the Ruach is witnessing about. The first is Romans 8:16, which states: *The Spirit himself bears witness with our spirit, that we are children of God*. The reason the believer is assured of his salvation in Yeshua the Messiah is because of the witness of the Spirit, who makes him conscious that he is a child of God.

The second passage is I Corinthians 2:9-16:

> *[9] but as it is written, Things which eye saw not, and ear heard not, And which entered not into the heart of man, Whatsoever things God prepared for them that love him. [10] But unto us God revealed them through the Spirit: for the Spirit searches all things, yea, the deep things of God. [11] For who among men knows the things of a man, save the spirit of the man, which is in him? even so the things of God none knows, save the Spirit of God. [12] But we received, not the spirit of the world, but the spirit which is from God; that we might know the things that were freely given to us of God. [13] Which things also we speak, not in words which man's wisdom teaches, but which the Spirit teaches; combining spiritual things with spiritual words. [14] Now the natural man receives not the things of the Spirit of God: for they are foolishness unto him; and he cannot know them, because they are spiritually judged. [15] But he that is spiritual judges all things, and he himself is judged of no man. [16] For who has known the mind of the Lord, that he should instruct him? But we have the mind of Messiah.*

Because the believer has the mind of Messiah, he can understand that which this mind has produced: Scripture.

Third, according to I Corinthians 12:3, the witness of the Spirit affirms the lordship of Yeshua the Messiah in that *no man can say* [He] *is Lord, but in the Holy Spirit*.

The fourth verse is II Corinthians 1:22, where the witness of the Spirit testifies that the believer has the seal of final redemption: *who also sealed us, and gave us the earnest of the Spirit in our hearts*. Just as the believer's immaterial part has been saved, even so, the material part of the believer will someday be saved as well. The believer will either be changed or resurrected at the rapture.

The fifth passage is II Corinthians 3:1-8, which deals with being called into the ministry:

[1] Are we beginning again to commend ourselves? or need we, as do some, epistles of commendation to you or from you? [2] Ye are our epistle, written in our hearts, known and read of all men; [3] being made manifest that ye are an epistle of Messiah, ministered by us, written not with ink, but with the Spirit of the living God; not in tables of stone, but in tables that are hearts of flesh. [4] And such confidence have we through Messiah to God-ward: [5] not that we are sufficient of ourselves, to account anything as from ourselves; but our sufficiency is from God; [6] who also made us sufficient as ministers of a new covenant; not of the letter, but of the spirit: for the letter kills, but the spirit gives life. [7] But if the ministration of death, written, and engraven on stones, came with glory, so that the children of Israel could not look stedfastly upon the face of Moses for the glory of his face; which glory was passing away: [8] how shall not rather the ministration of the spirit be with glory?

The reason some people feel they are called into the ministry is because of this witness of the Holy Spirit.

Sixth, Galatians 4:6 states: *And because ye are sons, God sent forth the Spirit of his Son into our hearts, crying, Abba, Father*. The Spirit gives the believer the consciousness of his relationship with God. Indwelled by the Ruach, the believer knows he has either a good or a bad relationship with God by means of this witness of the Spirit.

The seventh passage is Ephesians 1:17-21, which teaches that the Holy Spirit illuminates the believer in the understanding of God's program:

[17] that the God of our Lord Yeshua Messiah, the Father of glory, may give unto you a spirit of wisdom and revelation in the knowledge of him; [18] having the eyes of your heart enlightened, that ye may know what is the hope of his calling, what the riches of the glory of his inheritance in the saints, [19] and what the exceeding greatness of his power to us-ward who believe,

> *according to that working of the strength of his might* ^{20} *which he wrought in Messiah, when he raised him from the dead, and made him to sit at his right hand in the heavenly places,* ^{21} *far above all rule, and authority, and power, and dominion, and every name that is named, not only in this world, but also in that which is to come:*

The reason the believer can understand God's program, understand why God does things sometimes one way and sometimes another way, is because of the witness of the Spirit.

The eighth passage is Ephesians 3:16-19, which deals with knowing the love of Messiah:

> ^{16} *that he would grant you, according to the riches of his glory, that ye may be strengthened with power through his Spirit in the inward man;* ^{17} *that Messiah may dwell in your hearts through faith; to the end that ye, being rooted and grounded in love,* ^{18} *may be strong to apprehend with all the saints what is the breadth and length and height and depth,* ^{19} *and to know the love of Messiah which passes knowledge, that ye may be filled unto all the fulness of God.*

Because of this internal witness of the Spirit, the believer knows he has the love of the Messiah.

The ninth passage is I John 2:20-27, where the Holy Spirit witnesses to the believer concerning the truth of the teachings he has received:

> ^{20} *And ye have an anointing from the Holy One, and ye know all things.* ^{21} *I have not written unto you because ye know not the truth, but because ye know it, and because no lie is of the truth.* ^{22} *Who is the liar but he that denies that Yeshua is the Messiah? This is the antichrist, even he that denies the Father and the Son.* ^{23} *Whosoever denies the Son, the same has not the Father: he that confesses the Son has the Father also.* ^{24} *As for you, let that abide in you which ye heard from the beginning. If that which ye heard from the beginning abide in you, ye also shall abide in the Son, and in the Father.* ^{25} *And this is the promise which he promised us, even the life eternal.* ^{26} *These things have I written unto you concerning them that would lead you astray.* ^{27} *And as for you, the anointing which ye received of him abides in you, and ye need not that any one teach you; but as his anointing teaches you*

concerning all things, and is true, and is no lie, and even as it taught you, ye abide in him.

The reason the believer can be comfortable with a truth he has just received is because of the inner witness of the Holy Spirit.

The tenth verse is I John 3:24: *And he that keeps his commandments abides in him, and he in him. And hereby we know that he abides in us, by the Spirit which he gave us.* The verse talks about the witness of the Spirit to the believer that God is abiding in him.

The eleventh passage is I John 5:7-12:

7 And it is the Spirit that bears witness, because the Spirit is the truth. 8 For there are three who bear witness, the Spirit, and the water, and the blood: and the three agree in one. 9 If we receive the witness of men, the witness of God is greater: for the witness of God is this, that he has borne witness concerning his Son. 10 He that believes on the Son of God has the witness in him: he that believes not God has made him a liar; because he has not believed in the witness that God has borne concerning his Son. 11 And the witness is this, that God gave unto us eternal life, and this life is in his Son. 12 He that has the Son has the life; he that has not the Son of God has not the life.

This passage teaches that the Holy Spirit witnesses to the believer that he has eternal life in the Son.

It should be pointed out that this witness of the Spirit is not confirmed by feelings. Feelings can be very deceptive. A believer can feel very good about things which are very, very wrong. Fortunately, the Bible also explains just how this witness of the Spirit is confirmed. The witness of the Spirit and the conviction of its truth come through the Word of God. Ephesians 6:17 teaches that the *sword of the Spirit* is the Word of God. The witness is confirmed because it conforms to the teachings of the written Word of God. Revelation 2-3 is a good example. All seven letters written to the churches contain the statement: *what the Spirit says to the churches*, a reference to what had just been written. Hence, the witness of the Spirit does not come by means of feelings, but by means of the Word of God. The Spirit indwells the believer and illuminates his mind to understand the Scriptures. Illumination of the believer's mind is the means that the Spirit uses to witness to the believer concerning the truth or falseness of what has been heard.

g. The Ministry of the Fellowship of the Holy Spirit

The seventh ministry of the Holy Spirit in relation to spiritual growth is the fellowship of the Holy Spirit. There are two passages, which speak to this work. First is II Corinthians 13:14, which states: *The grace of the Lord Yeshua Messiah, and the love of God, and the communion of the Holy Spirit, be with you all*. Here, Paul calls the fellowship of the Holy Spirit "communion."

The second verse is Philippians 2:1, which reads: *If there is therefore any exhortation in Messiah, if any consolation of love, if any fellowship of the Spirit, if any tender mercies and compassions*. Here, Paul's words are translated as "fellowship of the Spirit." The Greek word used in both verses is *koinonia*, which means "fellowship" or "communion."

There are two aspects to the fellowship of the Spirit: a vertical aspect and a horizontal aspect. The fellowship *of* and *in* the Holy Spirit has two directions. The vertical aspect is the believer's fellowship with God the Father through the Holy Spirit. The horizontal aspect is the believer's fellowship with other believers through the Holy Spirit. This horizontal aspect of the fellowship of the Spirit makes fellowship among believers possible; without it, fellowship among believers would be impossible.

Concerning the vertical relationship, in order to have true fellowship with God, a personal walk with Him is required. This is where the ministries of fellowship and filling of the Holy Spirit come together.

Concerning the horizontal relationship, the fellowship with other believers necessitates the meeting of the church. For true *koinonia* to take place, the church must come together. This is why the Bible encourages believers to gather together into a local church, under the authority of elders and deacons. The horizontal relationship also necessitates the meeting of the congregants to be structured in a way that permits and encourages communication. It must not be so loosely formed that there is anarchy, and it must not be so tightly bound that the Spirit cannot be free to work through saints in the congregation. True fellowship requires a freedom of the Holy Spirit, necessitating a balanced structure which is both controlled by the elders and yet informal.

F. The Works in the Future

In this area of the ministries of the Holy Spirit, three things will be discussed: the great tribulation, the national regeneration of Israel, and the Messianic kingdom or millennium.

1. During the Great Tribulation

During the tribulation, the Holy Spirit will be working in three main ministries: the ministry of regeneration, the ministry of sealing, and the ministry of prophecy.

As to the work of regeneration, Revelation 7:1-17 points out that many will be saved during the tribulation. In verses 1-8, the 144,000 Jews are saved; in verses 9-17, myriads and myriads of Gentiles are saved. By the end of the tribulation, all Israel will be saved. Salvation is a work of the Holy Spirit. Salvation results from regeneration. The fact that both Jews and Gentiles will be saved during the tribulation shows that the Holy Spirit will be regenerating people during this time.

As to the work of sealing, Revelation 7:3 and 9:4 point out that the Holy Spirit will be sealing people during the tribulation. Sealing is always a guarantee of safety. In the present, believers are being sealed with the Spirit as a guarantee of spiritual safety. In the tribulation, those who have the seal of the Holy Spirit will not only be guaranteed eternal spiritual security, but also physical security from the judgments and persecutions of the tribulation. As a result of this sealing ministry of the Holy Spirit, they will survive the tribulation.

As to the work of prophecy, people will be given direct revelation from God during the tribulation. One example is the two witnesses in Revelation 11:3-6 who will prophesy in Jerusalem. These two witnesses are the two olive trees of Zechariah 4:11-14 and are connected with the Holy Spirit as the oil.

While these are the three key works the Holy Spirit will be performing during the tribulation, there is one ministry He will not perform: Spirit baptism. As emphasized earlier, Spirit baptism is a work reserved for the church only. While people will be regenerated, filled, sealed, and anointed with the Holy Spirit, no one in the tribulation will be baptized by the Spirit, because that is a work for the church age only, from Acts 2 until the rapture of the church.

2. On Behalf of the Nation of Israel

A second major future work of the Holy Spirit will be Israel's national regeneration. The national regeneration of Israel is consistently connected with the outpouring of the Holy Spirit. This is seen in a number of passages in the Hebrew Scriptures, the first one being Isaiah 32:9-20. This passage can be divided into three segments. First, verses 9-14 describe the period of the great tribulation. The second segment, in verse 15, describes the outpouring of the Holy Spirit: *until the Spirit be poured upon us from on high, and the wilderness become a fruitful field, and the fruitful field be esteemed as a forest.* In this verse, Isaiah speaks of an outpouring of the Holy Spirit upon Israel following the great tribulation (Isa. 32:9-14). The third segment, in verses 16-20, describes the Messianic kingdom, which follows the national regeneration of Israel.

Another passage that speaks of Israel's national regeneration is Isaiah 44:1-5. Verses 1-2 emphasize that Israel is the chosen people of God. In verses 3-5, Isaiah describes the outpouring of the Spirit upon the whole nation of Israel:

> [3] *For I will pour water upon him that is thirsty, and streams upon the dry ground; I will pour my Spirit upon your seed, and my blessing upon your offspring:* [4] *and they shall spring up among the grass, as willows by the watercourses.* [5] *One shall say, I am Jehovah's; and another shall call himself by the name of Jacob; and another shall subscribe with his hand unto Jehovah, and surname himself by the name of Israel.*

The third passage that speaks of Israel's national regeneration is Ezekiel 39:25-29. Verses 25-28 describe a world-wide regathering of the Jewish people for the Messianic kingdom. The basis for Israel's world-wide regathering is given in verse 29, which states: *neither will I hide my face any more from them; for I have poured out my Spirit upon the house of Israel, says the Lord Jehovah.*

This verse speaks of an outpouring of the Holy Spirit upon the whole nation of Israel. This outpouring will result in Israel's regeneration, which, in turn, will be the basis for Israel's final restoration and regathering.

The fourth passage that speaks of Israel's national regeneration is Joel 2:28-29. The prophet declares that in the last days of the great tribulation, the Holy Spirit will be poured out upon the whole nation of Israel:

> [28] *And it shall come to pass afterward, that I will pour out my Spirit upon all flesh; and your sons and your daughters shall prophesy, your old men shall dream dreams, your young men shall see visions:* [29] *and also upon the servants and upon the handmaids in those days will I pour out my Spirit.*

Peter quoted this passage in Acts 2:16-21. Yet, he did so only as an application to the experience of the believers, for there was a pouring out of the Spirit in a limited way—either upon the twelve apostles or on the one hundred twenty at the most, but certainly not on the whole nation of Israel. Hence, Acts 2 did not fulfill the prophecies of Joel 2:28-29. The outpouring of the Holy Spirit on Israel will occur only when the whole nation will be saved.[25]

The fifth passage that speaks of the national regeneration of Israel is Zechariah 4:1-14. The verses again picture Israel as a saved nation. The universal outpouring of the Holy Spirit will be on the nation of Israel only, and it is connected with the Holy Spirit in verse 6: *Then he answered and spoke unto me, saying, This is the word of Jehovah unto Zerubbabel, saying, Not by might, nor by power, but by my Spirit, said Jehovah of hosts.*

The sixth passage is Zechariah 12:10-13:1, and verse 10 reads:

> *And I will pour upon the house of David, and upon the inhabitants of Jerusalem, the spirit of grace and of supplication; and they shall look unto me whom they have pierced; and they shall mourn for him, as one mourns for his only son, and shall be in bitterness for him, as one that is in bitterness for his first-born.*

---

[25] For details as to how the New Testament quotes the Hebrew Scriptures, see Volume 1 of this series, pages 57-66.

In this passage, the outpouring of the Holy Spirit results in Israel's national regeneration, which, in turn, leads to the second coming of Messiah Yeshua described in Zechariah 14:1-15.

Summarizing the passages, in some future time, the Holy Spirit will minister in such a way that the whole nation of Israel will be saved by His regenerating work. This truth is reaffirmed by Paul in Romans 11:25-26. The universal outpouring of the Holy Spirit is on the nation of Israel only. This will, in turn, bring about the second coming of the Messiah.

3. During the Messianic Kingdom or the Millennium

The third future ministry of the Holy Spirit will be His work in the Messianic kingdom. Three main ministries should be mentioned. First will be the ministry of regeneration. People born during the millennium will continue to inherit the sin nature. That sin nature will need to be regenerated through faith in the substitutionary death, the burial, and the resurrection of the Messiah. According to Jeremiah 31:31-34, the Holy Spirit will be regenerating people in the millennial kingdom.

Second will be the ministry of indwelling. The Holy Spirit will indwell believers (Ezek. 36:27, 37:14).

Third, the Holy Spirit will be upon the Messiah. By means of the Holy Spirit, the Messiah will exercise His authority and rule with the attributes described in Isaiah 11:2-3:

> [2] *and the Spirit of Jehovah shall rest upon him, the spirit of wisdom and understanding, the spirit of counsel and might, the spirit of knowledge and of the fear of Jehovah;* [3] *and his delight shall be in the fear of Jehovah; and he shall not judge after the sight of his eyes, neither decide after the hearing of his ears;*

G. QUESTIONS AND STUDY SUGGESTIONS

Study Suggestion 1: The Spirit's ministry of illumination is taught in Nehemiah 9:20, I Corinthians 2:9-16, and Ephesians 1:15-18. Look up the verses and describe the exact character and content of this ministry. Then think about a moment in your life as a believer where you knew beyond the shadow of a doubt that the Ruach HaKodesh has performed this work in you.

Study Suggestion 2: Complete the graph Illustrating the Spirit's work in the life of Messiah.

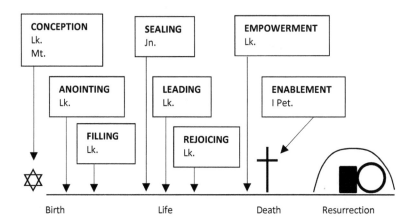

Ruach HaKodesh – God the Holy Spirit

Chapter VI

Sins Against the Ruach HaKodesh

This chapter is a study of specific types of sins that are committed against the Holy Spirit. The topic will be studied in two divisions: first, sins against the Holy Spirit committed by unbelievers; and second, sins against the Holy Spirit committed by believers.

A. Sins Committed by Unbelievers

Unbelievers can commit two types of sins against the Holy Spirit: They can vex or grieve Him, and they can blaspheme against the Holy Spirit.

1. The Vexing or the Grieving of the Ruach HaKodesh

The first type of sin committed against the Holy Spirit by unbelievers is the vexing or grieving of the Holy Spirit because of rebellion. This sin is mentioned in Isaiah 63:10: *But they rebelled, and grieved* [vexed] *his holy Spirit: therefore he was turned to be their enemy, and himself fought against them.* The context of this verse is the wilderness wanderings, during which the Israelites continually rebelled against God's authority administered through Moses. God viewed the rebellion as a vexing of His Holy Spirit.

The way unbelievers vex the Holy Spirit is by acts of rebellion against God's authority, especially God's authority through a specific individual. If God has placed someone in a position of authority and unbelievers defy that divine authority, this is the sin of the vexing of the Holy Spirit.

2. Blasphemy of the Ruach HaKodesh

The second sin committed against the Holy Spirit by unbelievers is the sin of blasphemy. This sin has been frequently misunderstood. Often people state that they have committed the "unpardonable sin" of blasphemy against the Holy Spirit. When asked what blasphemy against the Holy Spirit is, they are unable to give a clear answer and usually fall back on a specific sin they committed. They feel that this sin has put them beyond the hope of forgiveness.

Altogether, there are three passages of Scripture that deal with the blaspheming of the Holy Spirit. All three passages are in the Gospels: Matthew 12:22-45, Mark 3:22-30, and Luke 11:14-26. They deal with the same specific situation. Since Matthew 12:22-45 gives the most details concerning the blaspheming of the Holy Spirit, we will focus on his account. The other two passages do not go beyond what is given in the Matthew passage.[26]

a. The Rejection (Mt. 12:22-24)

> *²² Then was brought unto him one possessed with a demon, blind and dumb: and he healed him, insomuch that the dumb man spoke and saw. ²³ And all the multitudes were amazed, and said, Can this be the son of David?*

The incident began when Yeshua exorcised a demon that caused the possessed person to be both blind and dumb, meaning he could neither see nor speak (Mt. 12:22). Generally, exorcism was not all that unusual in the days of Yeshua's ministry. Even the Pharisees and their disciples practiced the casting out of demons, and Yeshua acknowledged it with His own challenging question: *by whom do your sons cast them out?* (Mt. 12:27). However, in rabbinic exorcisms, the exorcist would need to use a specific ritual that had distinctive steps. He would need to establish communication with the demon, who was using the vocal cords of the person under his control. Then the exorcist had to discover the demon's name. This was an important facet of the exorcism. Once he knew the demon's name, he

---

[26] For far greater details on this topic, see pages 366-402 in Volume 2 of the author's book titled *Yeshua: The Life of Messiah from a Messianic Jewish Perspective* (San Antonio, TX: Ariel Ministries, 2017). A shorter discussion of this topic is also found in the abridged version of the same book, pages 211-219.

could use it to order the demon out of the possessed person. There were times when Yeshua Himself used that method (e.g., Mk. 5:9). However, He normally just ordered the demon out without any ritual at all, which is what made His exorcisms so different. From the study of the rabbinic method of exorcism, one can deduce that, within the framework of Pharisaic Judaism, there was one kind of demon an exorcist could not cast out: the kind of demon that caused the person controlled to be mute. There was no way to communicate with that kind of demon, no way of finding out its name.

Before the event described in the verses above, Yeshua had cast out many demons, and the people were astounded, *for with authority and power he commanded the unclean spirits, and they come out* (Lk. 4:36). They wondered by what authority He was able to do this. When Yeshua cast out this particular demon, the multitudes reacted differently. They raised the question: *Can this be the son of David?* (Mt. 12:23). This is a very different question than the one they had asked before. "Son of David" is a Messianic title, so after witnessing this miracle, the multitudes were clearly asking if Yeshua could indeed be the Messiah. Something about this sign was so unique that they recognized that only Messiah could have performed it.

Their conclusion was correct; Yeshua had just performed the second Messianic miracle.[27] However, while the multitudes were willing to raise the question, they were not willing to answer it for themselves. From biblical times to the present, the Jewish people have labored under a "leadership complex," meaning, whichever way the leaders went, the people were sure to follow. This can be seen clearly in the Hebrew Scriptures. When a king did that which was right in the eyes of the Lord, the people followed. Conversely, when a king did that which was evil in the eyes of the Lord, they also followed. Even today, when believers speak to Jews about Yeshua's Messiahship, sooner or later, they will be confronted with the very same objection: "If Yeshua is the Messiah, why don't our rabbis believe in Him?" In New Testament times, the leadership complex was very strong because of the stranglehold Pharisaism had upon the masses

---

[27] The first Messianic miracle was the healing of a Jewish leper. The third such miracle was the healing of a man born blind. For details on all these miracles, see the author's *Yeshua: The Life of Messiah from a Messianic Jewish Perspective* series.

through the Mishnah, and so, while the Jewish people in this account were willing to raise the question, they were not willing to answer it for themselves. They were looking to their leaders to give them direction.

In light of the question by the multitudes concerning Yeshua's Messiahship, the Pharisees had only two options. The first option was to officially recognize Yeshua as the long-awaited Messiah, and this they did not want to do because He rejected Pharisaic Judaism and the authority of the Oral Law. The second option was to reject His Messianic claims. However, if they took that route, they would have to explain how Yeshua was able to perform miracles that had never before been done. In the end, the Pharisees took the second option and rejected Yeshua's Messianic claims. To explain His special abilities, they came up with a rather radical solution. They declared that Yeshua was able to cast out the demon that caused muteness because He Himself was controlled by *the prince of the demons* (Mt. 12:24), Beelzebub. The original form of the name Beelzebub was Beelzebul, meaning, "the lord of the royal palace." He was the god of the Philistine city of Ekron. After the Jews had finally been cured of idolatry by the Babylonian Captivity, the rabbis liked to poke fun at various pagan gods and apply some of their names to different demons. Here, they changed the last letter so that the name became Beelzebub, meaning "the lord of the flies" or "the lord of the dung," the demon in charge of diseases.

This explanation became the official basis for the rejection of the Messiahship of Yeshua: Because He was demon possessed, Yeshua could not be the Messiah. However, being under the control of the price of demons gave Him the power to perform signs and wonders never seen before. This explanation is not only reflected in the Gospels, but also in rabbinic literature. One passage in the Talmud elaborates on why Yeshua was executed on Passover. Executions were not permitted on feast days. However, in the case of Yeshua, an exception could be made because of the nature of His crime: He had seduced Israel by the practice of sorcery, which is closely connected with demonism. Another passage in the Talmud states that when Yeshua was in Egypt, He made cuts in the skin of His flesh. He inserted the four-letter name of God, *YHVH,* into these cuts, which gave Him the power to perform His unique miracles. Neither in the Gospels nor in rabbinic literature did the religious leaders ever deny the fact of His miracles. There were too many eyewitnesses to those signs. However, they ascribed the power of the miracles to a demonic source.

Therefore, the official basis for rejecting the Messiahship of Yeshua was that He was demon possessed. That was the given reason, but the real reason was that He did not do it their way.

b. The Defense (Mt. 12:25-29)

> *²⁵ And knowing their thoughts he said unto them, Every kingdom divided against itself is brought to desolation; and every city or house divided against itself shall not stand: ²⁶ and if Satan casts out Satan, he is divided against himself; how then shall his kingdom stand? ²⁷ And if I by Beelzebub cast out demons, by whom do your sons cast them out? therefore shall they be your judges. ²⁸ But if I by the Spirit of God cast out demons, then is the kingdom of God come upon you. ²⁹ Or how can one enter into the house of the strong man, and spoil his goods, except he first bind the strong man? and then he will spoil his house.*

Yeshua defended Himself against the charge of being demon possessed by declaring four things:

1. This accusation could not be true because it would mean a division in Satan's kingdom (Mt. 12:25-26; Mk. 3:23-26).
2. The religious leaders themselves had long recognized that the gift of exorcism was a gift of God, so to accuse Him of this was inconsistent with their own theology (Mt. 12:27).
3. This miracle authenticated the claims and the message of the Messiah (Mt. 12:28).
4. This miracle showed that He was stronger than, not subservient to, Satan (Mt. 12:29; Mk. 3:27).

c. The Judgment (Mt. 12:30-37)

> *³⁰ He that is not with me is against me; and he that gathers not with me scatters. ³¹ Therefore I say unto you, Every sin and blasphemy shall be forgiven unto men; but the blasphemy against the Spirit shall not be forgiven. ³² And whosoever shall speak a word against the Son of man, it shall be forgiven him; but whosoever shall speak against the Holy Spirit, it shall not be*

> *forgiven him, neither in this world, nor in that which is to come. ³³ Either make the tree good, and its fruit good; or make the tree corrupt, and its fruit corrupt: for the tree is known by its fruit. ³⁴ Ye offspring of vipers, how can ye, being evil, speak good things? for out of the abundance of the heart the mouth speaks. ³⁵ The good man out of his good treasure brings forth good things: and the evil man out of his evil treasure brings forth evil things. ³⁶ And I say unto you, that every idle word that men shall speak, they shall give account thereof in the day of judgment. ³⁷ For by your words you shall be justified, and by your words you shall be condemned.*

After having defended Himself against the accusation of being demon possessed, Yeshua pronounced a special judgment upon that generation of Israel (Mt. 12:41-42) for being guilty of a very unique sin, which has become known as the unpardonable sin or the blasphemy of the Holy Spirit (Mt. 12:31). Because it was unpardonable, a judgment that could never be removed or alleviated was set against *this generation*. That judgment came forty years later, in the year A.D. 70, when Jerusalem and the Temple were destroyed.

It is very important to understand what the unpardonable sin is in its exact context, because this is the *only* context in which this sin is found. Therefore, it must be interpreted accordingly. By definition, the unpardonable sin was the national rejection by Israel of the Messiahship of Yeshua on the grounds of demon possession while He was physically present on earth.

There are four ramifications of this definition. First, this was a national sin, not an individual sin. Individuals of that generation, like the Apostle Paul, could and did escape the judgment by becoming believers. Furthermore, the sin cannot be committed today. The Bible makes one point very clear: The individual who will come to God through Messiah's blood will be forgiven regardless of what sin he has committed. The nature of the sin is irrelevant. The Messiah did not die on the cross only for certain kinds of sins. He died for every type of sin and rendered all of them forgivable to the individual who will come to God through Messiah's blood. The term "whosoever" in Matthew 12:32 can have either an individual or a corporate meaning, depending on the context. In this context, it is defined by the term "this generation" of verses 41 and 42, which state: *The men of Nineveh shall stand up in the judgment with this generation, and shall condemn it . . . The queen of the south shall rise up in the judgment with this generation, and shall condemn it* (Mt. 12:41-42). This means that the word "whosoever" is corporate. The individual could be forgiven, but the nation is now unpardonable.

Second, this sin is unique to the Jewish generation of Yeshua's day, and it cannot be applied to later Jewish generations, a fallacy the Catholic Church, for example, has taught. It was to this particular generation that the Messiah came both physically and visibly. He offered to establish the Messianic kingdom for them, and He offered Himself as their Messianic King. It was also this specific generation that rejected Him. In carefully studying the Gospel accounts, it is quite evident that from this point on, the phrase "this generation" is frequently used. This generation alone was guilty of *the blasphemy against the Spirit* (Mt. 12:31). The work of the Holy Spirit was the final testimony of the Messiahship of Yeshua. It was possible to reject Yeshua's Messianic claims and still be convinced by the work of the Holy Spirit. However, to reject the witness of the Holy Spirit also meant rejecting the person of the Messiah. The sin, then, was the willful rejection of the person of the Messiah who had been authenticated by the signs of the Holy Spirit. To ascribe those signs to Satan was to blaspheme the Holy Spirit, which, in turn, led to the rejection of Yeshua's Messiahship. The Messiah needed to be present to perform these signs, which is why this sin was limited to that generation and cannot be committed today.

Third, no other nation could commit this sin. Yeshua was never visibly and physically present with any other nation, offering Himself as that nation's Messiah. This was a unique relationship He had with Israel. There is only one covenant nation: Israel.

There were two consequences for the generation that committed the unpardonable sin: First, it meant that the offer of the Messianic kingdom was rescinded, and that generation lost the opportunity, privilege, and benefit of seeing the kingdom established in their day. It is now destined to be reoffered to the future Jewish generation of the tribulation period, who will accept it, as detailed in Matthew 24-25. Yeshua used the phrases "this world" and "that which is to come" (Mt. 12:32). In the Judaism of His day, the world or age to come was the Messianic age. In other words, this generation was not going to see the kingdom established in their time, nor will they see it in an age to come. They will be long gone before it arrives.

Second, it meant that this generation was under a special divine judgment, a judgment of physical destruction, a judgment that was experienced forty years later, in A.D. 70, when Jerusalem and the Temple were destroyed. In rejecting Yeshua, this generation had reached the point of no return. In God's dealings with His covenant nation, once a generation reached the point of no return, nothing could be done to change the coming physical judgment.

This was the third time a specific generation had reached such a point. The first time this happened was when Israel committed the sin of Kadesh-Barnea, as recorded in Numbers 13-14. After marching through the wilderness, the Israelites finally arrived at Kadesh-Barnea, an oasis located on the border of the Promised Land. From there, Moses sent out twelve spies, who came back forty days later. They all agreed that the land was everything God had described, *a land flowing with milk and honey* (Ex. 33:3). Then came a sharp point of disagreement. Only two of the spies, Joshua and Caleb, had faith in God and believed the Israelites could conquer the land. The other ten men gave a discouraging report, that due to the numerical superiority and military strength of the inhabitants, they could not take the land. The people made the faulty assumption that the majority must always be right. There was a massive rebellion against the authority of Moses and Aaron, and the two men almost lost their lives in a mob scene, until God intervened and rescued them. At that point, the Exodus generation had reached the point of no return, and God decreed the judgment of forty years of wandering and death in the wilderness outside Israel. The people could do nothing thereafter to change the judgment. Numbers 14 does say that they repented and that God forgave their sins (Num. 14:20). The sin did not affect anyone's individual salvation. However, the people still had to pay the physical consequences of going beyond the point of no return, which was death outside Israel. The offer of the land was rescinded from the Exodus generation, and it was reoffered to the wilderness generation, who accepted it and entered Israel under Joshua. Even Moses died outside the land because of a sin he had committed, but that did not affect his individual, personal salvation.

The second time the nation reached the point of no return was in the days of Manasseh, one of the cruelest kings of Jerusalem, who practiced extreme forms of idolatry, including human sacrifice. Much innocent blood was shed throughout his lengthy reign (II Kgs. 21:16). He turned the Temple, built by Solomon for the glory of the true God, into a major center of idolatry (II Kgs. 21:1-9; II Chron. 33:1-9). Finally, he reached the point of no return, and God decreed judgment. Jerusalem and the first Temple were to be destroyed by the Babylonians, and the people were to go into captivity (II Kgs. 21:10-15). Nothing they did thereafter could change the course of judgment. Manasseh repented at the end of his life (II Chron. 33:10-13), and as an individual, he became a saved man. He was even followed by a good king, Josiah, who brought revival to Israel. The only thing God promised was that He would not bring the calamity during Josiah's day, but the judgment was still inevitable (II Chron. 34:22-28) because the people had reached the point of no return.

Now, for the third time, with the willful rejection of the person of the Messiah, that generation of Israel had reached the point of no return. Nothing they did thereafter could change the coming judgment. A study of the triumphal entry will show that a myriad of people proclaimed Yeshua to be the Messiah when He rode into Jerusalem on a donkey (Mt. 21:1-17; Mk. 11:1-11; Lk. 19:29-40; Jn. 12:12-19). However, in the midst of their Messianic acclamations, the words of the Messiah remained words of judgment, clearly stating that Jerusalem would be destroyed (Lk. 19:41-44). This is the nature of the unpardonable sin. Physical consequences must be paid. It meant that no matter how many Jews came to believe—and myriads did come to believe—it would not change the fact of the coming physical judgment of A.D. 70. But, again, this was a generational sin, not an individual one, and it was not applicable to subsequent Jewish generations.

d. The Conclusion

How is the national rejection of the Messiahship of Yeshua a blasphemy against the Holy Spirit? The answer to this question is that the work of the Holy Spirit is the final testimony of the Messiah's work. It is quite possible to initially reject the claims of the Messiah and still be convinced later by the work of the Holy Spirit, but to reject the work of the Holy

Spirit is to reject the person of the Messiah. Ultimately, this sin is the willful rejection of the person of the Messiah.

B. Sins Committed by Believers

The second division in the study of the sins against the Holy Spirit deals with sins committed by believers. Just as there are two sins against the Holy Spirit committed by unbelievers, there are also two sins committed against the Holy Spirit by believers: the grieving of the Holy Spirit and the quenching of the Holy Spirit.

1. The Grieving of the Holy Spirit

The first sin against the Holy Spirit that believers commit is that of grieving Him. This sin is found in Ephesians 4:30, which states: *And grieve not the Holy Spirit of God, in whom ye were sealed unto the day of redemption.* Ephesians was written to the church at Ephesus, so this is a sin committed by a group of believers. Furthermore, this verse states that the very ones who are capable of committing the sin of grieving the Holy Spirit are those who have already been *sealed unto the day of redemption*. Paul is speaking to the believers who have received the sealing ministry of the Holy Spirit. It is this ministry that "locks" or seals a believer into the body of the Messiah in such a way that he can never fall out. It is the sealing ministry of the Holy Spirit that guarantees the believer's eternal security. The believer who has been sealed unto the day of redemption is now eternally secured and is not to grieve the Holy Spirit.

How does a believer grieve the Holy Spirit? Any act of known sin committed by a believer grieves the Spirit, since He is the One who has sealed the believer into the body of the Messiah.

a. Sins of Speech

While it is true that any act of sin grieves the Holy Spirit, it is particularly true of the sins of speech, for this is the context of Ephesians 4. Verse 29 states, *Let no corrupt speech proceed out of your mouth, but such as is good for edifying as the need may be, that it may give grace to them that hear.* Paul admonishes the believer not to allow any corrupt speech out of his mouth. What he means by "corrupt speech" can be deduced from the second part of the verse. In place of corrupt speech, the believer should be speaking the kind of speech that is *good for edifying*, for the building up of the ones who are in need *that it may give grace to them that hear*. To build up someone is to say positive things about that person. To say negative things that are not true about a person is gossip and slander; this is corrupt speech.

There is nothing wrong with saying negative things about people if those charges are actually true, but one must ask the questions, "Do I know these charges to be true? Is it verified by the mouth of two or three witnesses? Is something being said on hearsay without knowledge of all the facts of the case?" If a believer is in public error, there is nothing wrong with publicly admonishing and denouncing his sins. It would not be corrupt speech, but the right way of handling things. Public sin is to be dealt with through church discipline.

Negative statements about others must be made out of pure motivation: to restore the sinner, not to destroy him or tear him down. In this verse, Paul is dealing with the kind of speech which is simply critical, tearing a believer down to make him less in the eyes of other believers. It is a sin of speech.

After writing about corrupt speech, in verse 30 Paul speaks about the grieving of the Holy Spirit. Immediately after that, verse 31 states, *Let all bitterness, and wrath, and anger, and clamor, and railing, be put away from you, with all malice*. This list of negative emotions may lead to the corruption of speech. Bitterness can lead to defamation of character; wrath and anger can result in cursing of other believers; clamor and railing are sins of the tongue and speech; the root cause of it all is malice.

b. Other Sins

As mentioned, the grieving of the Holy Spirit is caused by any act of known sin. Paul mentions other sins in Ephesians 4:25-28:

> [25] *Wherefore, putting away falsehood, speak ye truth each one with his neighbor: for we are members one of another.* [26] *Be ye angry, and sin not: let not the sun go down upon your wrath:* [27] *neither give place to the devil.* [28] *Let him that stole steal no more: but rather let him labor, working with his*

hands the thing that is good, that he may have whereof to give to him that has need.

Even in the wider context of Ephesians 4, the main sin is the sin of the tongue, but here, Paul mentioned other sins, such as the sin of stealing and the sin of giving a place to the devil.

c. The Remedy

Because believers still sin, every believer, at one time or another, grieves the Holy Spirit, but there is a remedy. When a believer has grieved the Holy Spirit by committing an act of known sin, the remedy is in I John 1:9, which states: *If we confess our sins, he is faithful and righteous to forgive us our sins, and to cleanse us from all unrighteousness.* The applied remedy is confession. The preventative remedy is to allow nothing in one's life contrary to the holiness of the Holy Spirit. If the believer walks this way, it will prevent him from grieving the Holy Spirit, but if a sin has been committed, the applied remedy is confession.

2. The Quenching of the Holy Spirit

The second sin committed against the Holy Spirit by believers is the quenching of the Holy Spirit. This sin is found in I Thessalonians 5:19, where Paul commands: *Quench not the Spirit.* What does it mean to quench the Holy Spirit? The word "quench" means "to put out a fire." For instance, Mark 9:48 reads, *where their worm dies not, and the fire is not quenched.* This point is made again in Hebrews 11:34: *quenched the power of fire.* As previously discussed, one of the symbols of the Holy Spirit is fire, as stated in Acts 2:3-4. The cloven tongues of fire are connected with the Holy Spirit, for fire is used as a figure of the Holy Spirit. Just as one can quench or put out a fire, it is also possible to quench or put out the Holy Spirit.

a. The Preventing of the Exercise of Spiritual Gifts

The best way to understand what it means to quench the Spirit is by studying the context of I Thessalonians 5:19. Verse 20 continues: *despise not prophesyings.* The gift of prophecy was one of the special gifts to be used in the public assembly (I Cor. 14). In the context of the quenching of the

Spirit, it is speaking specifically of quenching one of the gifts of the Holy Spirit in the meeting of the church. The purpose of the gifts of the Spirit is the edification of the body. The Scriptures do lay down specific rules as to how often and by whom these gifts can be used in the public assembly. Assuming all the rules of order are kept according to Scripture, to quench the Holy Spirit is to keep believers from exercising their spiritual gifts rightly in the meeting of the church.

The Thessalonians apparently were frowning upon any manifestation of the Holy Spirit that was out of the ordinary. In this case, their conduct was the opposite extreme of the Corinthians. The Corinthians' extreme was to let it all loose without any order, without any rules or regulations, without any elders exercising authority or restraint. Everyone was given free rein to exercise their gifts in any way they chose and as often as they chose. The gifts were exercised on the basis of the flesh, not on the basis of the proper rules and regulations found in the Scriptures. This created disorder, with no chain of command and a lack of the testing of the spirits, which is necessary in that kind of situation. While the Corinthians went to one extreme, the Thessalonians went to the other extreme by frowning upon any manifestation of the Holy Spirit that was out of the ordinary.

In local churches today, most services have a set format. Only a few people have total control of what may or may not go on, and only they give any input to the service. The authority and order exercised often quenches the Spirit. For instance, there is a prescribed time when the service must begin. It is opened with a song and prayer. Some announcements are made, followed by congregational singing, with every song chosen by one individual in the congregation. At some time during the congregational singing, the offering will be taken. Then the sermon is preached. The service often ends with an invitation, a closing hymn, and dismissal with a benediction. All must be concluded by about twelve o'clock lest the people get too restless. Because it is all so fixed, the Holy Spirit is quenched in that members of the congregation are not given an opportunity to share their spiritual gifts in the assembly.

There is no question that the free exercise of gifts must have a degree of control by spiritual elders. It would not be proper to let just anything go on, because that would lead to the Corinthian extreme, but the Corinthian extreme should not be avoided by the Thessalonian extreme. There must be a balance. There must be a time given at some point in the meeting of the church to let others use their spiritual gifts. Not to allow people to exercise their spiritual gifts is to commit the sin of quenching the Spirit.

From what has been said so far about the sin of quenching the Spirit, it is clear that this is not an individual sin, but a congregational sin. In the Greek text, the word "quench" is in the second person plural meaning: "Quench ye not the Spirit." Paul addressed his readers as a corporate body. As such, they were guilty of this sin. While an individual believer can be guilty of grieving the Holy Spirit, a local body, congregation, or assembly can also be guilty of quenching the Holy Spirit.

b. The Remedy

What is the remedy to quenching the Holy Spirit? The Greek form translated "quench not" is an imperative. It literally means, "Stop quenching the Spirit!" The command was to stop doing what the Thessalonians were doing, which was quenching the Spirit. The remedy was to allow for the exercise of the spiritual gifts in accordance with biblical rules and order (as those listed in I Cor. 12-14). An allowance must be made for the exercise of believers' spiritual gifts, whatever they may be, but in accordance with biblical order, rules, and regulations.

C. Conclusion

There is a parallel between the sins against the Holy Spirit committed by unbelievers and the sins committed by believers. The two sins committed by unbelievers are vexing the Holy Spirit, which is an individual sin, and the blasphemy against the Holy Spirit, which was a corporate sin. The sins committed by believers are grieving the Holy Spirit, which is an individual sin, and quenching the Holy Spirit, which is a corporate sin. All these sins need to be avoided, and there are remedies to deal with them in a biblical way.

D. QUESTIONS AND STUDY SUGGESTIONS

Question 1: Many believers struggle with the unpardonable sin and the blasphemy of the Holy Spirit. How would you explain in your own words the unpardonable sin? When was it committed? By whom? What were the consequences? What does this mean to the believer today?

Question 2: As a believer, we can grieve the Spirit. Is this sin the same as the unpardonable sin?

Question 3: Have you ever grieved the Spirit?

Question 4: Dr. Fruchtenbaum mentioned a remedy for the sin of grieving the Spirit. What is it?

Question 5: What does it mean to quench the Spirit? How is this sin different than grieving the Spirit?

Question 6: What is the proper response of the believer for having quenched the Spirit?

Chapter VII

The Gifts of the Ruach HaKodesh

A spiritual gift is a God-given ability to be used by the believer in serving others; it is a supernatural ability possessed by an individual. This is the emphasis of I Corinthians 12-14. Believers are placed by God into the church for the purpose of ministering to the body using their spiritual gifts, as Paul pointed out in Ephesians 4:11-12:

> *[11] And he gave some to be apostles; and some, prophets; and some, evangelists; and some, pastors and teachers; [12] for the perfecting of the saints, unto the work of ministering, unto the building up of the body of Christ:*

This chapter is on the gifts of the Spirit, and the various New Testament passages that deal with this subject will be studied.

A. THE GREEK WORDS

The New Testament writers used two Greek words when speaking of spiritual gifts. The first word is *charisma* and the second word is *pneumatikos*.

Charisma literally means "a gift of grace" or "grace gift." The plural of this Greek word is *charismata*. The word stems from the Greek root *cháris*, "grace," meaning that the gift is undeserved and cannot be earned. The power and operation of a spiritual gift is due to God alone. The word appears twelve times in the New Testament. Eleven times it is used by Paul. One time it is used by Peter. The following list summarizes the message of each of the twelve verses:

1. In Romans 1:11, Paul expressed his desire to go to Rome, so he could share his spiritual gift with the believers there.
2. In Romans 5:15-16, *charisma* is used in reference to the gift of justification, because that, too, is a grace gift; in this case, however, it has more to do with the believer's position of salvation[28] than with a spiritual gift to be used in the context of a church.
3. Romans 6:23 speaks of the gift of eternal life as being a grace gift. This, too, deals with the position of salvation.
4. In Romans 11:29, the gifts of God are without repentance. If God gives a gift as well as a calling, He does not take the gift or the calling away. For example, Israel received the calling to be the chosen people. Even in her unbelief, that status has never changed. Even so, since believers have been given spiritual gifts, those spiritual gifts are never taken away.
5. In Romans 12:6, Paul states that there is a variety of different gifts.
6. In I Corinthians 1:7, Paul expressed his desire that the Corinthian church would not fall behind in any spiritual gift but have all the gifts.
7. I Corinthians 7:7 deals with the use of spiritual gifts.
8. I Corinthians 12:9, 28, 30-31 deals with the use of spiritual gifts.
9. II Corinthians 1:11 details the believer's use of spiritual gifts.
10. In I Timothy 4:14, Paul encourages the believer to use his spiritual gift.
11. In II Timothy 1:6, the same point is made.
12. I Peter 4:10 teaches that all believers have spiritual gifts.

The word *charisma* should be distinguished from two other Greek words, namely, *pneumatikos* and *doron*. The adjective *pneumatikos* means "the things of the Spirit." The emphasis of this word is to point out the source and realm of spiritual gifts, the Holy Spirit. The second Greek word is *doron*, which simply means "gift." However, the connotation is a present, like that given at a birthday or an anniversary. Since this word has no

---

[28] See Messianic Bible Study # 110, available at www.ariel.org.

reference to spiritual gifts, this study will not be concerned with those passages that use the word.

B. ATTRIBUTES OF SPIRITUAL GIFTS

Spiritual gifts have specific attributes; altogether there are six attributes or characteristics that are true of all spiritual gifts. There are also several misconceptions as to what a spiritual gift is.

1. What Spiritual Gifts Are

The first attribute of spiritual gifts is that they are sovereignly bestowed upon the recipient. God decides who gets which gift, as I Corinthians 12:11 points out: *but all these works the one and the same Spirit, dividing to each one severally even as he will*. No matter how much one may personally pray for a specific gift, it will not be given based on that. God bestows the gifts sovereignly and chooses the gift or gifts each believer receives.

The second attribute concerns the timing of the giving. Spiritual gifts are given at the time of salvation, as I Corinthians 12:13 describes: *For in one Spirit were we all baptized into one body, whether Jews or Greeks, whether bond or free; and were all made to drink of one Spirit*. The gifts are not given at some time after salvation. The moment one believes and is baptized by the Spirit into the body of the Messiah, the believer receives his spiritual gifts.

The third attribute is that every believer has at least one gift (Rom. 12:6; I Cor. 12:7, 11).

The fourth attribute is that spiritual gifts differ in value. There is an order of importance, as I Corinthians 12:28 enumerates: *And God has set some in the church, first apostles, secondly prophets, thirdly teachers, then miracles, then gifts of healings, helps, governments, divers kinds of tongues*.

The fifth attribute is that these spiritual gifts are to be used in love. Between I Corinthians 12 and 14, which discuss the details concerning spiritual gifts, is chapter 13, the chapter on love, which emphasizes that these gifts are to be used in love.

The sixth attribute is that spiritual gifts follow a specific order of distribution. In discussing spiritual gifts in Ephesians 4:7-8, Paul quotes Psalm 68:18, saying:

> *⁷ But unto each one of us was the grace given according to the measure of the gift of Messiah. ⁸ Wherefore he says, When he ascended on high, he led captivity captive, And gave gifts unto men.*

This means that the Messiah is the ultimate source of spiritual gifts. However, the agent is the Holy Spirit. The extent of gift-giving is that each believer has at least one gift.

2. What Spiritual Gifts Are Not

In light of the attributes just mentioned, it is important to note that there are five things that a spiritual gift is not. First, there is no spiritual gift for serving in a specific place; therefore, no one is gifted for serving in Africa, Asia, this place, or that place. A spiritual gift is a God-given ability for service and can be used anywhere.

Second, a spiritual gift is not an office, though offices should be filled by spiritually gifted believers. For example, the gift of pastor is not the same as the office of a pastor. While every pastor should have the gift of pastoring, not everyone who has the gift of pastor needs to have the office of pastor. A counselor, for example, could have the gift of pastoring. Yet, he does not have to serve as a pastor in order to use his gift of pastoring. Likewise, according to Scripture, a woman cannot have the office of pastor, but she can have the gift of pastoring. A good place for a woman to use this gift would be in the position of Dean of Women at a Bible college. A spiritual gift is usable apart from the office. While the office may be limited, the gifts are not limited to either sex or any age group. The gift should fit the office. A deacon should have the gift of serving, an elder should have the gift of ruling, a teacher should have the gift of teaching, and a pastor should have the gift of pastoring.

Third, a spiritual gift is not a talent. Talents are innate to both believers and unbelievers, but spiritual gifts are limited to believers only.

Fourth, just as there is no gift for serving in a particular part of the world, there is no gift for ministry to a particular age group; no gift for "young people's work" any more than there is a gift for "old people's work." If someone has the gift of teaching or pastoring, they should be able to use it with any age group. A spiritual gift is simply a God-given ability for service and should be usable with every age level.

Fifth, spiritual gifts are not indications of spirituality. The possession of a spiritual gift is something God grants at the moment of salvation. Both spiritual and non-spiritual, carnal believers have spiritual gifts, and they can use the gift correctly or incorrectly. Hence, rules were laid down as to the proper use of spiritual gifts. The Corinthian church was the most active in the use of spiritual gifts; however, it was also the worst church in the New Testament record.

C. Main Bible Passages

There are five main passages that deal with spiritual gifts.

1. I Peter 4:10

according as each has received a gift, ministering it among yourselves, as good stewards of the manifold grace of God;

According to this verse, every believer has at least one gift. In this sense, every believer is truly "charismatic." This English word comes from the Greek term most frequently used for spiritual gifts, *charisma*. The biblical use of the term "charismatic" simply means that one has a spiritual gift, but it does not specify which gift it is. It is unfortunate that this word has been overused to describe a specific movement emphasizing one particular gift, the gift of speaking in tongues. The truth is that every believer has a spiritual gift. For this reason, every believer is charismatic whether or not he speaks in tongues. Therefore, in the biblical sense, all believers are truly charismatic, as they are all gifted.

According to the above verse, the believer must minister these gifts among the body of believers. As will be brought out later, the purpose of spiritual gifts is for building up the body.

Furthermore, a spiritual gift is a stewardship that God has given to the believer by His grace; therefore, the believer has the responsibility of using it wisely among believers.

2. Romans 12:4-8

The second passage can be divided into two sections.

a. The Body Doctrine (Rom. 12:4-5)

> *⁴For even as we have many members in one body, and all the members have not the same office: ⁵ so we, who are many, are one body in Messiah, and severally members one of another.*

The emphasis of these verses is on a doctrine one might call "body doctrine." This doctrine speaks of three facets: unity, diversity, and harmony. Paul writes that believers are *many members in one body*. The expression could also be worded as "many members of one single body." Furthermore, Paul says that the believers are *one body in Messiah*. Because this is so, there is unity. While believers may all be members of the same body, believers do not all have the same *office*, and the various spiritual gifts have different functions. Believers also do not all have the same gifts or number of gifts. Therefore, we are diverse. However, this diversity should not lead to division, but to harmony. Believers should use their gifts to minister to one another as they are *severally members one of another*. This is the "body doctrine," which teaches unity, diversity, and harmony. Believers are one. Therefore, there is unity in the body. Believers have different gifts. Therefore, there is diversity. In Messiah, individual believers are joined to each other. Therefore, there is harmony.

b. The Gifts of the Spirit (Rom. 12:6-8)

In the second section, Paul enumerates some of the specific gifts:

> *⁶ And having gifts differing according to the grace that was given to us, whether prophecy, let us prophesy according to the proportion of our faith; ⁷ or ministry, let us give ourselves to our ministry; or he that teaches, to his teaching; ⁸ or he that exhorts, to his exhorting: he that gives, let him do it*

with liberality; he that rules, with diligence; he that shows mercy, with cheerfulness.

Paul speaks of seven specific gifts here. In verse 6, he begins by stating the principle that believers have different gifts according to the grace that was given to them. One believer will never have all the gifts. On the other hand, no one gift will be given to every believer. Rather, God has ordained that believers have different gifts. Believers differ in the number and kinds of gifts they have, no one believer will ever have all the gifts, and no one specific gift is available to every believer.

After having stated the principle, Paul goes on to mention the first gift, which is the gift of prophecy. This gift was the ability to receive truth by direct revelation from God, and a prophet was one who received this gift. There are several examples of it in the New Testament: the prophets in the church of Antioch (Acts 13:1), Agabus (Acts 11:27-28; 21:10-11), and the daughters of Philip (Acts 21:8-9). As in the Hebrew Scriptures, a prophet needed to be tested by giving some near prophecies that came to pass. The prophecies of Agabus and Philip's daughters did come to pass, so they were proven to have the gift of prophecy.

Second is the gift of ministry or service. Serving is a specific spiritual gift. Since the office of a deacon is an office of serving, one who holds the office of deacon should have the gift of serving.

Third is the gift of teaching, which is the ability to organize the truth and present it in a clear manner, so the audience understands. It is the ability to communicate spiritual truth.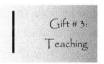

The fourth gift is the gift of exhortation, which is the divine ability to get people to apply the truth. Prophecy is receiving truth by direct revelation; teaching is the ability to organize the truth received and to present it in a clear manner; exhorting is the ability to move people to apply the truth so that they act on it.

Fifth is the gift of giving. Those who have this gift should do it with liberality. While everyone is responsible to give, those with this gift will be able to give to a far greater degree. Some people who have this gift have given away as much as 90 percent of their income to the work of the ministry.

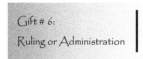

Sixth is the gift of ruling or administration. Those who have this gift are to exercise it with diligence. Since the position of elder requires ruling and administering, a person who wishes to have the office of an elder should have the gift of ruling or administration.

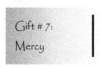

Seventh is the gift of showing mercy, a special gift of reaching out and comforting the sick and needy. Those who have this gift are to do it with cheerfulness.

3. Ephesians 4:11-16

Ephesians 4:11-16 emphasizes the gifts of the Holy Spirit as possessed by individuals, that is, gifted men. It also emphasizes the purpose of the gifts. Paul begins the passage by enumerating spiritual gifts, some of which are the same as those in Romans 12:4-8. There, Paul listed a total of seven spiritual gifts. Here, in Ephesians 4:11, he added a few to the list, stating: *And he gave some to be apostles; and some, prophets; and some, evangelists; and some, pastors and teachers.*

Since the gift of prophecy was part of the previous section, it will not be mentioned again in the discussion below.

a. The Gifts

(1) The Gift of Apostleship

The first additional gift Paul mentioned in this verse is the gift of apostleship. This was a unique gift, because, in order to receive this gift, one had to meet certain qualifications beyond that of being a believer.

While all believers were eligible for any other gift, though God alone determined the distribution of the gifts, only certa in believers were eligible for the gift of apostleship. There were two groups of apos-
tles; yet, both groups had in common that to receive this gift one had to have seen Yeshua after His resurrection. First was the closed g roup of the twelve apostles. To qualify for this group, one had to have been a follower of Yeshua from the baptism of John. In other words, this kind of apostle was first a disciple of John the Baptist; then he followed Yeshua; and then he saw the resurrected Messiah. This is seen in the selection of Matthias to replace Judas in Acts 1:22: *beginning from the baptism of John, unto the day that he was received up from us, of these must one become a witness with us of his resurrection*. Paul was not an apostle of the inner twelve because he had never undergone John's baptism. Neither had he been with Yeshua from the time He was baptized by John until His ascension.

The requirement for the second group of apostles was to have seen the resurrected Messiah. Paul fulfilled this requirement, for he saw the resurrected Messiah on the Damascus Road. On this basis, he defends his apostleship in I Corinthians 9:1, stating, *Am I not free? am I not an apostle? have I not seen Yeshua our Lord? are not ye my work in the Lord*? Paul proved his apostolic calling by claiming that he had seen the resurrected Messiah. Subsequently, he called himself an apostle in the first verse of nine of his 13 letters; namely, Romans, I and II Corinthians, Galatians, Ephesians, Colossians, I and II Timothy, and Titus. Barnabas was also an apostle of the second circle, according to Acts 14:14. James, the half-brother of Yeshua, was an apostle of the second circle because, according to I Corinthians 15:7, he had seen the resurrected Messiah. Galatians 1:19 also puts him in the category of an apostle.

So only those who saw the resurrected Messiah ever qualified for receiving the gift of apostleship. Therefore, this gift was only available to the five- or six-hundred men who saw the resurrected Messiah, and not every one of those received the gift of apostleship.

A second unique aspect of the gift of apostleship was the fact that this gift always included the power of miracles. In fact, the power of his miracles was the evidence of his apostleship. Paul says in II Corinthians 12:12,

Truly the signs of an apostle were wrought among you in all patience, by signs and wonders and mighty works. Again, Paul proved himself to be an apostle. Not only had he seen the resurrected Messiah on the Damascus Road, he also had the power of an apostle, as proven by his many miracles, signs, and wonders. The same point is made in Hebrews 2:3-4:

> ³ *how shall we escape, if we neglect so great a salvation? which having at the first been spoken through the Lord, was confirmed unto us by them that heard;* ⁴ *God also bearing witness with them, both by signs and wonders, and by manifold powers, and by gifts of the Holy Spirit, according to his own will.*

In verse 3, the writer points out that salvation was proclaimed by those who were eyewitnesses of the ministry of Yeshua. These eyewitnesses were the apostles who witnessed His resurrection and ascension. They proved their apostolic office by their power of miracles, signs, and wonders (v. 4). Apostles are seen using these powers of miracles in Acts 5:12-16, 16:16-18, and 28:8-9.

(2) The Gift of Evangelism

The second new gift Paul listed in Ephesians 4:11 is the gift of evangelism. The gift of evangelism is a unique, God-given ability to win people to the Messiah.

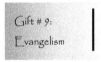
Gift # 9: Evangelism

Some people use the existence of the gift of evangelism as an excuse not to witness, claiming that they do not have the gift of evangelism, so they do not need to witness. However, Paul teaches otherwise in II Timothy 4:5. Timothy did not have the gift of evangelism, but he had the gift of teaching, so he became a teaching-elder in the church of Ephesus. When Paul wrote, he told Timothy to do the work of an evangelist. Although Timothy could not be an evangelist because he did not have the gift of evangelism, he could at least do the work of one, and that was to witness. Every believer has the responsibility of doing the work of an evangelist; every believer is responsible to witness concerning the truth of the gospel. Those who have the gift of evangelism will be able to enter into this kind of ministry full-time and will have a much higher number of people coming to the Messiah. Every believer can and should be leading people to the Lord, though those who do not have the gift will not have the same rate of success as those who do.

(3) The Gift of Pastor-Teacher

The third gift in Paul's list is the gift of pastor-teacher. Some translations read "pastor and teacher," but the word "and" is not in the Greek text. A proper translation of this should be "pastor-teacher." The gift of teaching was discussed earlier. It is the ability to organize the truth and present it. Not everyone who has the gift of teaching will necessarily have the gift of pastoring, but everyone who has the gift of pastoring will automatically have the gift of teaching, because the two go together.

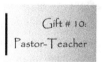

Pastoring involves shepherding. Shepherding involves guiding the flock, leading the flock, and feeding the flock. The means of feeding the flock is by the Word of God. If someone is guiding, leading, and feeding the flock, he is doing the work of pastoring, but he will only be able to do so by being able to teach the Word of God to the flock.

Again, while not everyone who has the gift of teaching will automatically have the gift of pastoring, everyone who has the gift of pastoring will automatically have the gift of teaching. Therefore, the spiritual gift mentioned here is the gift of pastor-teacher. This is a gift, not an office, though all who hold the office should also have the gift.

b. The Purposes and Goals of the Gifts

After having elaborated on the different gifts, Paul deals with their purpose, in Ephesians 4:12-14:

> [12] *for the perfecting of the saints, unto the work of ministering, unto the building up of the body of Messiah:* [13] *till we all attain unto the unity of the faith, and of the knowledge of the Son of God, unto a full-grown man, unto the measure of the stature of the fulness of Messiah:* [14] *that we may be no longer children, tossed to and fro and carried about with every wind of doctrine, by the sleight of men, in craftiness, after the wiles of error;*

In verse 12, Paul emphasizes the growing process concerning the body of the Messiah. The gifts are for the perfecting (equipping) of the saints, *unto the work of ministering*. Remember, the definition of a spiritual gift is "a God-given ability for service." Saints are to serve. The spiritual gifts equip them for the work of the ministry. Whether it is full-time, part-time, or as a lay person, *all* are to do the work of the ministry in the area of serving. The purpose of these spiritual gifts is not for the building up of oneself, but for *the building up the body of Messiah*.

Verse 13 points to the goals of these spiritual gifts. The growing process continues until *all attain unto the unity of the faith*, that is until all believers are united in the one body (v. 13a). Paul said in Romans 11:25 that this process would continue *until the fullness of the Gentiles be come in*. So, one goal of the spiritual gifts is to grow the church until everyone that is going to enter the body does so. Another goal is that the believers attain the *knowledge of the Son of God* (v. 13b). In I Corinthians 13:9, Paul said that believers only *know in part*. This means that they only have a dim and partial knowledge. Yet, there will be a time when believers shall know fully even as they are *fully known* (I Cor. 13:12). A third goal of the spiritual gifts is maturity (v. 13c). The purpose of the gifts is to help the believer in the growing process. This growing process will continue until the believer reaches maturity and until the body is complete. Once the body is complete, it will be removed by the rapture of the church. At that point, these gifts will no longer be necessary.

In verse 14, the spiritual gifts also have preventative purposes. They have the positive purpose of building up the body of Messiah, and they have the negative purpose of helping believers to avoid certain things. The first preventative purpose is that the believer will no longer be *tossed to and fro and carried about with every wind of doctrine*. A person is immature if he constantly goes back and forth between this doctrine or that doctrine or suddenly makes a particular doctrine into a fetish so that it becomes all he can talk about. The gifts are given to mature the believer and give him well-rounded knowledge. They are to teach the believer the whole counsel of God so that he will be stabilized in the faith. Only if he is stabilized is he reaching maturity. The second preventative purpose is that the spiritual gifts enable the believer to reject false doctrines caused *by the sleight of men, in craftiness, after the wiles of error*. Paul also used the term "wiles" in Ephesians 6:11. However, there he did so in reference to deception by Satan. Hence, any false doctrine caused by craftiness and error comes from the wiles of the devil and emphasizes the satanic counterfeit program. Because a counterfeit program looks like the real program, it would be very easy to deceive a believer if he is not grounded in the Word of God. Such a person can be caught up in "super spiritual" movements that sound really good and seem to give a great experience, but they are, nevertheless, false.

Summarizing the preventative nature of the spiritual gifts, they are given to prevent immaturity, instability, and gullibility. They are to promote knowledge, discernment, and stability. For these reasons, Ephesians 4:11-16 emphasizes gifted believers rather than the spiritual gifts in general. It is people with these particular gifts who are in leadership roles in the local church and in positions to feed the flock in order to stabilize others.

c. The Means of Maturity

Ephesians 4:15-16 then speaks of the means of maturity, stating:

> ^{15} but speaking truth in love, may grow up in all things into him, who is the head, even Messiah; ^{16} from whom all the body fitly framed and knit together through that which every joint supplies, according to the working in due measure of each several part, makes the increase of the body unto the building up of itself in love.

According to verse 15, the means to maturity is doctrinal adherence. Doctrine is learned because people with the spiritual gifts of teaching and exhortation teach the truth. If a believer holds on to the truth he has learned from his teachers, if he has doctrinal adherence, he will grow into maturity. The teachers are to speak this truth in love. This expression refers to holding the truth in the right spiritual love. To grow to maturity, one must hold the truth, not as "an axe to grind," but in spiritual love.

In verse 16, Paul emphasized the building up of the body by each one using his spiritual gift. The body, the church, must be built up by each believer using his spiritual gift or gifts in love. Each member has a gift. With that gift, he has been placed by God in the proper place in the body. In whatever part of the body he may be placed, he is responsible for using his spiritual gift for the purpose of building up the body. Each member, with his gift, is in his proper place, and for that reason, each member is indispensable.

4. I Corinthians 7:1 and 7

First Corinthians 7:1 and 7 speak of the gift of singleness:

¹ Now concerning the things whereof ye wrote: It is good for a man not to touch a woman.

⁷ Yet I would that all men were even as I myself. Howbeit each man has his own gift from God, one after this manner, and another after that.

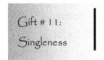

The gift of singleness is a spiritual gift. Those who have this gift have their sexual appetites totally under control and would not need to have an outlet in that area through marriage; therefore, they can devote their time entirely to the ministry. A married person can never devote as much time to the work of the Lord as a single person can. A married person with children cannot devote as much time to the ministry as a married person without children. The gift of singleness is given to those people who are called by God to serve Him on a truly full-time basis, with no other obligations in the realm of marriage.

The gift of singleness is a specific gift. In I Corinthians 7:1, Paul suggested that singleness is the better option. In verse 7, he stated that he himself had this particular gift. He desired that everyone would be like him so that everyone could devote all their energies to the work of the ministry, but he realized that was not the way God ordained it. He recognized that not all believers have this gift, and he stated as much. Only those who have the gift of singleness should remain single.

5. I Corinthians 12-14

The most extensive treatment on the gifts of the Holy Spirit is I Corinthians 12-14. The chapters will be dealt with one by one.

a. The Doctrine of the Gifts of the Spirit: I Corinthians 12

This passage deals with the doctrine of the gifts of the Spirit. While Paul had spoken of spiritual gifts in other passages, this is his most extensive treatment.

(1) The Topic of Gifts and the Test (I Cor. 12:1-3)

Paul begins the chapter by introducing the topic of spiritual gifts in I Corinthians 12:1-3:

> ^{1} Now concerning spiritual gifts, brethren, I would not have you ignorant. ^{2} Ye know that when ye were Gentiles ye were led away unto those dumb idols, howsoever ye might be led. ^{3} Wherefore I make known unto you, that no man speaking in the Spirit of God says, Yeshua is anathema; and no man can say, Yeshua is Lord, but in the Holy Spirit.

In Greek, the introductory words "Now concerning" are *peri de*. The phrase has become known as the "peri de formula" and is a mark that Paul is starting a brand-new topic—in this case, the topic of spiritual gifts.

The Corinthian church was by far the most Pentecostal and charismatic church on record in the New Testament. It was also the most carnal church in the New Testament record, and it showed its carnality in a number of different ways, which Paul addressed in the first eleven chapters of his epistle. In I Corinthians 1, for example, it becomes clear that the church was split by various political parties and religious divisions. Some were saying, "I am of Paul"; others, "I am of Apollos"; still others claimed they were of Peter; and the "super-spiritual" were saying, "I am of Messiah" (I Cor. 1:12). In chapter 5, Paul chastised the church for tolerating immorality. In chapter 6, he addressed the fact that believers of this church were taking fellow believers to court. In chapters 12-14, the carnality was also evident in the misuse of spiritual gifts. The problem of the Corinthian church was not that they emphasized the usage of the gifts. Usage of gifts is good. Every church should emphasize the use of spiritual gifts. The trouble was that they played up the less important gifts and played down the more important ones, and by so doing they showed their carnality. This proves one thing: The usage of spiritual gifts is not by itself a mark of spirituality of a local church. One can have a manifestation of spiritual gifts and still be sinful and carnal.

Going back to the verses above, in verse 2, Paul reminded the Corinthian believers of their former state. In their unbelieving state, they had not experienced what they are now experiencing as believers in the body of the Messiah. However, spiritual gifts, especially those of the more sensational type, need to be tested. The test is by the declaration of the

Lordship of the Messiah (v. 3). The purpose or result of using these spiritual gifts is for the exaltation of Yeshua the Messiah.

(2) *The Distribution of the Gifts (I. Cor. 12:4-6)*

In the next verses, I Corinthians 12:4-6, Paul pointed out that the distribution of the gifts is of the whole Triune God:

> [4] Now there are diversities of gifts, but the same Spirit. [5] And there are diversities of ministrations, and the same Lord. [6] And there are diversities of workings, but the same God, who works all things in all.

The role of the Holy Spirit is in verse 4: He is the One who produces the *diversities of gifts*. The Greek word for "diversities" is *diaireseis*, which could also be translated as "distributions" or "apportions." These distributions of the gifts come from *the same Spirit*. The point is that the Holy Spirit distributes the spiritual gifts directly to the believer, which is why they are called "the gifts of the Holy Spirit."

The role of the Son is in verse 5. Here, Paul talked about the distributions of "ministrations," a term that refers to external offices. As stated earlier in this study, several of the spiritual gifts lend themselves to external offices, such as those mentioned in Ephesians 4:11. For instance, the gift of serving lends itself to the office of a deacon. The gift of ruling or administration lends itself to the office of an elder. The gift of evangelism lends itself to the office of an evangelist. Hence, there are diversities of ministrations, but every appointment to a ministration of office is of the same Lord. "The Lord" here is the Yeshua the Messiah. While the gifts themselves come from the Holy Spirit, the appointment of a gifted person to a specific office comes by means of the Son. For example, the Holy Spirit bestows the gift of pastor-teacher upon a believer. Later, this believer is offered a position of pastor-teacher in a congregation. The One who placed him there is the Son.

Verse 6 gives the role of the Father: *diversities of workings, but the same God*. The Greek word translated "workings" is *energēmatōn*, which means "an effect" and "powers." It deals with the results of God's power and the effects of seeing the gifts exercised. The results come from God the Father. This is the Father's role in these spiritual gifts.

To summarize: The believer receives his gifts from the Holy Spirit. If these gifts lend themselves to a specific office (not all gifts do), the believer is brought into this office by the Son. The results which come from the use of the gift in a specific office are a product of God the Father. In those cases where the spiritual gifts do not lend themselves to a specific office, the results are still the work of God the Father. Spiritual gifts are called the gifts of the Holy Spirit because these gifts come to the believer from the Holy Spirit; He is the One who distributes them to the individual believer.

(3) *The Gifts of the Spirit (I Cor. 12:7-11)*

So far, eleven gifts of the Spirit have been listed from previous passages. In I Corinthians 12:7-11, Paul enumerates some additional gifts:

> *⁷ But to each one is given the manifestation of the Spirit to profit withal. ⁸ For to one is given through the Spirit the word of wisdom; and to another the word of knowledge, according to the same Spirit: ⁹ to another faith, in the same Spirit; and to another gifts of healings, in the one Spirit; ¹⁰ and to another workings of miracles; and to another prophecy; and to another discernings of spirits; to another divers kinds of tongues; and to another the interpretation of tongues: ¹¹ but all these works the one and the same Spirit, dividing to each one severally even as he will.*

In verse 7, Paul notes that *to each one*, meaning to each and every believer, *is given the manifestation of the Spirit*. Every believer receives at least one spiritual gift. Therefore, every believer has a God-given ability *to profit withal*, meaning for the good of all. The one common principle true of all the spiritual gifts is unity. This unity does not mean that any one person ever receives all the gifts, nor is the unity that one gift is given to every believer. Rather, unity is seen in that every believer has gifts, and the source of those gifts is always the same: the Holy Spirit. Hence, unity is found in the source of the gifts, not in the gifts themselves.

Having stated the common principle, Paul begins to list some specific gifts in verses 8-10. First is the gift of wisdom. This gift is the ability to use spiritual and biblical knowledge for the best results. Someone with

Gift # 12: Wisdom

this gift can take the Word, given by the prophet and communicated by the teacher, and apply it correctly in a particular situation.

Gift # 13: Knowledge

Next, Paul mentions the gift of knowledge. According to I Corinthians 13:2, knowledge refers to knowing the *mysteries* of God. Hence, the gift of knowledge is the ability to comprehend the Scriptures and to see unifying principles in the Word of God. It is the ability to put the doctrines of Scripture into a meaningful whole. Obviously, several of the spiritual gifts are corollary and go together. For someone to have the gift of teaching also requires him to have the gift of knowledge. He needs to know what he needs to communicate. However, not everyone who has the gift of knowledge would also have the gift of teaching. The gift of knowledge is the gift of being able to understand the truth of God, to understand the mysteries of God, to understand the Scriptures. When someone also has the gift of wisdom, he can then apply the knowledge for best results. Those who have the gift of wisdom would naturally also have the gift of knowledge. However, not everyone who has the gift of knowledge would necessarily also have the gift of wisdom. It is quite possible to have knowledge without wisdom.

Gift # 14: Faith

The next gift mentioned is the gift of faith. This spiritual gift is not the same as saving faith. While all believers have saving faith, not all believers have the gift of faith. The gift of faith is the God-given ability to trust God in any and all circumstances without a shadow of a doubt. Perhaps one of the best examples of those who had the gift of faith was George Mueller of Bristol, England. George Mueller was a man of God, a great man of faith who was led to set up an orphanage. One day, the orphanage was totally out of food. Nevertheless, he believed God would provide the food when mealtime came, but when mealtime came, no food had yet arrived. In spite of this, he had the children sit down at the table and proceeded to say grace. No sooner had he finished praying than there was a knock on the door, and there stood a farmer with an abundance of food for the orphanage. Other men who had the gift of faith were Hudson Taylor, the founder of the China Inland Mission, and Rabbi Leopold Cohn, the founder of the American Board of Missions to the Jews (which later became Chosen People Ministries).

The next gift mentioned is what Paul calls the *gifts of healings*. Both words are in the plural, which makes this gift different than all the other gifts. The word "heal-

ings" is plural because there are various classes of sicknesses; therefore, there are various classes of healings. However, why would the word "gift" be in the plural? In Greek, the plural often emphasizes repeated action. The phrase "gifts of healings" indicates that this is a gift that comes and goes. While all the other gifts stayed with the believer once he had received them, the gifts of healings cannot be used all the time. They come and go. Another way to put it is that those who were given the gift always had it but were not always free to use it. They could only use it when God willed it. This explains why Paul on one occasion was able to raise someone from the dead (Acts 20:10), but on another occasion, he was not able to heal Trophimus of a sickness and had to leave him behind (II Tim. 4:20). Paul did not say Trophimus was sick because he was sinful. He did not say he could not heal Trophimus because he did not have enough faith. Paul was not able to heal him on that occasion because the Bible does not teach that it is God's will to heal everyone. In those cases where He wishes to perform a healing of some person, He will provide someone with the gifts of healings. It was not God's will to heal Trophimus, so Paul had to leave him behind, still sick. There are gifts of healings, and sometimes Paul had it, and sometimes he did not. When Paul did have it, he could proceed to heal regardless of the sick person's faith. Healing came by the will of the healer. Examples of healings based on the will of the healer, not on the faith of the one being healed, include Acts 3:1-7; 9:32-34, 36-42; 20:9-12; and 28:8.

The next gift mentioned is the *workings of miracles*. Again, both words are in the plural. The word "miracles" is plural, emphasizing that there are various categories

of miracles. The word "workings" is also plural, emphasizing that, like the gifts of healings, it is not with a person all the time. It comes and goes as God wills it.

Paul then mentions the gift of prophecy, something already discussed earlier, as gift number one.

Gift #17: Discernment of spirits

The seventeenth gift is the gift of *discernments of spirits*. This is the God-given ability to identify the true source of a teaching or a problem. Most believers have to test the spirits to see if something is demonic or not. Someone who has the gift of discernment of spirits will be able to identify immediately whether someone else has a demonic problem.

Gift #18: Tongues

The eighteenth gift mentioned is *divers kinds of tongues*, or, in Greek, *heterō genē glōssōn*. Speaking in tongues is not some kind of gibberish, some type of ecstatic speech, or just the constant repetition of three or four syllables. The Greek word *glōssōn* means "languages." Someone may have a talent for languages and can easily learn languages, but that is not the gift of tongues. The gift of tongues is a God-given ability to speak a language one has never studied or learned. The fact that the word *glōssōn* simply means "languages" is evident from Acts 2:4. The believers there were given the gift of tongues and began speaking *with other tongues*. The result was that the Jews who had come to Jerusalem from all over the world for the observance of the Feast of Pentecost could hear the gospel proclaimed in their own languages. The one who is using the gift of tongues may not understand what he is saying and probably will not in most cases. However, he is speaking a real, known language with all the rules of grammar, syntax, and diction that every language requires. He is not speaking mere gibberish. The gift of tongues is just **one** of the 19 gifts of the Spirit; and again, it is the ability to speak a language one has not studied or learned.

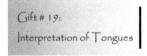

Gift #19: Interpretation of Tongues

The corollary gift to speaking in tongues is the gift of *interpretation of tongues*. This is the God-given ability to interpret a language being spoken by someone who has the gift of tongues. In Acts 2, this gift was not necessary because there were Jews from all parts of the world who understood the languages being spoken. In the case where the whole congregation speaks the same language, for the gift of tongues to be used requires also the presence of someone who has the gift of interpretation.

In I Corinthians 12:11, Paul again emphasizes the source of the gifts. The three truths spelled out in this verse should not be missed: *but all these works the one and the same Spirit, dividing to each one severally even as he will*. First, the source of these spiritual gifts is the Holy Spirit, something that Paul emphasized earlier.

Second, the Spirit sovereignly distributes the gifts as He wills and decides who gets which gift. There is no need for the individual believer to seek a specific gift, and the Bible does not encourage such seeking. Rather, the Holy Spirit decides who will receive which gift. He sovereignly distributes the gifts *even as he will*. He is the *one and the same Spirit*. The word "one" contrasts with the many believers: There is only *one* Holy Spirit. The word "same" contrasts with the diversity of the gifts: They all come from the *same* Holy Spirit. The Holy Spirit does not haphazardly distribute the gifts. He knows each individual, He knows God's calling for each individual, and He provides the necessary spiritual gifts accordingly.

Third, the verse states: *to each one severally*. This phrase repeats an already established concept, namely, that there is no such thing as a believer who has no gifts; at least one gift is given to every believer.

This completes the list of the 19 gifts of the Spirit.

(4) One Body, Many Members: Unity in Diversity (I Cor. 12:12-31)

The list of gifts is followed by I Corinthians 12:12-31, where Paul again shows the relationship of the spiritual gifts to the so-called "body doctrine." This doctrine was studied in connection with Romans 12 and was defined in the following manner: There is one body and many members, meaning there is unity in diversity.

(a) The Body (I Cor. 12:12-13)

In I Corinthians 12:12-13, Paul expresses the concept this way:

> *[12] For as the body is one, and has many members, and all the members of the body, being many, are one body; so also is Messiah. [13] For in one Spirit were we all baptized into one body, whether Jews or Greeks, whether bond or free; and were all made to drink of one Spirit.*

The point of verse 12 is that there is only one body which is made up of many members. This emphasizes unity. There is only one body of the Messiah, and every believer without exception is a member of the body of the Messiah. Because there are many believers, there are many members; yet they are not members of "many bodies," but of one body, the body of the Messiah. The body of the Messiah is the universal, invisible church (Col. 1:18).

In verse 13, Paul explains the means by which one enters into the body: Spirit baptism. The clear point made by this verse should not be missed: Every believer is baptized by the Holy Spirit. The result of Spirit baptism is not one specific gift (such as the gift of tongues). The result of Spirit baptism is membership in the body of the Messiah.[29] The other point the verse teaches pertains to the moment the believer receives his spiritual gift(s). At the very moment when the believer gets baptized by the Spirit, he also receives all the spiritual gifts he will ever have. Gifts are not something given subsequent to salvation, after one believes. Hence, if someone testifies and says, "I received this gift five years after I believed," whatever it was he might have received, it was not a spiritual gift. The moment one accepts Yeshua as his Savior, at that very moment he is baptized by the Spirit into the body of the Messiah, and at that very moment, he receives his spiritual gifts. Remember, the purpose of spiritual gifts is service in the body. One is placed in a specific part of the body when he believes. Therefore, the gifts must be given at that specific point in time.

Summarizing the verses, we note that the result of Spirit baptism is the same for every believer: He becomes a member of the body of the Messiah. Also at that time, he receives his gift or gifts; however, no one particular gift is given to every believer.

(b) The Many Members (I Cor. 12:14-26)

Next, Paul deals specifically with the many members, in I Corinthians 12:14-26. The emphasis is on diversity within the unity. The basic truth of verse 14, that there is one body with many members, is explained in verses 15-26 with two illustrations and two applications.

---

[29] See Chapter VII for details on the Spirit baptism.

The basic truth is spelled out in I Corinthians 12:14: *For the body is not one member, but many*. The body of the Messiah, meaning the church (Col. 1:18), has many members.

The first illustration is given in I Corinthians 12:15-17:

> *[15] If the foot shall say, Because I am not the hand, I am not of the body; it is not therefore not of the body. [16] And if the ear shall say, Because I am not the eye, I am not of the body; it is not therefore not of the body. [17] If the whole body were an eye, where were the hearing? If the whole were hearing, where were the smelling?*

The point Paul makes in these verses is twofold. First, every part of the body, no matter how insignificant, is still part of the body (vv. 15-16). Second, the body would never be able to function if it were only one part (v. 17). If the whole body were merely an eye, it would see well, but it could not hear. If the whole body were an ear, it could hear well, but it could not walk. If the whole body were feet, it might walk well, but would not see where it was going.

Paul then follows the first illustrations with the first application, in I Corinthians 12:18-20:

> *[18] But now has God set the members each one of them in the body, even as it pleased him. [19] And if they were all one member, where were the body? [20] But now they are many members, but one body.*

The application is threefold. First, God has placed each believer in the body where He wills (v. 18). Some are eyes, some are ears, some are hands, and some are feet. Where the believer has been placed is also the basis for what kind of gifts he was given when he believed. Second, if all were the same member, there would not be a proper functioning of the body (v. 19). For the body to function properly, some believers must be the eyes, the ears, the hands, or the feet. Third, the basic truth is reiterated: There are many members, but only one body (v. 20).

Paul gives the second illustration of the body in I Corinthians 12:21-23:

> *[21] And the eye cannot say to the hand, I have no need of you: or again the head to the feet, I have no need of you. [22] Nay, much rather, those members of the body which seem to be more feeble are necessary: [23] and those parts of the body, which we think to be less honorable, upon these we bestow*

more abundant honor; and our uncomely parts have more abundant comeliness;

One part of the body cannot easily do without another part of the body (v. 21). The hand cannot say to the feet, "I don't need you." The head cannot say to the hands, "I don't need you." The importance of every part of the body is seen in the way the body is treated (vv. 22-23). Some parts of the body may be more important than other parts at certain times, but sooner or later, every part of the body is used for some purpose. All these different parts are needed for a proper functioning body.

The second illustration of the body is followed by the second application, in I Corinthians 12:24-26:

[24] whereas our comely parts have no need: but God tempered the body together, giving more abundant honor to that part which lacked; [25] that there should be no schism in the body; but that the members should have the same care one for another. [26] And whether one member suffers, all the members suffer with it; or one member is honored, all the members rejoice with it.

In the second application, three points are made. First, more honor is given to those parts that lack, because that is where the lack is felt more consciously (v. 24). When people lose their hands, they are more conscious of their missing hands than they are conscious of the feet they still have.

The second point is the reason why it is necessary to realize that every part of the body is important: *that there be no schism in the body*. The goal is that members should *care one for another* (v. 25). There is a twofold purpose in recognizing the importance of every believer with his spiritual gifts, one negative and one positive. The negative purpose is *that there should be no schism in the body*. If one believer feels that because of his gifts he is more important than someone else, that he is indispensable but someone else is dispensable, that kind of attitude will cause church splits and schisms. If it is acknowledged that every believer is important, not just verbally but honestly and inwardly, then that will accomplish the negative purpose: There will be no schisms in the body. The positive purpose is to develop a caring attitude toward all fellow believers. If one really thinks that every believer is important, he will exercise care for fellow believers.

The third point is the principle that if one member suffers, the whole body suffers (v. 26). For example, when someone slices off a finger, the main center of pain is in that finger. Yet, the whole body is feeling the pain of the injury. It affects the thinking and actions of the person. Even so, if inferior gifts are despised and not used, the whole body cannot help but feel it. On the other hand, if lesser gifts are emphasized while the greater gifts are ignored, the body will also suffer for it, and there will be an obvious lack of maturity. In the next segment, Paul will teach that there are lesser and greater gifts, yet they are all important for the building up of the body. If the inferior gifts are despised and not used, it will cost the church. On the other hand, if the greater gifts are ignored in favor of lesser gifts, the church will suffer. If one member is honored, all are honored. If greater gifts are honored and put in their proper perspective, lesser gifts are also honored. If lesser gifts are honored in their proper perspective, so are the greater gifts.

(c) The Application to the Gifts (I Cor. 12:27-31)

In the next passage, I Corinthians 12:27-31, Paul now turns to the lesser and the greater gifts:

> *²⁷ Now ye are the body of Messiah, and severally members thereof. ²⁸ And God has set some in the church, first apostles, secondly prophets, thirdly teachers, then miracles, then gifts of healings, helps, governments, divers kinds of tongues. ²⁹ Are all apostles? are all prophets? are all teachers? are all workers of miracles? ³⁰ have all gifts of healings? do all speak with tongues? do all interpret? ³¹ But desire earnestly the greater gifts. And moreover a most excellent way show I unto you.*

Verse 27 contains the application of the truth of I Corinthians 12:12-26. The phrase "Now ye are the body of Messiah" summarizes verses 12-13; the phrase "severally members thereof" summarizes verses 14-26.

Having said this, Paul next states that while there are various kinds of gifts, which he emphasized earlier in the chapter, not all gifts are of equal importance (v. 28). There is an order of importance. Notice the numbers: *first, secondly, thirdly*. These numbers are not mere enumerations; they indicate a ranking system. This is followed by the word "then," which indicates that the following gifts are also listed in descending order. The most important gift is the gift of apostleship, and the second most important is the gift of prophecy. Ephesians 2-3 indicates that these two gifts are no longer available, because their purposes have been fulfilled.[30] The third most important gift is the gift of teaching. Of the gifts that are available today, this is the highest-ranking gift. However, in the order of the 19 gifts of Paul's day, teaching was the third most important gift.

The fourth most important gift is the gift of miracles.

The fifth most important gift is the gifts of healings. The gifts of miracles and healings may be more spectacular than the gift of teaching, but they are less important. The reason is in Ephesians 4:11-16, which spoke about those gifts of the Spirit that were especially useful for the maturing of the saints, a major purpose of the gifts. The lesser gifts do not go as far as the greater gifts in the maturing of the saints. A believer will mature faster by sitting under a person who has the gift of teaching than he will sitting under a person who has the gifts of miracles or healings.

The sixth most important gift is the gift of helps. This is a category of gifts that include the gift of serving, the gift of showing mercy, the gift of giving, and the gift of discernment of spirits.

The seventh most important gift is the gift of governments or administrations, which is the gift of ruling.

The eighth and last gift on the list is the gift of tongues. First Corinthians 12:27-31 clearly teaches that the gift of tongues is the least important gift. Yet, this was the gift that the church in Corinth was emphasizing most. In I Corinthians 3:1-3, Paul pointed out that the Corinthians were exercising their gifts by means of carnality. Because of their carnality, they were stressing the lesser gifts and ignoring the greater gifts. This was the reason they were still in a state of spiritual immaturity, for the gifts they were emphasizing were not those that could mature them, such as the gift of teaching.

---

[30] More will be said about the end of these gifts in "D. The End of the Gifts of Apostleship and Prophecy."

Having given the order of gifts and letting it be known that the gift of tongues is the least important, Paul shows that not all can have the same gift, in I Corinthians 12:29-30. The form of the questions in Greek requires negative answers. The New American Standard Bible reflects the Greek the best:

> [29] *All are not apostles, are they? All are not prophets, are they? All are not teachers, are they? All are not workers of miracles, are they?* [30] *All do not have the gifts of healings, do they? All do not speak in tongues, do they? All do not interpret, do they?*

Every question requires a negative answer. The clear teaching is that no single gift is given to every believer. In I Corinthians 12:13, Paul taught that every believer is baptized by the Holy Spirit. Here, in verse 30, he now states that all do not speak in tongues. Not all can have the same gift. The questions in these verses correspond to the illustrations concerning the body: Not everyone can be an eye; not everyone can be an ear; not everyone can be a hand or a leg. By the same token, not everyone can have the same gift, be it teaching or tongues.

The obligation of the believers is spelled out in verse 31: *But desire earnestly the greater gifts. And moreover a most excellent way show I unto you.* Paul starts out with the word "but," which is contrastive. Their obligation is to desire earnestly the greater gifts. In the Greek text, Paul used the second person plural: "you all desire." He is not telling the Corinthians that individual believers should seek a specific gift. He has already stated earlier in the chapter that the Holy Spirit sovereignly distributes these gifts to individuals. He is not speaking about seeking a gift by an individual. The second person plural means Paul is telling the church that, as a group, as a congregation, as a local body, they should be seeking earnestly the exercise of the greater gifts. Paul is not saying the Corinthians should not use the lesser gifts, but they were emphasizing the lesser gifts and ignoring the greater gifts. Therefore, they are to seek after higher gifts. Since the gift of tongues has been relegated to last place, what this passage clearly means is that, as a congregation, they should not be seeking to exercise the gift of tongues, but seeking to exercise the greater gifts, such as teaching.

After telling the Corinthian church that, as a body, they need to seek to exercise the greater gifts and not the lesser ones, as they had been doing, Paul then states in verse 31b: *And moreover a most excellent way show I unto you.* What he will be discussing in chapter 13 is the most important element of his teaching on the gifts.

(5) *Summary of the Doctrine of the Gifts*

In chapter 12, several things have been clearly taught which will be listed here in summary form:

1. Every believer has been baptized by the Holy Spirit into the body of the Messiah at the moment they believe.
2. Every believer has at least one spiritual gift, possibly more.
3. No one is to be excluded from the use of his gift(s). There is a proper way and a place to use the gifts. This is dealt with in I Corinthians 14.
4. No one believer is going to have all the gifts because God has ordained the members of the body to be interdependent.
5. No one gift is given to every believer, for the body cannot be composed of just one thing. For example, the gift of tongues is not available to every believer, no matter how much one may try to sanctify himself to gain it. On one hand, no one has all the gifts; but on the other hand, no one gift is given to every believer.
6. No one should hinder the use of gifts that he himself does not possess.
7. There is an order of importance in the gifts. Therefore, we can conclude: If a believer does not speak in tongues, it automatically means that he has been given a superior gift. He should not go seeking after the lesser gift. Instead, he should discover the greater gift or gifts he has been given and seek opportunities to exercise them in the local body. The local church's obligation is to emphasize the greater gifts, not the lesser ones.

b. Love and the Gifts of the Spirit (I Cor. 3:1-13)

The theme of chapter 12 was the doctrine of the gifts of the Holy Spirit. The theme in chapter 13 is love, for love is the means of exercising these gifts. The Greek word Paul used for "love" is *agape*, which is "love of the will." This chapter can be divided into five units.

(1) Love and the Gifts (I Cor. 13:1-3)

In the first unit, I Corinthians 13:1-3, Paul deals with love and the gifts. Without love, the exercise of these gifts is pure carnality.

> *¹ If I speak with the tongues of men and of angels, but have not love, I am become sounding brass, or a clanging cymbal. ² And if I have the gift of prophecy, and know all mysteries and all knowledge; and if I have all faith, so as to remove mountains, but have not love, I am nothing. ³ And if I bestow all my goods to feed the poor, and if I give my body to be burned, but have not love, it profits me nothing.*

If one speaks with tongues and has not love, the speaking in tongues is worth about as much as a clanging sound. The expression "tongues of men and of angels" has given rise to the teaching that there is a difference between an angelic or heavenly language and human languages, so when one speaks in tongues, he speaks in a heavenly language. Yet, Paul does not say that there is a difference between human language and heavenly language. Notice the word "if." Paul is using an extreme hypothetical case to drive a point home. "If I speak in different types of languages, whether heavenly or earthly, and have not love, it profits absolutely nothing." It is like saying, "I would not marry her if she were the last person on earth." Obviously, she will never be the last person on earth. Yet, the expression is used as an extreme hypothetical example to drive a specific point home. The heavenly language is Hebrew. Therefore, the language that angels speak is Hebrew. Angels do not speak a different language than humans do. The rare angelic names (Michael, Gabriel, Satan) are Hebrew names. Jewish history only begins as of Genesis 12, but all names recorded in the previous chapters are Hebrew names. God's name, *YHVH* or *YHWH*, is a Hebrew name. All the word plays before Genesis 12 are Hebrew word plays.

All that Paul is saying is that *if* there were such a distinction, and *if* he could speak both tongues, it would still be worthless *if* it were not exercised in love. Acts 2 makes it very clear that speaking in tongues is not a heavenly language distinct from human language. In Acts 2:4, the believers spoke *with other tongues*. Were they heavenly languages distinct from human language? Were they "languages of angels" distinct from the languages of humans? They were not. The Jewish audience who came to Jerusalem from various parts of the world was able to understand what the apostles were saying as they spoke with other tongues. Hence, I Corinthians 13:1 does not teach that those who speak in tongues are speaking a heavenly language. If it is the real gift, it will be an earthly language, a real, spoken language. Most of what passes for the gift of tongues today is not what is described in Scripture.

Concerning prophecy, Paul says in verse 2 that even if one has the gift of prophecy and can understand all mysteries, it is worthless without the exercise of love. As for the gift of knowledge, despite the great achievements this gift may attain, it too is worthless without love. As for the gift of faith, one might have the faith to move mountains, and still it would be worthless without the exercising of love.

As for the gift of giving, in verse 3, one might have this gift to the point of being able to give away everything, but still it would profit nothing apart from love.

(2) *The Attributes of Love (I Cor. 13:4-7)*

After introducing the topic of love in relation to spiritual gifts, Paul lists 15 attributes of love, in I Corinthians 13:4-7:

> *⁴ Love suffers long, and is kind; love envies not; love vaunts not itself, is not puffed up, ⁵ does not behave itself unseemly, seeks not its own, is not provoked, takes not account of evil; ⁶ rejoices not in unrighteousness, but rejoices with the truth; ⁷ bears all things, believes all things, hopes all things, endures all things.*

The following is a list of the 15 characteristics of love:

1. *Love suffers long*, meaning it is patient.
2. Love *is kind*. It is a type of love that exercises good manners.

3. Love *envies not*. It is characterized by generosity.
4. *Love vaunts not itself*. It does not boast. True love is shown by humility.
5. Love *is not puffed up*. It is not ostentatious or arrogant.
6. Love does *not behave itself unseemly*. True biblical love shows respect, politeness, and courtesy.
7. Love *seeks not its own*. It is characterized by unselfishness.
8. Love is not easily *provoked*. It is good-natured.
9. Love *takes not account of evil*. It is charitable, kindly, and lenient.
10. Love *rejoices not in unrighteousness*. It is characterized by sincerity.
11. Love *rejoices with the truth*. This expression emphasizes the goodness of love.
12. Love *bears all things*. It is willing to suffer in the face of insults and is characterized by graciousness.
13. Love *believes all things*. It has confidence in other believers.
14. Love *hopes all things*. It has assurance.
15. Love *endures all things*. It exercises patient endurance.

(3) The Relation to Time (I Cor. 13:8)

In the third unit, which encompasses I Corinthians 13:8, Paul makes a distinction concerning the element of time: *Love never fails: but whether there be prophecies, they shall be done away; whether there be tongues, they shall cease; whether there be knowledge, it shall be done away.* The love described in I Corinthians 13 is permanent and will last forever. It never fails because it is eternal. This is not true of the spiritual gifts. Concerning the gift of prophecy, it will someday be rendered inoperative, as shown by the use of the Greek passive voice in this verse. According to Ephesians 2:17-3:6, the gift of prophecy became unavailable when the New Testament was completed and the last apostle died. As for the gift of tongues, it will cease in and of itself, as indicated by the use of the Greek middle voice. As for the gift of knowledge, it too will be rendered inoperative, because the Greek passive voice is used again. A time will come when these gifts will no longer be necessary, and they will all be done away but love will remain forever.

(4) The Relation to Maturity (I Cor. 13:9-12)

In the fourth unit, which encompasses I Corinthians 13:9-12, Paul draws some distinctions in maturity, as he explains why these gifts will not be needed when a certain time comes.

> *⁹ For we know in part, and we prophesy in part; ¹⁰ but when that which is perfect is come, that which is in part shall be done away. ¹¹ When I was a child, I spoke as a child, I felt as a child, I thought as a child: now that I am become a man, I have put away childish things. ¹² For now we see in a mirror, darkly; but then face to face: now I know in part; but then shall I know fully even as also I was fully known.*

In these verses, Paul draws distinctions in maturity to explain that a day will come when all the gifts will no longer be necessary (v. 8).

The gifts are partial and not perfect (v. 9). A time will come when they have done their job and have matured the church as far as it could go, and then something else must happen.

This something else is described in verse 10. The imperfect, or *that which is in part*, are the spiritual gifts of verse 9; but when the *perfect* comes, the imperfect will come to an end.

First Corinthians 13:10 has become a battleground between pro-Charismatics and anti-Charismatics, between pro-Pentecostals and anti-Pentecostals. The issue is: "What is the 'perfect' that Paul is speaking about?" Charismatics and Pentecostals claim that the "perfect" is the *parousia*, the Greek term for the "return of the Lord." They interpret the verse to mean that when the *parousia* comes, when the Lord returns, only then will these gifts be done away. The anti-Charismatics/anti-Pentecostals point out that this cannot be, for *parousia* is a feminine term. However, the Greek word translated as "perfect," *teleios*, is a neuter term, and by the rules and laws of Greek grammar, a neuter cannot modify a feminine. Therefore, it cannot be the *parousia* that Paul is talking about. On this score, the anti-Charismatics/anti-Pentecostals are correct. However, what do they claim the "perfect" is? Their answer, in most cases, is that the word refers to the New Testament. When the New Testament was complete, the perfect came and the "sign gifts" (tongues, healings, and miracles) came to an end. Usually Charismatics and Pentecostals do not know how to answer this claim, because, unfortunately, most never bother to study the Greek language. However, the anti-Charismatics/anti-Pentecostals cannot be correct either, because the Greek term for "New Testament" is *kainei didachei*, which is also feminine. So, the reason that "perfect" cannot refer to the *parousia* is the same reason it cannot mean *kainei didachei*. By the rules of Greek grammar, both the pro-Charismatic/pro-Pentecostal and the anti-Charismatic/anti-Pentecostal are wrong. They both misinterpret the verse.

As always, the context is the best answer to understanding a specific verse. Paul began his discussion of spiritual gifts with chapter 12, where he dealt with the concept of the one body with many members. The Greek word for "body" is *soma*, which is a neuter noun. Within the same context, Paul now speaks of the "perfect," which, like *soma*, is a neuter in Greek. The "perfect" is the *soma*, and when the *soma*—the body—is complete, that is when these gifts will end. When is the body complete? The body is complete at the rapture of the church. When the full number that God has planned to bring into the church is reached, the church is complete and removed from the earth at the rapture. At that point, the spiritual gifts will end.

As mentioned, the gifts of apostleship and prophecy are no longer available today. As for the other 17 gifts, there is no basis for teaching that any of them have been done away. However, the gifts must always be tested to see if they really are the gifts of the Holy Spirit. God can still give the gift of tongues today if He chooses. However, it must be the biblical gift, which is the speaking of a known language. It must come on the day that the person believes in the Messiah and not some "afterglow" experience.

There is a need for balance in the area of spiritual gifts, and the extremes must be avoided. One extreme is that everyone needs to have the gift of tongues in order to be "spiritual." The other extreme dogmatically states that the gift of tongues cannot be given today. This view is based on an overreaction to the former extreme rather than on a sound exegesis of the Word. There is a balance. If it is remembered that tongues is the least important of the gifts, and that a congregation should be striving to exercise the greater gifts, the extremes that have hit the church in this and the previous century can be avoided.

In verse 11, Paul uses the illustration of growing up, saying that a child will always do *childish things*; the implication might be that the desire for gifts such as tongues can be seen in young, immature believers. At maturity, the lesser gifts become less important to them as they begin to learn from the greater gifts, and it is the greater gifts that bring them to maturity, not the lesser gifts.

In verse 12, Paul makes a distinction between *now* and *then* in relation to sight and knowledge. In relation to sight (the gift of prophecy), *now we see* vaguely; but when *the perfect is come*, we will *then* see clearly, as *face to face*. As for knowing (the gift of knowledge), we are *now* in the imperfect state, so we have partial knowledge. When the perfect is come, we will then know fully.

(5) The Present State (I Cor. 13:13)

The chapter ends with verse 13, in which Paul discussed the present state, saying, *But now abides faith, hope, love, these three; and the greatest of these is love*. Paul speaks of three things that will abide, in contrast to those that will be made inoperative or that will cease of themselves. Even after the coming of that which is perfect, even after the gifts will be done away, three things will abide:

1. *Faith* will continue to abide. This is not the gift of faith, but salvation faith.
2. *Hope* will abide, hope for that part of salvation yet to be accomplished.
3. *Love* will continue to abide.

Although faith, hope, and love will continue forever, Paul makes the point that the greatest of the three is love.

c. Practical Rules for Tongues and Prophecy (I Cor. 14:1-40)

In I Corinthians 14, Paul deals with some practical rules for the exercise of the gifts of tongues and prophecy. This chapter will be covered in five divisions.

(1) The Contrasting of Tongues and Prophecy (I Cor. 14:1-5)

The first division is I Corinthians 14:1-5. In these verses, Paul contrasts the gifts of tongues and prophecy, listing them from the lesser to the greater:

> ¹ *Follow after love; yet desire earnestly spiritual gifts, but rather that ye may prophesy.* ² *For he that speaks in a tongue speaks not unto men, but unto God; for no man understands; but in the spirit he speaks mysteries.* ³ *But he that prophesies speaks unto men edification, and exhortation, and consolation.* ⁴ *He that speaks in a tongue edifies himself; but he that prophesies edifies the church.* ⁵ *Now I would have you all speak with tongues, but rather that ye should prophesy: and greater is he that prophesies than he that speaks with tongues, except he interpret, that the church may receive edifying.*

The two gifts of tongues and prophecy were the least and the greatest of the gifts available to believers in general in Paul's day. Apostleship, the greatest gift, was available only to those who had seen the resurrected Messiah. Prophecy was still available during the apostolic period. In relation to seeking, Paul says: *follow after love* (v. 1), which is the love he had just finished dealing with in chapter 13. Then he states: *yet desire earnestly spiritual gifts*. With this statement, he picks up at the point where he left off at the end of chapter 12. Again, there is no basis for the individual believer to seek a specific gift. Paul has already said in chapter 12 that the Holy Spirit decides who gets which gifts. In this passage, he is now speaking to a congregation; as a congregation, they should *desire earnestly spiritual gifts*. The emphasis, as he said at the end of chapter 12, should be on the greater gifts and not on the lesser gifts. Paul now details the point made at the end of chapter 12 concerning the desire for greater gifts as over against lesser gifts. In chapter 14, he goes back and forth between the least important gift (tongues) and the most important gift (prophecy) available to all believers. He uses the gift of tongues to represent all the lesser gifts, and he uses the gift of prophecy to represent the greater gifts. Apostleship was the most important gift, but it was limited to those who saw the resurrected Messiah and was not available to believers in general as prophecy was.

In verse 1, the preferable gift to seek as a congregation is prophecy, because it is superior to tongues. As a brief overview of what follows this introductory verse, in I Corinthians 14:2-25, Paul draws a distinction between the comparative usefulness of the gifts of tongues and prophecy in two ways: first, in relation to the edification of the church (vv. 2-20); and second, in relation to the conversion of people outside the church (vv. 21-25). Then in verses 26-40, Paul gives specific rules for the exercising of these gifts.

In verses 2 and 3, Paul draws a distinction between tongues and prophecy in relation to understanding the means by which they operate. In verse 2, he focuses on tongues. The one who speaks in tongues is not speaking to other people, but to God. The reason is that when one has the gift of tongues, he does not himself understand what he is saying. Paul writes: *in the spirit he speaks mysteries*. The Greek text does not have the definite article "the" before "spirit," which means that Paul is not speaking of the Holy Spirit but of the human spirit. Some teach that when one speaks in tongues, it is the Holy Spirit who is actually doing the speaking. However, if the Holy Spirit were doing the speaking, it would be impossible to misuse the gift. Yet, the Corinthians were misusing the gift, and that is why Paul had to lay down certain rules in chapter 14 for when and how the gift of tongues could be exercised. While the gift of tongues comes from the Holy Spirit, the individual believer who has been given this particular gift exercises his own will in using the gift. So, it is the human spirit that is speaking. When one prays in tongues, it is the human spirit that is praying and not the Holy Spirit. That is why the individual has control of this gift. That is why he has the choice to use it either correctly or incorrectly. It is the human spirit that is praying, and because the believer who has the gift can choose when and how to exercise it, the gift of tongues can be used correctly or misused. The Corinthians were misusing it.

On the other hand, Paul says that *he that prophesies speaks unto men* (v. 3). Included within the gift of prophecy are *edification, exhortation, and consolation*. These three correspond to the three eternal things of I Corinthians 13:13. Edification corresponds to faith; it is a new development of or a confirmation of the truth of faith. Exhortation corresponds to love; it involves encouragement that is applied to the will. Consolation corresponds to hope; it means "to soothe" or "to put pain to sleep." Merely edifying, merely exhorting, and merely consoling is not prophecy.

The gift of prophecy means receiving direct revelation from God. One who receives direct revelation from God and communicates it to men does the work of edification, and exhortation, and consolation, but these things without direct revelation from God are not prophecy. That is why there is a separate gift of exhortation, distinct from the gift of prophecy.

Verse 4 deals with the two gifts in relation to edification. Tongues are for self-edification, but prophecy edifies the church. In chapter 12, Paul clearly emphasized that the primary purpose of the gifts is for building up the church. Prophecy edifies by itself, but tongues does not, which is another reason the former is superior to the latter.

Verse 5 deals with the importance of the two gifts and summarizes the results of what has been said in verses 1-4. Paul states: *I would* [wish] *have you all speak with tongues*. Some teach that Paul's statement means that everyone could speak in tongues. Some draw a distinction between the gift of tongues and tongues as "a sign," claiming that everybody can have the sign of tongues, but they cannot all have the gift of tongues. However, that is only an attempt to get around the obvious teaching of I Corinthians 12, when Paul taught that all do not speak in tongues. In this verse, all Paul is saying is that his own personal preference is that everyone would have the gift of tongues and everyone would have the gift of prophecy. That was his personal wish, but in chapter 12, he has already shown that this is impossible. The way to understand this verse is to go back to I Corinthians 7:1-7, where Paul discussed the superiority of the single state as over against the married state. In verse 7, Paul said: *Yet I would that all men were even as I myself*. Paul's own personal preference was that everyone had the gift of celibacy. That was his personal wish, but he knew God had chosen not to do that. Here, in I Corinthians 14:5, using the same terminology as in I Corinthians 7:7, Paul said he wished everyone could speak in tongues and have the gift of prophecy; but as he indicated in chapter 12, he already knew that God had chosen not to do that. Another example is in Romans 9:3, where Paul states that he would wish to end up in *anathema* if that would result in Israel's national salvation, but he already knows that this is not the will of God. So, verse 5 should not be used to teach that everyone who is a believer can, if he really had the faith, speak in tongues. Paul was simply expressing a personal desire. Furthermore, if he had to make a choice, he would prefer prophecy to tongues, because greater is the one prophesying than the one who speaks in tongues. The only time tongues are useful for the congregation is when there is the corollary gift of interpretation.

(2) Tongues in the Public Assembly (I Cor. 14:6-19)

The second division is I Corinthians 14:6-19, in which Paul deals with the subject of tongues in the public meeting of the church. In the first part of this section, verses 6-11, Paul talks about the necessity for understanding:

> *⁶ But now, brethren, if I come unto you speaking with tongues, what shall I profit you, unless I speak to you either by way of revelation, or of knowledge, or of prophesying, or of teaching? ⁷ Even things without life, giving a voice, whether pipe or harp, if they give not a distinction in the sounds, how shall it be known what is piped or harped? ⁸ For if the trumpet give an uncertain voice, who shall prepare himself for war? ⁹ So also ye, unless ye utter by the tongue speech easy to be understood, how shall it be known what is spoken? for ye will be speaking into the air. ¹⁰ There are, it may be, so many kinds of voices in the world, and no kind is without signification. ¹¹ If then I know not the meaning of the voice, I shall be to him that speaks a barbarian, and he that speaks will be a barbarian unto me.*

In verse 6, the point is made that tongues are without profit unless it also includes things that are understandable, namely, revelation, knowledge, prophesying, and teaching. In the context, "teaching" refers to doctrine.

In verses 7-8, Paul gives the illustration of musical instruments. Such instruments must make clear notes in order to create harmonious music (v. 7). In the military, there is also a necessity for instruments to make clear military calls, so a soldier knows what he is to do: march forward, turn, or retreat (v. 8).

Having given the illustration of musical instruments both in orchestral and military terms, in verses 9-11, Paul then applies the illustration. Unless one speaks in a clear language, he will not be understood (v. 9). The means of rendering the gift of tongues into a clear language is by the gift of interpretation. The only one who can understand a person who is speaking in tongues is the one who understands and speaks the language being spoken, as the audience in Acts 2 did. Since most local congregations use a single language, someone with the gift of interpretation is needed, who can clearly translate for the congregation what had been spoken in tongues.

In verse 10, Paul states that there are many voices and not any *without signification*. In other words, no language exists without articulate words. Mere babbling and repetitions of the same syllables is not speaking in tongues.

In verse 11, Paul points out that if the spoken word remains unclear, the speaker and the one spoken to will appear to each other as being merely barbarians. Therefore, it is necessary that the gift of tongues be understood before it serves any useful ministry. To make it understood, for it to edify the body, it is necessary to have someone with the gift of interpretation.

Having spelled out the necessity of understanding, Paul next deals with the usage of tongues in the assembly itself in I Corinthians 14:12-19:

> [12] *So also ye, since ye are zealous of spiritual gifts, seek that ye may abound unto the edifying of the church.* [13] *Wherefore let him that speaks in a tongue pray that he may interpret.* [14] *For if I pray in a tongue, my spirit prays, but my understanding is unfruitful.* [15] *What is it then? I will pray with the spirit, and I will pray with the understanding also: I will sing with the spirit, and I will sing with the understanding also.* [16] *Else if you bless with the spirit, how shall he that fills the place of the unlearned say the Amen at your giving of thanks, seeing he knows not what you say?* [17] *For you verily give thanks well, but the other is not edified.* [18] *I thank God, I speak with tongues more than you all:* [19] *howbeit in the church I had rather speak five words with my understanding, that I might instruct others also, than ten thousand words in a tongue.*

In verse 12, Paul states what the proper aim should be: to speak clearly for the edification of the assembly so that one will not be like a barbarian to another. The proper aim is to edify the church, not the self.

The principle of verse 12 is now applied in verse 13: The one who speaks with tongues should pray that someone is there who has the gift of interpretation.

The reason is given in verse 14: If one prays *in a tongue*, it is the spirit of the man praying but the understanding of the man's mind *is unfruitful*. Again, "spirit" is not the Holy Spirit, but the human spirit. When one speaks in tongues, it is the human spirit that is praying, but the human mind remains unfruitful, for the one who speaks in tongues does not understand what he is saying.

If someone has the gift of tongues, he should learn the balance of verse 15, which is the conclusion of what was said in verse 14. If one has the gift, he could pray with the human spirit and with the mind of understanding. In singing, he can sing with the human spirit, and he can sing with the mind of understanding. Those who might have the gift of tongues should not go overboard by using tongues only. Again, it is the human spirit that is using the gift in prayer and singing. Speaking, praying, and singing in tongues are not separate types of tongues. If one has a specific gift, it can be used in various ways. When one has the gift of teaching, he can use it in a lecture, during praying, and many other ways. The one who has the gift of tongues can use it to speak, to pray, to sing, but it is still the one gift used in various ways.

In verses 16-17, Paul points out that one of the reasons tongues are useless in the assembly apart from interpretation is that without understanding, no one can *say the Amen*. The word "Amen" means, "let it be true" or "so be it." The Amen should never be said after someone else's prayer unless one agrees with what has been said. If someone prayed in tongues and it is not known what was said, the last thing anyone should do is say Amen, because one does not know if it is true or if he agrees.

In verses 18-19, Paul provides his preference. Paul himself spoke in tongues more than the others did (v. 18). He does not mean to disdain the gift of tongues. He is not saying that the gift of tongues is totally unimportant; but in the public meeting of the church, in the assembly, it is far more important to *speak five words with* the mind of understanding *than ten thousand words in a tongue* (v. 19). Once again, Paul points to the order of priority among the gifts. Some gifts are more important than others are. The proper place for the gift of tongues is in the private domain rather than in public worship.

(3) The Problems of Tongues in the Assembly (I Cor. 14:20-25)

The third division is I Corinthians 14:20-25. In it, Paul deals with specific problems that arose from speaking in tongues during the assembling of the church:

> [20] Brethren, be not children in mind: yet in malice be ye babes, but in mind be men. [21] In the law it is written, By men of strange tongues and by the lips of strangers will I speak unto this people; and not even thus will they hear me, says the Lord. [22] Wherefore tongues are for a sign, not to them that believe, but to the unbelieving: but prophesying is for a sign, not to the unbelieving, but to them that believe. [23] If therefore the whole church be assembled together and all speak with tongues, and there come in men unlearned or unbelieving, will they not say that ye are mad? [24] But if all prophesy, and there come in one unbelieving or unlearned, he is reproved by all, he is judged by all; [25] the secrets of his heart are made manifest; and so he will fall down on his face and worship God, declaring that God is among you indeed.

In verse 20, Paul admonishes the readers to act maturely. The Corinthians had become like children, preferring the gifts which were more amusing and entertaining rather than the gifts which were more useful. They showed their carnality, their immaturity, by preferring the lesser gifts to the greater gifts.

Having given this admonition, in verses 21-22, he deals with the purpose of tongues and prophecy in relation to the unbeliever. In verse 21, Paul quotes Isaiah 28:11-12, but what he is teaching is often misunderstood. Isaiah 28 speaks of an historical event, the divine judgment by means of the Assyrian invasion. Isaiah had called and warned the people of Israel to repent, but they refused to listen and failed to repent and obey. They remained in a state of unbelief to Isaiah's message. Because Israel remained in unbelief, the judgment God sent was the Assyrian invasion. When the Assyrians came, they spoke their own language. When the Jewish people of Jerusalem heard the Assyrian language, they knew that they had been invaded. The Assyrian language was a sign that they were in a state of unbelief and disobedience. Isaiah went on to say that even then, Israel would not obey the prophets, and indeed, they did not. Had Israel obeyed the voice of Isaiah, there would not have been an

Assyrian invasion, and the Israelites would not have heard the Assyrian language in the land. When they heard the Assyrian language, the tongue of Assyria became a sign to them. This sign was not meant to get them to believe, for even then they did not believe. It was a sign of their unbelief.

After quoting Isaiah 28:11-12, Paul gives the application regarding the gift of tongues, in verse 22. The gift of tongues is meant to be a sign for the unbeliever. They hear other languages being spoken, but they do not understand; and because they do not understand, they will not believe. Speaking in tongues is also a sign to Israel, showing her that she is in unbelief. Israel rejected the Messiahship of Yeshua, and because of this rejection, God brought in a new entity. This time, the new entity was not an invasion by the Assyrians, but was the church, the body of the Messiah. It is with the church, in the church, and through the church that the gifts of the Spirit are to be exercised. Had Israel accepted Yeshua as the Jewish Messiah, had they believed on Him, then the Messianic kingdom would have been established and God would not have brought in this new entity with its gifts of the Spirit. The existence of the church with the gifts of the Spirit shows that God is again working in a new way. He brought in the church, this body made up of Jews and Gentiles together, because Israel as a nation rejected the Messiahship of Yeshua. The nation was set aside, and God said that He would provoke Israel to jealousy with that which is not a nation (Rom. 10:19), namely, the church. The church is composed of Jews and Gentiles; it is a distinct body, different and separate from Israel. The gifts of the Spirit are unique to the church and a part of the church age. When the church is complete, the gifts will cease. One of the more vocal of the gifts is, of course, the speaking in tongues. Now notice that the speaking of tongues in the church is a sign of Jewish unbelief. It is not for the purpose of bringing Jews to Messiah or for bringing any unbeliever to Yeshua. Here, in I Corinthians 14, it is the same as what it is in Isaiah 28: The existence of tongues means that God brought in a new element. This new element comes to be only because of the national unbelief of the Jews, so the existence of tongues within this new body is a sign of Jewish unbelief. Had Israel accepted the Messiah, there would have been no church; therefore, there would have been no gifts of the Spirit. So, just as Israel's disobedience led to the existence of the Assyrian language being spoken in the land, her new disobedience led to the new body and the existence of the speaking of tongues.

In saying this, it must be made clear that God has in no way cast off His people, Israel (Rom. 11:1); but God's plan or program for Israel as a nation has been temporarily set aside until the rapture occurs, which will remove this new entity, the church. Then God will once again resume His plan for the nation of Israel, until all Israel will be saved.

Summarizing this very important verse, I Corinthians 14:22, when Paul stated that tongues are a sign to the unbelieving, he did not mean that the sign was given for the purpose of bringing the unbelievers to faith, because verse 21 states: *not even thus will they hear me*. Tongues are a sign of Jewish unbelief. Had Israel believed, tongues would not exist; since the gift of tongues does exist, it is a sign of Israel's unbelief. While tongues are a sign for the unbelievers of their unbelief, prophecy is a sign for the believer, because it communicates God's message to the believer.

In verses 23-25, Paul draws the application for the assembly. Concerning tongues and the unbeliever, verse 23 notes that if *all speak with tongues*, the unbeliever who walks into the meeting hall will declare them to be insane, because they are all speaking that which has no meaning.

In verses 24-25, Paul shows why prophecy is superior to tongues. Earlier in the chapter (vv. 6-19), he showed why prophecy is superior to tongues for the believer who is in the assembly. Now he is going to show why prophecy is superior to tongues for the unbeliever who happens to walk into the meeting of the church. Prophecy is superior to tongues because if all the unbeliever hears is tongues, he will merely conclude that these believers are insane. If he comes in and someone receives a direct revelation from God and applies it to him, the unbeliever will then be convicted of his sin (v. 24). He will be judged as his inner being is searched out.

The reasons are given in verse 25. The unbeliever's heart is revealed when his life is illuminated by someone who is receiving a direct revelation from God—the mark of a prophet—and he will then *worship God*. Rather than declaring these believers to be insane, he will have to admit and declare, *God is among you indeed*.

To summarize what has been discussed so far, four points should be made:

1. With respect to usefulness, the gift of tongues is inferior to prophecy (vv. 1-5).
2. Without interpretation, the gift of tongues becomes entirely useless in the public assembly (vv. 6-15).
3. To exercise tongues without the gift of interpretation creates real confusion and impropriety in the church (vv. 16-19).
4. To emphasize tongues, as is often done, is simply childish and shows immaturity rather than maturity (vv. 20-25).

(4) Further Rules for Tongues and Prophecy (I Cor. 14:26-33a)

The fourth division is I Corinthians 14:26-33a. In these verses, Paul lists more rules for the proper use of the gifts of tongues and prophecy:

> *26 What is it then, brethren? When ye come together, each one has a psalm, has a teaching, has a revelation, has a tongue, has an interpretation. Let all things be done unto edifying. 27 If any man speaks in a tongue, let it be by two, or at the most three, and that in turn; and let one interpret: 28 but if there be no interpreter, let him keep silence in the church; and let him speak to himself, and to God. 29 And let the prophets speak by two or three, and let the others discern. 30 But if a revelation be made to another sitting by, let the first keep silence. 31 For ye all can prophesy one by one, that all may learn, and all may be exhorted; 32 and the spirits of the prophets are subject to the prophets; 33a for God is not a God of confusion, but of peace.*

These rules are frequently disobeyed by those who claim to have the gift of tongues. In verse 26, Paul spells out the basic rule: *Let all things be done unto edifying.* All gifts must be used to edify the body.

Having laid down this basic rule for all spiritual gifts, Paul then lays down specific rules for the use of tongues, in verses 27-28. The first rule concerns the number of speakers: No more than two or three people should give a message in tongues during any single meeting of the church.

The second rule is that it should be done in order. If two or more people are speaking publicly in tongues at the same time, it is a violation of this rule.

The third rule concerns the mode: *let one interpret*. This rule reiterates that there must be an interpreter and specifies that it must be *one* interpreter. In other words, there must not be three interpreters for three different people speaking in tongues. Since these gifts are given when one believes, one will know his gift before he uses it publicly in a church. One person who is known to have the gift of interpretation is assigned to interpret the message given by the gift of tongues. While there may be as many as three people giving a message in tongues, only one person is to do the interpreting for all three.

The fourth rule is that if there is no one with the gift of interpretation present, those who have the gift of tongues must remain silent. They can speak quietly to God and to themselves, but they must remain silent.

Having given the rules for speaking in tongues in the public assembly, Paul turns to rules that pertain to the gift of prophecy in the assembly, in verses 29-31. The first rule concerns the number of speakers: *by two or three*.

The second rule concerns the mode: others are to discern which spirit is at work. A person with the gift of prophecy may believe they have a word from God when they do not. Even prophets, when they are not being inspired by God, can make mistakes. One key example is that of the prophet Nathan in the Hebrew Scriptures. King David told Nathan that he would like to build God a temple, and Nathan, without consulting God, told David to go ahead. Then God revealed Himself to Nathan and told him to go back to David and tell him not to build the Temple (II Sam. 7:1-7; I Chr. 17:1-6). The prophets were not always under inspiration, so they could make mistakes. Therefore, when there is a claim of prophetic inspiration, others are to discern which spirit is at work. Those with the gift of discernment are to determine the source of the message. There are three possible sources: the Holy Spirit, the human spirit, and demonic spirits. The rule is that the words of the prophets must be tested.

The third rule concerns the order: If a revelation is given to a second man, the first man should immediately sit down, because the latest revelation is always the purest and most complete. When a person stands, it signals that he has a message and wants to speak. The one who is speaking should heed the signal and sit down.

The fourth rule concerns timing: Those speaking should not lengthen their discourse so that another prophet or two may have a chance to speak; they should give a succinct message and conclude it.

The fifth rule concerns procedure: *all* [may] *prophesy one by one, that . . . all may be exhorted* (v. 31). The "all" is the "two or three" of verse 29. Paul does set a maximum, but both or all three prophets should be given the opportunity to speak.

In verse 32-33a, Paul gives the principle upon which the rules for the exercise of the gifts of tongues and prophecy are based, and the point must not be missed: *the spirits of the prophets are subject to the prophets*. All these gifts, including the gifts of tongues and prophecy, can be controlled by the person possessing the gift. Those who claim that they could not help themselves but were suddenly "taken over" by the Holy Spirit to utter tongues or prophecies are contradicting what the Bible teaches. It is the human spirit that speaks in tongues, not the Holy Spirit. The human spirit is subject to the possessor. Prophets and those who speak in tongues can and should exercise the control necessary to restrain mere outbursts of so-called "prophetic inspiration." True prophetic inspiration does not "carry away" the prophet without his consent or against his will. What Paul said here in verse 32 is in opposition to I Corinthians 12:2, which states that when the Corinthians were unbelieving Gentiles, they were carried away with *dumb idols*. Demonism is the root of idolatry. The biblical gift of prophecy or tongues, or any spiritual gift, does not carry away the person without his consent. So, prophetic inspiration cannot be used as a pretext to discard the rules of order laid down by an apostle. Those who claim that they could not help themselves, for they were simply "caught up in the Spirit," are deceiving themselves. It was not the Holy Spirit in whom they were caught up, but their own human spirit. When they disobey these rules and regulations laid down by the Scriptures, they are sinning.

The evidence of the principle is in verse 33a: *God is not a God of confusion*, but a God of order. Therefore, all these things can be kept in check and under control so that these rules are obeyed. The principle of the public assembly is that all should be able to participate in the use of the spiritual gifts. However, they are not to be carried away to the point that it results in confusion. If these rules are obeyed, there will be order instead of confusion.

(5) *Conclusion (I Cor. 14:33b-40)*

In the fifth and final division of chapter 14, which encompasses verses 33b-40, Paul concludes his lengthy discussion concerning spiritual gifts which began in chapter 12:1:

> [33b] *As in all the churches of the saints,* [34] *let the women keep silence in the churches: for it is not permitted unto them to speak; but let them be in subjection, as also says the law.* [35] *And if they would learn anything, let them ask their own husbands at home: for it is shameful for a woman to speak in the church.* [36] *What? was it from you that the word of God went forth? or came it unto you alone?* [37] *If any man thinks himself to be a prophet, or spiritual, let him take knowledge of the things which I write unto you, that they are the commandment of the Lord.* [38] *But if any man is ignorant, let him be ignorant.* [39] *Wherefore, my brethren, desire earnestly to prophesy, and forbid not to speak with tongues.* [40] *But let all things be done decently and in order.*

In verses 33b-35, Paul deals with the topic of women in the public meeting. In verse 33b, he states that what he is about to say to this church is true for all churches: *As in all the churches of the saints*. In other words, he is not laying down rules that are applicable only to the culture of the Corinthian church. The rules he lays down here are rules to be followed by every church no matter where it is and no matter what its culture. These rules, which were true for the first century church, are still applicable today. The 21st century church has no right to discard scriptural rules and regulations on the pretense of "culture" or any other reason.

The basic rule concerning women in the meeting of the church is that women are to keep silent in the assembly (v. 34). Because of the context in which this verse is found, the primary thrust is that a woman must not speak in tongues in the assembly. A woman can have the gift of tongues, but she cannot use that gift in the meeting of the church. Even with an interpreter present, women are not to speak in tongues in the church.

Paul then shows that he is not limiting the rule of silence for women in the assembly only to speaking in tongues. In verse 35, he goes on to say that if women wish to learn anything, they are to wait and *ask their husbands at home*. In other words, they are not even allowed to ask questions in the meeting of the church. Obviously, a woman would not ask questions in tongues, because she would not understand the language that she is speaking. The fact that she is not even allowed to ask questions in the meeting of the church shows that the rule of silence applies in every category, not only in the area of speaking in tongues. Concerning women, then, the Bible teaches that women are to keep silent in the church; they are not to speak in tongues in the church; they are not even to ask questions. It means total silence as far as speaking is concerned.

In verse 36, Paul reminds the Corinthian church that although they had people there with the gift of prophecy, the Word of God did not come to them alone. In other words, the Corinthian church cannot follow their own course of action apart from other churches. They do not have the right to put themselves above the rules followed by other churches. The rules the apostle spelled out for the Corinthian church are rules which must be obeyed by all churches. Since these are rules given in the dispensation of grace, these are rules given for the church age. These rules which were true of the first century are also true of the 21st century. One should judge today's culture by the Word of God, not interpret the Word of God by 21st century culture.

Having stated that not to them alone came the Word of God (v. 36), in verses 37-38, Paul develops further what the Word of God is, especially as it applies to spiritual and non-spiritual believers in the local church.

He first discusses the *spiritual* believers (v. 37). These are the mature believers, those controlled by the Holy Spirit, in the Corinthian church (I Cor. 2:14-3:6). They will recognize that what Paul said and wrote is the Word of God. Paul was not expressing just a personal preference or opinion here, as he did in two other places in the epistle. What he stated here are divine commands coming through his apostolic authority. He had the gift of apostleship, and like a prophet, he too received direct revelation from God. The rules he spoke were not rules of preference, but rules that God Himself gave him, the rules of the Word of God. Those who were spiritual would recognize that what Paul said and wrote is the Word of the Lord. He is addressing those believers who, on the grounds of a "higher revelation," might want to change these rules he has just given as well as those he had given earlier in discussing the gifts of the Holy Spirit. Someone in the Corinthian church may say, "I have the gift of prophecy. As a prophet, I have authority to change the rules that have been handed down by the apostles." But that would be wrong. No matter how much higher revelation anyone may claim to have, no matter how great a prophet, even if all his prophecies have come true, he has no authority to change the directions given by God Himself.

In Old Testament times, the test of a prophet was always twofold: First, he had to predict near events that came to pass to authenticate his prophetic office; second, even if all the events he prophesied came to pass, when he taught things contrary to the written Word of God, he was not to be followed. Paul said that if some of those who have the gift of prophecy in the Corinthian church began to teach things contrary to that which was handed down through apostolic authority, they are not to be believed nor followed. Those who are true prophets and those who are truly spiritual will recognize that what Paul taught is indeed the Word of God.

Then, in verse 38, Paul addresses the non-spiritual believers. He calls them *ignorant*, and Paul says that those who chose to remain ignorant are to remain ignorant. Their ignorance will be evident by their immaturity, their carnality, their misuse of spiritual gifts, and their claims of authority to change the rules of the Word of God. They remain in ignorance though they claim to have all knowledge.

Having said this, Paul then draws the proper balance concerning spiritual gifts (I Cor. 14:39-40). He begins in verse 39 by stating two things. First: *desire earnestly to prophesy*. The word "desire" means "to covet." As a congregation, this is what they should be seeking. They had been emphasizing the gift of tongues and de-emphasizing the greater gifts. While the sensational gifts are more amusing, they are not the gifts that bring believers to maturity. It is the greater gifts, such as the gift of teaching, that bring believers to maturity. As a congregation, the Corinthians should not desire the lesser gifts but the greater gifts. Second: *forbid not to speak with tongues*. The biblical emphasis on the greater gifts does not mean that the lesser gifts should be dismissed or ignored. They, too, have their proper place. "Forbid not" simply means "to let it happen." However, it does not encourage the seeking of it. Furthermore, "forbid not" means "it cannot be prohibited," as long as the rules which Paul listed earlier are obeyed. Tongues can be forbidden if the gift is used contrary to the rules of I Corinthians 14: If two or more people speak at the same time, it can be forbidden; if more than three desire to speak, it can be forbidden; if a woman is speaking in tongues in the church, she can be forbidden from doing so; if there is no interpreter, it can be forbidden. But if all the rules are obeyed, then *forbid not to speak in tongues*. Let it happen, but do not seek it.

The balance concerning tongues is: seek not—forbid not. Seek not: If you are a believer who does not speak in tongues, then you have a superior gift, so do not seek after a lesser gift like tongues. Forbid not: I there is someone who has the true gift of tongues, and it can be used within the rules of I Corinthians 14, then it should be allowed.

In verse 40, the whole discussion ends with the rules Paul has been emphasizing throughout: *let all things be done decently and in order*.

D. The End of the Gifts of Apostleship and Prophecy

Of the 19 spiritual gifts Paul introduced in his epistles, two were the gifts of apostleship and prophecy. These two gifts are no longer available. The gift of apostleship was given only to selected people sent by God. To be an apostle, one had to have seen the resurrected Messiah and have the power of miracles. The gift of prophecy was the ability to receive direct revelation from God. A prophet could even write Scripture which would be inspired and without error.

In his epistle to the Ephesians, Paul states two purposes for these gifts.

1. Laying the Foundation of the Church

In Ephesians 2:19-22, Paul explains that the gifts of apostleship and prophecy were needed to lay the foundation of the church:

[19] So then ye are no more strangers and sojourners, but ye are fellow-citizens with the saints, and of the household of God, [20] being built upon the foundation of the apostles and prophets, Messiah Yeshua himself being the chief corner stone; [21] in whom each several building, fitly framed together, grows

into a holy temple in the Lord; ^{22} *in whom ye also are built together for a habitation of God in the Spirit.*

According to this passage, the two gifts of apostleship and prophecy in the New Testament were for the purpose of laying the foundation of the church. The picture is that Yeshua is *the chief corner stone*. From the cornerstone, two lines were marked out along which the stones were laid for the foundation. One line of stones represents the apostles, and the other line of stones represents the prophets. In this passage, the prophets are not those of the Hebrew Scriptures, but those of the New Testament. The purpose of the New Testament apostles and prophets was for laying the foundation of the church. By the time of the death of John (the last apostle, who died circa A.D. 90), the foundation of the church had been laid.

What is happening today is described in verses 21-22: Believers are stones that are being fitly *framed together*, one on top of the other, building up the house of God. That is the purpose for the other gifts. The other gifts are being used to lay stone upon stone in building up the house of God, but the foundation is comprised of the apostles and prophets.

2. Recording New Testament Revelation

The second purpose of the gifts of apostleship and prophecy is described in Ephesians 3:1-9:

> ^{1} *For this cause I Paul, the prisoner of Messiah Yeshua in behalf of you Gentiles,—* ^{2} *if so be that ye have heard of the dispensation of that grace of God which was given me to you-ward;* ^{3} *how that by revelation was made known unto me the mystery, as I wrote before in few words,* ^{4} *whereby, when ye read, ye can perceive my understanding in the mystery of Messiah;* ^{5} *which in other generations was not made known unto the sons of men, as it has now been revealed unto his holy apostles and prophets in the Spirit;* ^{6} *to wit, that the Gentiles are fellow-heirs, and fellow-members of the body, and fellow-partakers of the promise in Messiah Yeshua through the gospel,* ^{7} *whereof I was made a minister, according to the gift of that grace of God which was given me according to the working of his power.* ^{8} *Unto me, who am less than the least of all saints, was this grace given, to preach unto the Gentiles the unsearchable riches of Messiah;* ^{9} *and to make all men see what*

is the dispensation of the mystery which for ages has been hid in God who created all things

It is within these verses that Paul spells out a second purpose for the spiritual gifts of apostles and prophets: They were to receive and record new revelation concerning the teachings on the dispensation of the grace of God. The term "mystery" refers to things unrevealed in the Hebrew Bible but revealed for the first time in the New Testament (Eph. 3:3-5, 9; Col. 1:25-27). Verse 5 makes it clear which prophets are meant: not the prophets of the Hebrew Scriptures, but the New Testament prophets. Paul expresses it this way: *it has now* [in Paul's day] *been revealed*. Just as the Hebrew Scriptures had to be recorded by the prophets of that era, the New Testament had to be recorded by New Testament prophets.

3. Conclusion

The two purposes for the gifts of apostleship and prophecy were to lay the foundation of the church, which has now been laid, and to record New Testament revelation, which has now been recorded. With these two things accomplished, the clear teaching is that these two gifts are no longer given.

In the case of apostleship, people today are not seeing the resurrected Messiah, which was a prerequisite for the gift of apostleship. In the case of prophecy, people today are not receiving direct revelation from God. If they were, they could record Scripture. There are many people claiming to receive direct revelation, and therefore claiming to be "prophets of God," yet none of them are claiming the ability to write inerrant Scripture, nor are any of them willing to take the test of a prophet according to Deuteronomy 18:20-22. If they are prophets and are receiving direct revelation from God, they should be able to predict some clear events that would come to pass within a short period of time.

E. Questions and Study Suggestions

Question 1: How do the Greek words *charisma* and *doron* differ from each other?

Question 2: What is a spiritual gift?

Question 3: What is it not?

Study Suggestion 1: Many people are eager to learn which gifts the Ruach HaKodesh may have bestowed upon them when they became believers. Dr. Fruchtenbaum teaches that there are three principles in discovering one's spiritual gift. The first principle is to know what the spiritual gifts are. As mentioned, there are 19 gifts of the Holy Spirit. Make a list of these 19 gifts.

Study Suggestion 2: A second principle in discovering a spiritual gift is based on the purpose of the gifts: the building up of the body. This principle presupposes that the believer is actively involved in a local body. Are you involved in a local congregation?

One of the reasons why believers are responsible to become part of a local body and to be in subjection to the spiritual authorities of that body is because it is by means of the local body that believers can discover what their spiritual gifts are. By being involved in a local body, other believers will discern which gift or gifts the individual has and ask him to function in it. In this way, one can discover his spiritual gift. We suggest you make a point to ask your brothers and sisters in the Lord to think about what gift they see in you.

Study Suggestion 3: The third principle is discovering other gifts. Frequently, believers have more than one gift. The way someone can discover other gifts is by being faithful in using the gifts he knows he has. For example, in Acts 6, Philip was recognized to have the gift of serving and was asked to take the office of a deacon. Because he was faithful in performing the office of a deacon and using his gift of serving, God showed him another gift—the gift of evangelism—and he went to Samaria to evangelize the Samaritans (Acts 8). On the list you prepared, make sure to correlate the gifts that belong together. Then ask your brothers and sisters of your church to brainstorm and see if they can detect any other gifts in you.

CPSIA information can be obtained
at www.ICGtesting.com
Printed in the USA
JSHW012305210723
45229JS00003B/9

9 781935 174820